PENGUIN BOOKS
NEPAL 2043

Sujeev Shakya is a thought leader who traverses many worlds. He earned the title of Nepal's CEO, 'chief eternal optimist', for the optimism he projected in his book, *Unleashing Nepal* (2009) and subsequently in *Unleashing the Vajra* (2019). He writes and speaks extensively on business, development, economy and leadership. In 2008, after spending two decades in one of Nepal's leading business groups, he founded beed, an international management consulting and advisory firm based in Kathmandu, Nepal. He is also founder and chair of the Nepal Economic Forum.

ADVANCE PRAISE FOR THE BOOK

'This book by Sujeev Shakya is an audacious attempt to reimagine Nepal's future as an economic bridge between China and India. Breaking out of existing stereotypes of Nepal as a Himalayan (geo-)political battleground, it re-focusses Nepal as a substantive contributor and beneficiary of the Asian twenty-first century—**Kishore Mahbubani, a distinguished fellow at the Asia Research Institute, National University of Singapore and author of *Living the Asian Century***

'Sujeev Shakya is a masterful storyteller who weaves a vibrant tapestry of Nepal's growth and development through careful study of its history, societal patterns, economic data, industry trends and geopolitics. This is an artful examination of Nepal's past, present and future, broadly framed by the rich lived experience of a Nepali builder, entrepreneur, writer, scholar, executive, thought leader and consummate global citizen. Count me as one who believes in the dream of *Nepal 2043*'—**Jack McCarthy, associate professor, Babson College, US**

'Land-linked Nepal is deeply integrated in the global economy, mainly thanks to the mobility, the ingenuity and the working ethics of its diverse population. Its future is promising. It could reach high-income status by mid-century if it seizes the opportunities created by its citizens [who are] studying and working abroad. This is the inspiring message sent by Sujeev Shakya in his analytical assessment of Nepal's historical trajectory and of its manifest destiny. Friends and economic partners of Nepal will learn from this book how to support the country's development by recognizing, respecting and engaging the many talents of young and dynamic Nepali citizens'—**Jörg Frieden, chairman, Swiss Investment Fund for Emerging Markets**

'Sujeev Shakya has given us a book to savour, telling us how Nepal has changed in this century and how it can achieve the national ambition of becoming a high-income country by 2043. This book, [written] by an optimist with practical experience, who is firmly grounded in economic and social reality, is easily one of the best guides to Nepal's and South Asia's complex reality and potential future'—**Shiv Shankar Menon, former foreign secretary of India and national security advisor of India**

'*Nepal 2043* generates infectious enthusiasm about the economic and political prospects of the long-underestimated Himalayan Republic. Shakya's optimism is grounded in documented economic facts and social trends in Nepal that make his latest book a compelling read. This book has a place on the bookshelves of all those who are interested in the geo-economics of this vital Himalayan region nestling between a China that has risen to be a great power and an India that is emerging as a major regional force'—**Professor C. Raja Mohan, Institute of South Asian Studies, National University of Singapore**

'Sujeev Shakya's book reintroduces Nepal to the world as a rising economy, challenging stereotypes of poverty and irrelevance. It is remarkable that despite political turmoil, natural disasters and a pandemic, Nepal's GDP grew sixfold from 2004 to 2024. With increasing remittances, a growing banking sector, strong real estate and strategic links to India and China, Nepal shows immense economic potential. Sujeev draws from decades of work in strategy and development to make this book a strong advocate for reimagining Nepal's promising future'—**Shamika Ravi, member, Economic Advisory Council to Prime Minister, Government of India**

'Every country needs to pause once in a while and try to reimagine its future. In Nepal's case, there is no one better qualified than its chief optimist, Sujeev Shakya, to play that role. You may disagree with his conclusions, but you will find the journey informative and worthwhile'—**Gurcharan Das, author**

'This is a remarkable book. As Sujeev Shakya embarks on an extraordinary journey to his country's future, we suddenly find ourselves not just in the centre of the world but in the centre of the future. In this book, Nepal is an unavoidable country. Located between India and China, with privileged connections to both, it is already an image of future geopolitics. The challenges it faces are the challenges of a fractured world: demography, climate change and migration. Sujeev Shakya is an entrepreneur, a policy wonk, a visionary. Here, he takes us to the heights of Nepal and shows us how the world below truly works'—**Bruno Maçães, author, journalist and politician**

'*Nepal 2043* is a compelling and hopeful vision of a country ready to defy outdated stereotypes. Despite years of political and natural upheaval, Nepal has shown extraordinary resilience, which I have noticed during my visits. With the right investments and leadership, it has the potential to harness that same resilience to become a high-income nation within a generation.

'With sharp analysis and practical insights, Shakya highlights the role of transformative sectors such as hydropower, tourism, agriculture and technology in Nepal's growth. This vision document is not just a road map for Nepal—it's an inspiring read for leaders everywhere committed to sustainable, inclusive development'—**Helen Clark, former prime minister of New Zealand (1999–2008), former United Nations Development Programme administrator and patron, New Zealand Himalayan Trust**

'I have travelled to and been a fan of Nepal since a young age—simply for its immense natural beauty and people's hospitality. The country's multidimensional attributes, including culture, race, language and ethnicity, resemble those of Southeast Asia, albeit different in scale.

'Being the fiftieth-most populous nation, land-linked as opposed to landlocked and wedged by Asia's two largest countries, inevitably and forcefully motivates Nepal to tell its story to the world with the right tone, cadence, frequency and elegance. A storytelling that needs to resolutely capitalize on the country's demographic dividends for educational attainment in line with the evolution of geopolitics, technology, climate change and movement of people.

'A fourfold growth of economic size from 2006 to 2024 is capital for the country to better embrace ambition, imagination and serendipity to attain its 2043 ambition. A prosperity shared'—**Gita Wirjawan, former trade minister of Indonesia; visiting scholar, Doerr School of Sustainability, Stanford University; host,** *Endgame* **podcast and author,** *What It Takes*

'This book is an antidote to the gloom-and-doom narrative of "Nepal is *khatam* (over)" by many professional pessimists. Author Sujeev Shakya makes a plausible case for Nepal reaching an upper-middle income status by 2043 by leveraging its strategic location between two of the world's largest and rapidly growing economies, and the dynamism of its upwardly mobile, globally adaptable and increasingly digitally savvy youthful population'—**Kul Chandra Gautam, former assistant secretary general, United Nations, and author** *Global Citizen from Gulmi* **and** *Lost in Transition*

'Nepalis frequently bemoan the state of their country's economy and politics. Premature announcements of Nepal as a "failed state" have been made many times. I have long thought that these doom-laden discourses seriously underestimate both ordinary Nepalis (their ingenuity, determination, hard work, etc.) and the substantial achievements of Nepalese politics (democracy, republicanism, federalism, secularism, negotiating relations with Nepal's two giant neighbours). Here, at last, in the pages of *Nepal 2043: Road to Prosperity*, covering everything from hydropower to climate change, from tea gardens to trans-Himalayan trade, is an informed insider's

view explaining—with manifold supporting evidence and deep personal experience—why the glass is indeed half full, not half empty, and why Nepal, with its surplus of dynamic and educated young people, has a bright future ahead of it'—
Professor David N. Gellner, FBA, emeritus professor, social anthropology and Fellow of All Souls College, University of Oxford

Nepal 2043
The Road to Prosperity

SUJEEV SHAKYA

PENGUIN BOOKS
An imprint of Penguin Random House

PENGUIN BOOKS

Penguin Books is an imprint of the Penguin Random House group of companies whose addresses can be found at global.penguinrandomhouse.com

Published by Penguin Random House India Pvt. Ltd
4th Floor, Capital Tower 1, MG Road,
Gurugram 122 002, Haryana, India

First published in Penguin Books by Penguin Random House India 2025

Copyright © Sujeev Shakya 2025

All rights reserved

10 9 8 7 6 5 4 3 2 1

The views and opinions expressed in this book are the author's own and the facts are as reported by him which have been verified to the extent possible, and the publishers are not in any way liable for the same.

Please note that no part of this book may be used or reproduced in any manner for the purpose of training artificial intelligence technologies or systems.

ISBN 9780143467106

Typeset in Adobe Caslon Pro by MAP Systems, Bengaluru, India
Printed at Replika Press Pvt. Ltd, India

This book is sold subject to the condition that it shall not, by way of trade or otherwise, be lent, resold, hired out, or otherwise circulated without the publisher's prior consent in any form of binding or cover other than that in which it is published and without a similar condition including this condition being imposed on the subsequent purchaser.

www.penguin.co.in

To all those who believe in the future of Nepal

Contents

Introduction   xiii

Section 1

Chapter 1: Reimagining Nepal   3
Chapter 2: Advantage Location   27
Chapter 3: Federalism and Further   59
Chapter 4: Thriving in Chaos   83
Chapter 5: Climate Change   111

Section 2: The Enablers

Chapter 6: The Himalayan Powerhouse   139
Chapter 7: Agricultural Revolution   161
Chapter 8: Towards Sustainable Tourism   186
Chapter 9: Digital Transformation   207
Chapter 10: Reaping the Demographic Dividend   229
Chapter 11: The Global Nepali   242
Chapter 12: Towards Transformation   253

Acknowledgements   267
Notes   271

Introduction

In 2023, after the pandemic ended and in-person meetings resumed, I decided to embark on a mission: to reintroduce and reimagine Nepal. I travelled to India, Europe, Singapore and the United States of America to conduct rapid eight- to ten-minute sessions in front of entrepreneurs, development practitioners and academics. These are sessions I continue to conduct even today. Now, you might ask why there is a need to reintroduce or reimagine Nepal—particularly to investors, businessmen and businesswomen, development partners, financial institutions and even young job seekers.

Well, the sad truth is that Nepal continues to languish under stereotypes and the stubborn misconception of being a poor, landlocked country that has lost its relevance. The truth of the matter is that in 2024, Nepal's gross domestic product (GDP) was US$44 billion[1]—a sixfold increase from US$7 billion in 2004.[2] The past two decades have seen unprecedented growth despite the challenges posed by frequent changes in government, tumultuous political transitions from 2006 to 2015, earthquakes, floods, blockades and, to top it all, the pandemic.

With a population of 30 million, Nepal is hardly a small country—it is the fiftieth most populous nation in the world. It is not 'land-locked' but 'land-linked' to two of the world's fastest-growing economies—China and India. Furthermore, Nepal has an incredible diaspora, with four million Nepalis working or settled in 180 countries across the world.[3]

That's not all. In the sessions I host, I highlight other lesser-known facts. For instance, Nepal has the highest tax-to-GDP ratio in South Asia.[4] Nepalis pay nearly the same taxes as residents of Singapore when purchasing vehicles.[5]

One fact I repeat ad nauseam is that 81 per cent of Nepalis live in houses they own,[6] which means they do not have to pay rent like many others in South Asia. This raises the disposable income available for consumption.

In 2023, the capital formation–to–GDP ratio in Nepal was second only to India.[7] The size of the banking sector has also grown manifold. For example, if we compare Nepal with Bangladesh, Nepal's banking industry is twice the size of Bangladesh's—despite Nepal having just one-fifth of Bangladesh's population.

Let's talk about remittances. Initially, Nepalis went abroad to work only in India. In more recent times, they have started finding work and settling in countries around the world. The remittances they send from formal channels have increased from US$2 billion in 2008 to US$10 billion in 2024.[8] In a study undertaken by beed management—a management consulting company I founded and manage—we found that, in 2022, informal remittances[9] were also approximately the same amount.[10]

There is a general perception that a large number of Nepalis work in India—and this is true, given the US$1.5 billion that comes from India. However, what is equally interesting is that many Indians now work in Nepal, filling roles vacated by Nepalis migrating to other countries, and the remittances from Nepal to India also amount to approximately US$1.5 billion.[11] During the pre-pandemic period, remittances from Nepal to India were even higher. An article in the Indian newspaper the *Economic Times* in 2019 cited World Bank data to point out that there was an outflow of US$3 billion in remittances from Nepal to India. At the time, this was double the remittance inflow from India to Nepal.[12]

With the exchange rate fixed to the Indian rupee, Nepal has also benefitted from the rupee's stability. In 2014, the exchange rate of the US dollar to both the Nepali and Pakistani rupees was 100, while the dollar traded at 130 Sri Lankan rupees. By October 2024, the Sri Lankan rupee was hovering around 300, and the Pakistani rupee stood at 275 to the dollar. When you compare Nepal with these countries, you realize how its exchange rate has remained fixed at 1.60 Nepali rupees (NPR) to one Indian rupee for the past thirty-five years. During this period, Nepal has been able to leverage India's steady growth trajectory.

The real estate sector in Nepal offers a distinct picture of the kind of growth taking place in the country. In February 2025, journalist Ramesh Kumar wrote in the *Nepali Times*: 'The price of real estate is doubling every two to three years here because of the soaring demand for land due to migration to the cities, plains and valleys from the mountain districts.'[13] In 2021, the Nepal Rastra Bank released a report citing a 26.45 per cent rise in real estate prices.[14] In fact, real estate prices in Nepal are very high, comparable with those in some of the world's most expensive cities. For instance, consider the area around Durbar Marg in central Kathmandu: about 100 acres or 800 *ropanis* (8 ropanis to an acre),[15] of land would be valued at US$8 billion. That is nearly a fifth of Nepal's GDP. I do not see this trend stagnating or reversing, and by the time you finish reading this book, you will understand why.

At the Nepal Economic Forum (NEF), we have been doing many events in partnership with different embassies and agencies to highlight how Nepal is a country with a high potential for economic growth; it is a sought-after investment destination and a place to settle in the future, especially for the Nepali diaspora. In fact, there are many potential investors in the bordering areas of Nepal apart from small family trust offices in Canada, Europe and US that seek investments into emerging markets. Nepal should ideally leverage these investment opportunities.

I constantly remind people that Nepal is graduating to a middle-income country in 2026 and therefore, the lens through which we look at Nepal—as a 'small poor country'—needs to change. In more ways than one, this is therefore the central aim of this book: to reimagine, reintroduce and re-situate Nepal for a global audience.

Why 2043?

In 2019, when the government of Nepal, in its fifteenth five-year plan, announced its ambition of transforming Nepal into a high-income country by 2043,[16] I decided to investigate whether this was a possibility at all. Additionally, as someone engaged in the economic development space, I wanted to assess whether my vision for Nepal aligned with the government's.

The government has chosen the year 2043 to coincide with the turn of the century to 2100 in the Bikram Samvat (Era), the official calendar used in Nepal. When formulating a national vision, it is essential to set a reasonable timeframe. A period of fifteen to thirty years is generally considered good enough to study the impact of initiatives and policy interventions.

My preliminary investigation suggests that the government of Nepal's ambition isn't so far-fetched. For instance, let's refer to the Asian Development Bank report, *Asia 2050: Realizing the Asian Century*. It argues that Asian economies are projected to double their share of global gross domestic product (GDP) to 52 per cent by 2050, enabling Asia to regain the dominant economic position it held some 300 years ago, before the Industrial Revolution. The report further argues that China and India will be the dominant economies, with 36 per cent of the global population and a 30 per cent share of global GDP.[17]

China will celebrate 100 years of the founding of the People's Republic of China in 2049, having set its goal to 'build a modern socialist country that is prosperous, strong, democratic, culturally advanced and harmonious'.[18] Similarly, India has articulated its vision for Viksit Bharat (Developed India) by 2047, coinciding with 100 years of independence. Why can't, then, Nepal, align with the vision of its neighbours, who are expected to be the first- and second-largest global economies by 2050?

By 2043, the global population is projected to reach 9.3 billion, with Nepal's population estimated at 35 million.[19] The government's vision document states that 'Nepal will be established as a high-income country with a per capita national income of 12,100 US dollars.'[20] This would imply a GDP of US$423 billion—an ambitious figure, but not an unachievable one. We need to remind ourselves that the income from remittances alone consistently accounts for around 25 per cent of GDP. The estimate is also in line with the report produced by the Observer Research Foundation (ORF) in India. Its publication, *Nepal: Leap to the Himalayas*, suggests that Nepal's GDP could potentially reach US$200 billion by 2032.[21] Even in a conservative scenario—assuming Nepal grows only at the same rate as in the past twenty years (600 per cent)—GDP would still reach US$225 billion, with remittances at around US$50 billion. Thus, the government's vision is not so far-fetched after all.

I have always believed in Nepal's long-term potential, given my own workaround vision and strategy. However, writing a book that looks at the future is not an easy one, especially due to the paucity of data. The government's *Nepal Vision 2043* document continues to be the driving vision as endorsed in the 16th Five-Year Plan released in June 2024. The data in these documents provides me with the necessary tools to substantiate my own vision, thoughts and research.

Vision Documents

I have been fascinated by vision documents since my early days of work, when I was part of teams working on building long-term plans for businesses and not-for-profit organizations. My career began in 1989, at a time when the world was pursuing economic liberalization, and countries, individuals and organizations were envisioning what the scenario might be like in ten, twenty or thirty years.

In 1993, I joined a team that was tasked with drawing up long-term plans for Soaltee Hotel Limited, at a time when the company was going public through Nepal's first public offering of shares at a premium. Between 1992 and 1996, I was a part of team involved the vision for the Annapurna Conservation Area Project (ACAP), Nepal's award-winning conservation programme. In 1997, I was involved in preparing financial projections for the Upper Bhote Koshi Hydroelectric Power Project. We were looking into handing over the power plants to the government in twenty-five to thirty years from the time of writing the document. In 1996, I worked with the Quality Tourism Project team, which was given the responsibility, to shape Nepal's tourism sector. I continued to be involved in the country's tourism vision well into 2005.[22] In 2015, when the Government of Nepal began drafting its Vision 2030 document, I contributed by writing a chapter titled 'Leveraging Private Sector Growth and Investments'.[23] I argued that for Nepal to become a US$100 billion economy by 2030, annual investments of US$7 to 8 billion would be necessary. Although the 2015 earthquake, border blockade and COVID-19 pandemic disrupted these plans, Nepal could easily inch towards becoming US$75 billion economy by 2030.

All these years of working on such projects have equipped me with skills that have proved invaluable as I embark on an ambitious task: envisioning the future of my country.

Throughout my career, whether through newspaper columns or books, my writings have consistently explored Nepal and its place in the world in the years to come. *Unleashing Nepal: The Past, Present and Future of the Economy* was published in 2009, with a revised edition released in 2013. *Unleashing the Vajra: Nepal's Journey between India and China* was published in December 2019. These two books give a good understanding of the history and journey of Nepal from the sixth century CE to 2020. I believe they also offer perspectives that can help readers grasp Nepal's potential for the future.

In these works, I have attempted to articulate a vision for Nepal and urge the reader to think ahead about the multiple scenarios for economic growth and national prosperity.

By 2023, I felt it was right again to pause, evaluate and look at the future. There were two main reasons for this. First, the world had begun talking about 2050 as the next big milestone year, especially in terms of economic indicators, as China and India are expected to become the world's two largest economies. Second, the target of net-zero emissions by 2050 set by the Paris Agreement is another concern for the global community. I want to examine how Nepal will be influenced by both these pivotal developments.

Forecasting the Future

Writing about the future is complicated and presents a completely different set of challenges when compared to describing the past. In a country where data is sparse and individuals leading institutions are not used to thinking about the long-term future, it is very difficult to weave a vision for the future. From conversations with business leaders, civil society leaders, academics, people in government and politicians in Nepal, I was yet unable to get a detailed answer to the question: What is your long-term vision, or where do you see yourself or your institutions in 2043? I therefore turned to literature outside Nepal. Since I have been a long admirer of vision documents, I started to re-read some of the seminal ones that have influenced me. The vision statement by Lee Kuan Yew, the prime minister who led Singapore's transformation, had deeply impressed me. In a lecture in 1965, he had famously said, 'Over 100 years ago, this was a mud-flat, swamp. Today, this is a modern city. Ten years from now, this will be a metropolis. Never fear.'[24]

In 1992, I had read about the 'Malaysia Vision 2020' document and was keen on finding a copy. In pre-Internet days, I had to spend a good amount of money to get a copy that had arrived at the chairman's office at Soaltee, which was meant for the then-palace. While the vision articulated by Prime Minister Mohammad Mahathir of a per capita income of Malaysian $19,500 per citizen was not achieved, I was intrigued by the thought process that went behind such a vision. The copy still sits in my office library.

It was around this time that, in my own career, I graduated to leading teams and guiding them in preparing vision documents for companies. In 2000, as vice president, business development, I was assigned to work on a business plan for the Soaltee Hotel. I spent a few months interviewing people, researching vision documents of other companies and organizations and eventually emerged with one. I articulated the vision of building a leading hotel chain that managed multiple hotels within the country and potentially built a brand that would be recognized outside Nepal too. When I visit the hotels that are now managed by Soaltee across Nepal, I look back at those moments of writing about creating Nepal's premium and largest hotel chain.

According to me, the key skills required to execute such a plan are strong strategic thinking, the ability to see the big picture, undertaking deep research and analysis, building potential models after extrapolating data, following innovations happening around the world and being able to talk to key people who are subject experts. Apart from being able to imagine future scenarios, it is also important to articulate a vision in a simple but compelling way.

My interest in vision and trends forecasting has also pushed me to create a tool to envision the future path of organizations. When I started to teach strategic management at the Kathmandu University School of Management, I created a proprietary tool called 'Vision Mandala', which combines brand vision and strategic management tools. The Vision Mandala can be described as 'A geometric figure of an organization's dream, capturing the power of charting what will come to be.' I used this tool in many institutions, but I look at the Rwanda tourism vision mandala as one of the major successes, as the focus was to help Rwanda emerge as a high-end tourist destination. When beed management started work in Rwanda in 2012, there were limited tourism products, and tourism revenues were US$282 million.[25] In 2023, tourism in Rwanda was recognized globally, with revenues crossing US$630 million.[26] Working in Rwanda also taught me how to align one's work with the country's vision.

The Megatrends

Taking off from the government's ambition, this is a book that puts forward my vision for Nepal. But I also want this book to be more. I want it to be a playbook for other emerging markets and developing economies (EMDE) around the world. In 2024, the United Nations Trade and Development lists forty-five countries as least developed countries (LDCs).[27] Of these, five, including Nepal, will graduate out of LDC by 2027.[28] The rest of the forty could learn many lessons from Nepal's journey.

The future of the world and many EMDE countries hinges on multiple issues, but I have chosen four in particular: geopolitics, climate change, technology and the movement of people.

The world has seen unprecedented geopolitical polarization since 2016, and nobody knows this better than Nepal, situated as it is between India and China, right at the centre of geopolitical impact. The global discourse on climate change has moved from being a distant possibility to a challenge that requires collective action. All countries' futures, especially Nepal's, hinge on how they adapt to or mitigate climate change.

Further, the first quarter of the twenty-first century has seen unprecedented technological advancement around the world. There is little doubt that, for a country like Nepal, leapfrogging through digital transformation and digitalization will accelerate its economic growth and development.

Finally, globally, there is a large movement of people internally within their countries and to countries outside one's own. With Nepalis in 180 countries, the 'Global Nepali' today is charting Nepal's future transformation. In this book, I use these four lenses to look at Nepal's future. I believe these could also help any EMDE country looking to catapult itself towards a better tomorrow.

Pracademic Approach

In writing this book, I have combined my interests in reading and writing with real-life experiences as a practitioner of running a business, a consulting firm and a think tank. I also rely on the continuous fortnightly column I have been writing for over two and a half decades: the 'Economic Sense' column in *Nepali Times* from 2000 to 2011 and 'The Other View' in the *Kathmandu Post* from 2013 to 2023. The work at beed since 2009, as a consultant working across ten countries covering both for-profit and not-for-profit organizations has helped me gain a wealth of insights. Living in the cosmopolitan city of Kathmandu, one is fortunate to meet people from all walks of life and engage in conversations that provide varied perspectives. I also learn a lot when I travel around the world for events, work and leisure. For me, a week's travel packs the same learning as a semester at a university.

For geopolitics, my association with the National University of Singapore—Institute of South Asian Studies as a senior fellow has given me perspectives on how Asia is moving and how we can find a place for Nepal in this evolving scenario. I never look at the Rwandan experience in isolation; I look at Rwanda's aspiration of becoming the Singapore of Africa—a thought leader for the continent of fifty-four countries—and take inspiration from it.

For climate change, hosting the Himalayan Consensus Summits and the Himalayan Future Forum has given me a chance to re-imagine the future of the Himalayas.

Through the Centre for Digital Transformation at NEF, I am looking at the past and future transition of Nepal through digitization and digitalization. And lastly, through the Nepal and World Program that includes the Global Nepali Network at NEF, I try to understand the different facets behind the movement of people and the world of remittances. These diverse experiences and network have guided the insights, anecdotes and views in this book.

Context and Enablers to Nepal's Transformation

This book is organized into two sections. In the first, I re-introduce Nepal by providing fresh lens, which looks at the history and development of over two thousand years. This, I hope, will set the context to understand Nepal's future potential. I then look at Nepal's future, situated as it is between China and India. Thereafter, I provide some perspectives on three key areas that are critical to Nepal's future: the Nepali's ability to thrive despite being surrounded by chaos, the political transformation and tumult in the country, and the discourse around climate change.

In the second section, I discuss the enablers that will help Nepal achieve the transformation it needs in order to become a high-income country in 2043. I deep dive into the potential of hydropower, agriculture and tourism. Thereafter, I discuss how digital transformation, reaping the demographic dividend and the emergence of the force term 'Global Nepalis' will accelerate the pace of growth and development. I end the book by explaining why I believe in the potential of Nepal's transformation in 2043, reflecting on my own personal journey and providing a list of perceived risks that might derail the transformation.

The Wish

When I was writing the concept note for this book, I was sitting outside a manager's bungalow at Gisovu Tea Estate in Rwanda. I was reflecting on what the year 2043 means to me personally. I will be seventy-five years old in 2043. I would like to be holding the book, sitting in a Himalayan perch, looking at the breathtaking view of the stunning landscape on a sunny morning. The birds are chirping, and a light wind is blowing. The mountains are clearly visible after a light shower the previous night. There is a sense of calm and contentment as I reflect on the wonderful journey that Nepal has had. There has been equitable prosperity for all its citizens, and Nepal has emerged as the centre of Asia in terms of both attention and action. I think about having taken this playbook to the world and seeing not only Nepal, but many other countries and their citizens benefitting from this thought process.

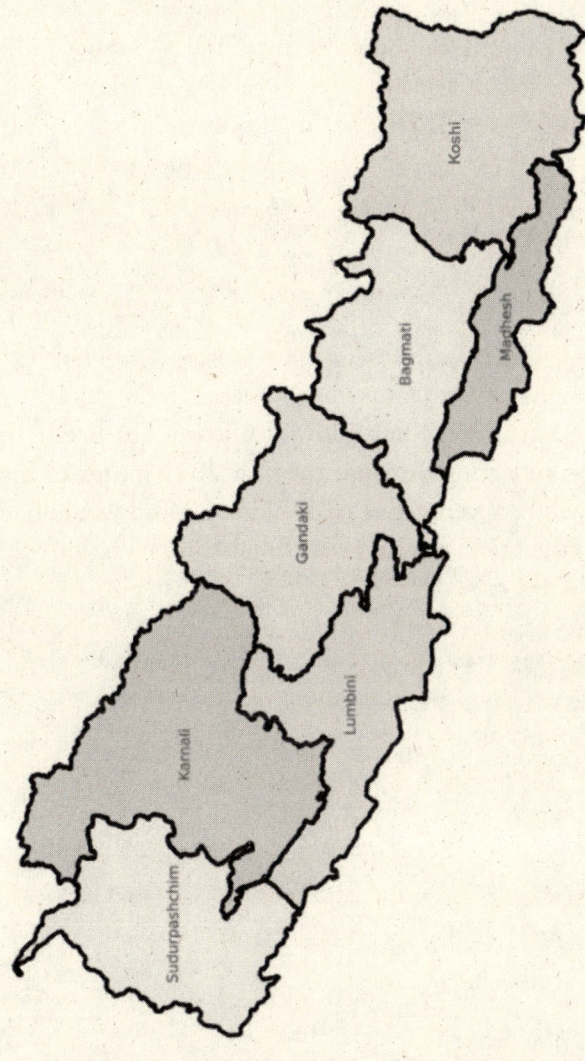

A map of Nepal with its seven provinces.

Source: Government of Nepal, https://nationalgeoportal.gov.np/#/map

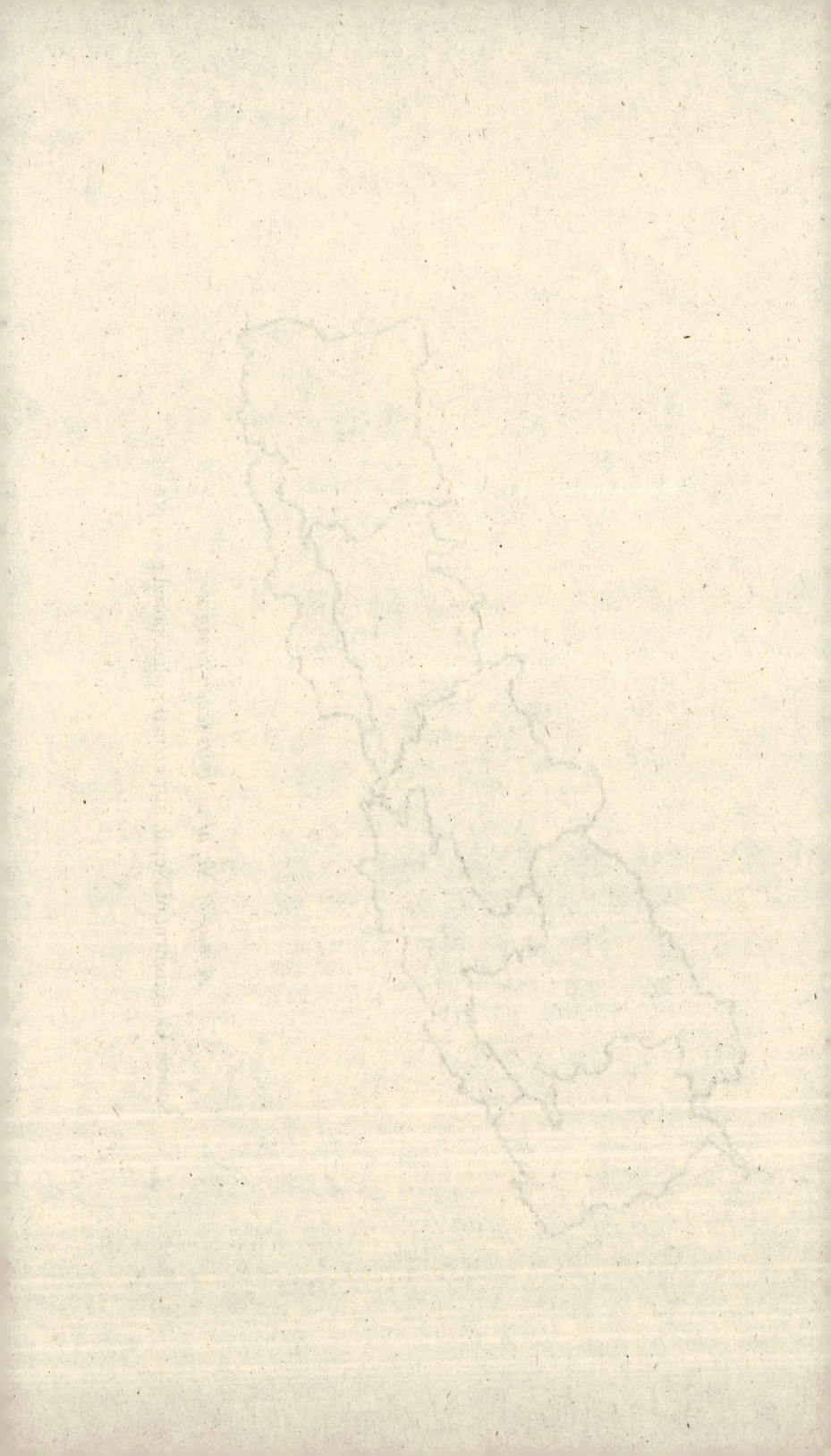

Section 1

Chapter 1

Reimagining Nepal

Every year since 2020, in his annual course on entrepreneurial leadership, Prof. Jack McCarthy at Babson College, US, shows his students a map of Asia that places Nepal at the centre. No, he isn't making a provocative geopolitical argument. His simple point is that sometimes the only way people can truly begin to gauge and forecast a country's potential is by reimagining it. What if Nepal were at the centre of Asia? What would it be capable of at the height of its potential? And if that's the ambition, then what would it take to get to that potential?

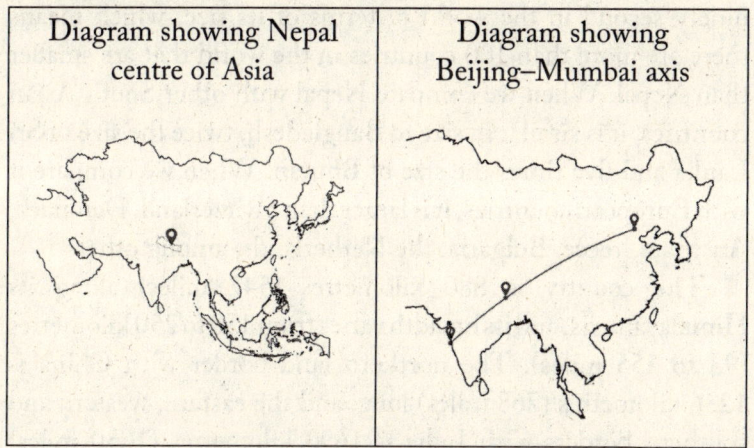

Illustrations: Courtesy of author

Nepal Is Not Small

When we draw a line from Mumbai to Beijing, Kathmandu falls right in the middle. This is a great way to look at Nepal, actually. A country of 30 million people, situated between three billion people in China and India, poised to graduate from a low- to a middle-income country by 2026 and eventually to a high-income country in 2043.

Seventy-five years ago, Nepal was a poor country trying to open itself up to the world; it was also situated between two poor neighbours. China was just at the beginning of the People's Revolution and India had just gained independence after nearly two hundred years of colonial rule. Nepal has witnessed steady economic growth since then, and as its neighbours are poised to become the two largest economies of the world by 2050, Nepal too, I believe, can tag along in this golden run.

But truth be told, this is not how Nepal is viewed in the world today.

In between two tall skyscrapers, even a ten-storey building looks small. The same is true for Nepal. With 1,47,516 square kilometres (56,956 square miles) of surface area, Nepal is ranked ninety-second in the world in terms of its size, which means there are more than 100 countries in the world that are smaller than Nepal. When we compare Nepal with other South Asian countries, it is similar in size to Bangladesh, twice the size of Sri Lanka and five times the size of Bhutan. When we compare it with European countries, it is larger than Switzerland, Denmark, Austria, Greece, Bulgaria, the Netherlands, among others.

The country is 880 kilometres (547 miles) along its Himalayan axis, and its breadth varies from 150 to 250 kilometres (93 to 155 miles). The northern land border with China is 1236 kilometres (768 miles) long, and the eastern, western and southern borders with India is 1690 kilometres (1050 miles) long. Nepal is connected to China through twenty-one border points and to India through twenty-four border points.

The country is divided into three major terrains. The Himalayan high mountains take up 15 per cent of the area, the lowland Terai takes up 17 per cent and the remaining 68 per cent are mid-hills. Therefore, the infrastructure and development challenges are huge and require large resource outlays. At the same time, what this also means is that there is a huge opportunity for investment here. For instance, there are opportunities to redefine mobility by using mass transit solutions powered by the abundant electricity available.

Additionally, any new piece of infrastructure will need to take into consideration the impact of natural disasters; it will also need to mitigate and adapt to climate change, but again, what this also means is that there is an opportunity to start new trends in terms of aesthetics and design.

Nepal is the fiftieth most populated country in the world. It has more people than Australia and one-fifth fewer than Canada. If Nepal were in Europe, it would be the sixth most populated country. In Latin America, with the same population as Venezuela, it would be ranked fifth, just behind Peru.

When one thinks from a market perspective, Nepal has five times more people than Denmark, three times more than Portugal, and is similar in numbers to Malaysia, Ghana and other emerging economies. If one compares it with US states, Nepal would be the second largest in terms of population, behind California and closer to the size of Texas. If we compare it with Indian states, Nepal has 10 per cent fewer people than Andhra Pradesh, Orissa or Gujarat and is equivalent to the size of the twelfth-largest state in India. In China, it compares with Chongqing, the twentieth most populated administrative area, four times the size of Hong Kong's population and nine times the size of the Tibet Autonomous Region (TAR).

My quest for reintroducing and reimagining Nepal began during my time at the Hubert Humphrey Fellowship at Boston University in 2002 when I was asked to make a presentation about my country. It was then that it struck me that Nepal was not small. We have been conditioned to think of Nepal as 'tiny' based on reports by international agencies. When I wrote *Unleashing Nepal* in 2009, back then, Nepal ranked forty-first in terms of population in the world. It was hard for people to believe the size of the population, and at presentations, I was repeatedly asked to reconfirm. In between two countries with 1.4 billion people, interestingly, Nepal just constitutes 1 per cent of the population of the world, but in absolute terms, it is not small at all. Perhaps, because of our Nepali psyche of comparing ourselves with Bhutan, a country of 8,00,000 people approximately, and the Indian state of Sikkim with half a million people, we tend to mentally shrink the size of our country. But this needs to change. When we are looking at the future of Nepal, it is very important to view the population of the country as one that is sizeable both in terms of market and workforce.

Youth Are the Future

Nepal's biggest asset in its journey towards 2043 and the future is its young population. With 5.7 million, or 20 per cent of the population, in the age group between fifteen and twenty-four, Nepal is experiencing a 'youth bulge' as per the report by the United Nations Population Fund (UNFPA).[1] The 2021 census puts the number of young people under 25 at 50 per cent, and 73 per cent of the population is under forty.[2] The median age of Nepalis is 24.4 years. If we extrapolate the data from the Labour Survey Report (2017–18) by the Central Bureau of Statistics,[3] according to which half a million people are entering the job market each year, we can assume that in 2024 alone, 6,00,000 people entered the job market.

Until 1990, women represented only 19 per cent of the workforce due to societal structures, but today school enrolments for boys and girls are equal, and women are seeking jobs and entrepreneurial opportunities on par with men.[4] Young Nepali men and women are increasingly taking up jobs around the world and engaging in entrepreneurial pursuits. The UNFPA report states that 'the working-age population between 15–64 years is 64.6 per cent, and this will peak in 2051 at 69.4 per cent before starting to decline to 66.7 per cent in 2061'.[5]

Won Young Hong, who is the Country Representative for UNFPA Nepal, says: 'The large proportion of the population that is young can potentially bring an enormous demographic dividend with investments in education, healthcare and infrastructure. There is, however, a limited time window to seize this opportunity—of about thirty years—after which the population dynamic momentum will reverse as the lower rates of fertility start to impact working-age groups and the percentage of the elderly will continue to increase.'[6]

The time to focus on Nepal's youth is quite literally now.

Land-linked not Landlocked

Ever since Prithivi Narayan Shah, the first King of the Shah dynasty, proclaimed Nepal to be a yam squeezed between two boulders, Nepalis have grown up thinking that being landlocked is a big curse. I have continuously been trying to change this narrative and urge people to think of Nepal as being 'land-linked' to two of the largest populated countries in the world and two of the fastest-growing economies in the world. Being landlocked is not necessarily a difficult challenge to surmount. Being sea-locked can be equally challenging.

François-Xavier Léger, who served as the French ambassador to Nepal between 2018 and 2021, was posted in Fiji during the COVID-19 pandemic. He would talk about how many island nations, like Fiji, faced challenges when they tried to reach out to other countries for supplies and medical emergencies during the COVID-19 pandemic in 2020. He would say, 'Being sea-locked is a bigger challenge than being landlocked.'

While being land-linked to markets comprising over half a billion people within twelve hours' driving distance in South Asia is one way to look at it, one also needs to think of the possibilities that aerial connectivity opens up. A billion people are within the radius of a three-hour flying distance from airports in Nepal. This can help redefine not only tourism by air but also fly perishables and other high-value items to and from Nepal. Waterways, too, are currently completely unexplored, despite the ecosystem available for transportation via rivers to India and onward to Bangladesh. On 7-April-2018, the governments of Nepal and India issued a joint statement on 'expanding rail linkages, agreeing to construct a new electrified rail line, with India's financial support, connecting the border city of Raxaul in India to Kathmandu in Nepal'.[7] Similarly, work has begun on the feasibility study for railway connections between Kathmandu and the Chinese city of Kyirong and thereafter to the vast network of the Chinese Railway system too.[8] Hari Bansh Jha, a visiting fellow at the Observer Research Foundation, India, says that 'such a rivalry between Nepal's two neighbours, India in the south and China in the north, might help Nepal develop its linkages with the two countries'.[9]

Nepal Is Very Diverse

When I tell people that Nepal has the highest diversity in terms of people, language and culture in Asia, it is hard for people to believe me. Nepal is a multi-cultural, multi-racial, multi-linguistic and multi-ethnic country. It is a melting pot of Tibeto-Mongoloid and Indo-Aryan cultures. There are 142 caste/ethnic groups reported in the census in 2021. Chhetri is the largest caste/ethnic group, comprising 16.45 per cent of the population, followed by Hill Brahmins (Bahun) (11.29 per cent), Magar (6.9 per cent), Tharu (6.2 per cent), Tamang (5.62 per cent), Biswakarma (5.04 per cent), Newa (4.6 per cent), Musalman/Muslim (4.86 per cent), Yadav (4.21 per cent) and Rai (2.2 per cent). The Bahun–Chhettri ethnic groups dominate major political, government and social service delivery functions like healthcare, education and citizen support.

There are 124 languages in Nepal, and Nepali is the mother tongue of 45 per cent of the people and the official language recognized by the Nepal Constitution in 2015. English is not an official language, but with the proliferation of private education since the 1990s, English is understood and widely spoken across the country. Tourism in the earlier decades and thereafter, technology, the Internet and the aspiration to go abroad have accelerated the pace of adoption of the English language too.

The Shah and Rana rulers tried to present a pan-Nepali identity by imposing a common religion, language, festivals, national dress and symbolism. Until 2006, Nepal was a Hindu kingdom. In 2024, secular Nepal has 81.19 per cent Hindus, followed by Buddhists (8.21 per cent), Muslims (3.17 per cent) and Christians (1.76 per cent). Religious tolerance has been Nepal's hallmark, unshaken by the communal divisions in the region. The fact that two large mosques are located at a prime location in downtown Kathmandu, very close to the former palace, and the fact that large Sikh Gurudwaras were built with the royal patronage of the Malla Kings back in the day prove that there is a history and tradition of religious tolerance in Nepal.

Nepal continues to be a pilgrimage destination for Buddhists, Hindus and Jains. What makes it unique is the preservation of intangible heritage around day-to-day religious practices and cultural festivals that cannot be distinguished as a Buddhist or a Hindu practice or festival alone.

Nepal also has a special relationship with the idea of peace and harmony. The excavation of Lumbini began in 1896 and picked up speed when the world was reeling under the world wars. It helped resurrect Buddhism in Nepal. This establishment of historical evidence, of Buddha being born in current-day Nepali territory, and the spread of Buddhism in the latter part of the twentieth century in the West, has helped Nepal build its image as a harmonious country with peace-loving people. Late King Birendra even went around with a proposal to declare Nepal a zone of peace.[10]

That's not all.

People filling the visa application for Nepal are surprised to see that the forms mention Male, Female and Others in the gender box.[11] Nepal has been accepting towards LGBTQIA+ communities. Some laws protect sexual minorities, and the Nepal Constitution recognizes rights to such minorities.[12] Nepal also recognises same-sex marriage. State protection, along with societal tolerance, has made pride parades possible since 2019. Nepal, therefore, has become a preferred destination to travel and live for members of these communities and is only expected to grow exponentially in the future too.[13]

When the rule of the Shahs ended, people felt free to discover the plurality of Nepal. With local governments supporting local art, culture, cuisine, attire and festivals—and with the help of social media—Nepalis started to discover their rich history, heritage and diversity. In a blog published by the NEF, team member Nasala Prajapati examined the participation of youth in preserving the intangible cultural heritage of the Kathmandu

Valley. She argues, 'Youth bring a unique perspective to preserving cultural heritage, guided by nuances of maintaining culture and adapting to modernity.'[14]

In our meetings at beed, we continue to discuss how the youth will be the link to Nepal's past and future. During the Shah period, Newa festivals in the Kathmandu Valley were about a few old men playing some traditional instruments. In the Indra Jatra of 2024, it was wonderful to watch thousands of young men and women take to the streets in colourful attire, playing the traditional instruments. It was fascinating to see how young women would play the Dhime, the traditional drum. Then pause to take a selfie and post it on Instagram immediately and then take a quick moment to explain to a tourist in English what they were celebrating and then finally take a break for a quick café latte before calling it an evening.

The Cosmopolitan Capital of South Asia

Among the fun things I like doing in Kathmandu is taking my friends on gastronomical journeys across the Kathmandu Valley before visiting numerous art galleries and attending music and other cultural events. The opening up of Nepal to high-end tourism in the early 1950s brought to Kathmandu the European café culture and food from around the world. The city has some of the best Japanese, Korean and Italian restaurants. I tell my friends from Delhi and Mumbai that in their cities, authentic global cuisine is expensive, but in Nepal, one can eat a good bowl of Japanese Ramen noodles at the price of a local meal. Many art, film and music festivals dot the yearly calendar, bringing international artists and fans from around the world. There is a rise in student exchange and visiting programmes from around the world. If it was the 'hippy cult' in the 1970s that put Nepal on the global tourist map for young people, in the future, youth will throng to Nepal to discover the cosmopolitan nature of Kathmandu alongside its natural and cultural diversity. As a young student visiting Kathmandu from the US once told me, it felt like you were travelling through Europe at one-fifth of the cost, so you do tend to overlook things like bad roads, traffic etc.

Understanding 2500 Years of Nepal's History

When I introduce Nepal as the country with a traceable history of over 2500 years in South Asia, people get a bit baffled. Most of them would have read about Nepal's history starting from 1769, at the beginning of the rule of Prithvi Narayan Shah. While Nepal's history goes back nearly 2500 years, generally, 1776 is referred to as the starting point. The main reasons for this are the history books written during the Shah's rule. But let me provide a rapid summary of the important events in Nepal's history to give you an idea of how far back the story actually goes.

Nepal's traceable history goes all the way back to the pillars constructed by King Ashoka of the Maurya dynasty, who ruled between 268 and 232 BCE. On the pillar at Lumbini, there is an inscription that records the visit of King Ashoka to Lumbini, the birthplace of Buddha. Lumbini, which is located around 300 kilometres south-west of Kathmandu and about 20 kilometres away from the Indian border, is the birthplace of the Newa[15] prince Siddhartha Shakya (born 583 BCE), who went on to become Gautama Buddha. Much of Nepal's earlier history can be gleaned from the travels of Ashoka, his daughter Charumati, who settled in the Kathmandu Valley and the travelogues of Chinese pilgrims who travelled to the subcontinent at that time.

Nepal was originally referred to as 'Nepa: Mandala' in the Newa language or 'Nepal Mandala' in present-day Nepali. Prof.

David Gellner, an anthropologist at Oxford University, in his book *Idea of Nepal*, talks about how the Nepa: Mandala was imagined around 1500 years ago during the Licchavi dynasty's rule. He writes that the 'valley was conceived both religiously and politically as a mandala, that is to say, as a sacred space with a centre and geometrically arranged divinities in the cardinal directions'.[16] He further explains how the Vajracharya priests used this phrase in their rituals, and the term is also found in inscriptions from the Licchavi era.[17]

The history before Buddha's time can be found in the annals of the Kirats,[18] a tribe whose descendants live in present-day Eastern Nepal. The Yeledong era celebrated by the Kirats goes back 5000 years; they celebrated their 5085th year in 2025.[19] However, popular history accounts refer to the Kirats as having ruled Nepal from 1200 BCE until the Licchavis[20] defeated them in the third century. The Licchavis ruled the country from the third century CE until the ninth century CE. One important consequence of this rule is the marriage of Princess Bhrikuti to the Tibetan King Songtsen Gompo in the sixth century. This alliance marked the spread of Newa culture, script and the advent of Buddhism in Tibet.

From the tenth to the twelfth centuries, Nepal was ruled by Thakuri kings.[21] There is very little known about their rule apart from a few inscriptions with the names of the kings in a few temples in the Kathmandu Valley. Then, the Mallas,[22] a group within the Newa tribe, ruled Nepal from the twelfth century until 1769. Many of the Kathmandu Valley's palaces and temples were built during their era. The Mallas were defeated by the Gorkha King Prithvi Narayan Shah, who then went on to establish the Shah dynasty, which ruled Nepal from 1769 to 2006.

The Shah dynasty's 240-year rule from 1769 to 2006 can be divided into five phases. First, the unstable reign between 1769 and 1846 saw many intra-family squabbles within the Shah family. In 1850, Jung Bahadur Kunwar, a general during the rule of Rajendra Bikram Shah, initiated a massacre dubbed the 'Kot Massacre' to kill all his opponents. He usurped power and became the prime minister, taking on the title 'Jung Bahadur Rana'. He and his family ruled the country until February 1951. This second phase, between 1850 and 1950, which saw the Shah Kings relegated to titular heads, is otherwise popularly known as the Rana regime.

The third phase began with the Shahs regaining power in 1950, with King Tribhuvan Shah as a constitutional or parliamentary monarch at the head of a democratically elected government. However, Nepal's experiment with democracy was short-lived, with Tribhuvan's son, Mahendra, imprisoning democratic government leaders and imposing an autocratic, party-less *panchayat* system in 1960, which can be referred to as the fourth phase.

Mahendra died in 1972, and his son Birendra was named king. Birendra survived a referendum against the panchayat in 1980, but ten years later, he had to give up his autocratic rule after a popular uprising called Jana Andolan I in 1990. He agreed to become a constitutional monarch under a new constitution. However, he was killed by his son Deependra in a palace massacre in June 2001, along with ten other family members. This led to an unforeseen situation, and the only surviving brother of Birendra, Gyanendra, became king.

Around this time, a Maoist insurgency movement that had begun in 1996 was already crippling Nepal's politics. Gyanendra made the grave mistake of usurping power like his father. In October 2002, he dissolved the parliament. The proclamation of direct rule by Gyanendra in February 2005 brought the democratic forces and underground Maoists together. They signed a twelve-point agreement in New Delhi in November

2005. They had a common agenda—oust the king, reinstate the parliament, declare Nepal a republic and hold elections to a constituent assembly that would write a new constitution. The last Shah king was finally ousted by a second popular uprising, the Jana Andolan II, in April 2006. This was the final phase of the 240 years of rule by the Shah dynasty.

Nepal was declared a federal democratic republic in 2008, and elections to the Constituent Assembly were held to write a new constitution. The first constituent assembly, which served from May 2008 to May 2012, was not successful in drafting the constitution. After a year of a technocrat government led by a former chief justice of the Supreme Court, a second constituent assembly was elected in 2013. They were also not progressing well. The Gorkha earthquake of April 2015 gave a big jolt to the complacency of politicians and political parties. People demanded more from their government and had had enough. This forced a hurried promulgation of the new constitution in 2015.

Nepal Constitution 2015

The Constitution that was promulgated on 24 September 2015 was the seventh in sixty-five years. However, this Constitution was historic as it helped Nepal transition from an autocratic kingdom to a republic. Power was transferred from the king to the people, from a unitary government to a federal one, and from a Hindu kingdom to a secular country. The new Constitution recognized 'multi-ethnic, multi-lingual, multi-religious, multi-cultural and geographically diverse characteristics' of the country, which was a stark departure from the Hindu king-led kingdom that Nepal was before and which imposed the doctrine of 'one religion, one language and one people' on all its people.[23] This is a big milestone for Nepal because the diversity of Nepal is one of the key pillars to fall back on as we embark on unleashing Nepal's potential.

The 2015 Constitution was not a perfect document as it had many drawbacks. For instance, it did not address the concerns of some of the marginalized communities in Nepal. The people of Madhes living in the southern plains, popularly known as the Terai, felt left out in the final draft of the Constitution. They felt that issues around the citizenship of the Madhesis were not addressed adequately.[24] People could only get citizenship if the father was Nepali. In many cases in Terai, the mothers could be from India. Similarly, if Nepali women married men from India, their children would not get Nepali citizenship. They had hoped that this constitution would end years of discrimination, but it did not. India, too, was unhappy with the new constitution and thought it was discriminatory against the Madhesis. It slapped a blockade. This was the third blockade India had imposed since 1950, and it crippled the supply lines into a country that was already reeling under the impact of an earthquake.

Nevertheless, despite its shortcomings, in South Asia, Nepal's Constitution has been hailed as a progressive one, especially when it comes to guaranteeing the rights of women through reservation and the devolution of power to the local levels. Former assistant secretary-general of the United Nations, Kul Chandra Gautam, who currently occupies the highest position a Nepali has reached in the global sphere, has highlighted the significance of Nepal's Constitution to the world. In an opinion piece for *Inter Press Service*, he said, 'It is a constitution that enshrines many positive and progressive principles for the first time in Nepal's history. These include republicanism, federalism, secularism and an inclusive democracy. The themes of social justice, gender equality and inclusion run through different parts of the document, including specific affirmative actions for the benefit of historically marginalized and deprived communities, especially women and Dalits'.[25] It does institutionalize Nepal as a secular, federal republic with multi-party democracy, thus relegating the Hindu kingdom to the history books.

The new Constitution provides for a governance structure with separate branches for the legislative, executive and judiciary. The bicameral federal parliament, therefore, comprises the House of Representatives and the National Assembly. In the 275-member House of Representatives, 165 members are elected through the first-past-the-post electoral system, and 110 members through the proportional representation electoral system. The National Assembly, or the upper house, comprises fifty-nine members. Inclusion was a prime agenda, as the constitution provides mandatory representation for women and people from different communities and regions. For the first time, the constitution was written by the people of Nepal rather than one imposed by the rulers. For the first time, there is diversity in the parliament that reflects the diversity of the nation.

Nepal and the World

Nepal was never colonized by the British, even though it did lose approximately one-third of its territory to the British when it signed the Treaty of Sugauli in 1815.[26] The end of the British Empire in India and other parts of the world reinforced the sovereignty of Nepal as well. It signed the special India–Nepal Treaty in 1950 and got itself admitted to the United Nations. Until the 1990s, when the means of communication were limited to just the telephone—and even that was not something many people could afford—air travel was also restricted, and passport issuance was a privilege, Nepalis interacted mostly with India. Apart from tourists who visited Nepal, there was little other interaction with the outside world back then. Nepalis could not invest outside Nepal due to a draconian law that prohibited them from doing so.[27] Foreigners were also not allowed to invest in Nepal, except for a few who were pre-approved thanks to the involvement of members of the royal family. After passports started to be issued to Nepali citizens in 1996, global mobility became a reality for Nepalis within a week. One could even get a passport within a day by paying extra fees—and in their own districts—compared to the long, tardy Kathmandu-centric process. While Nepalis could travel freely outside, they still could not invest.[28]

Today, the growth of airlines in India and Asia and the emergence of Bangkok, Doha, Dubai, Kuala Lumpur and Singapore as hubs make the world accessible to Nepalis in one hop. The Internet and digital revolution have made the world a smaller place as one can buy tickets from one's phone, book hotels and travel the world for education, leisure or work. Nepalis today study, work or live in 180 countries around the world. We will discuss more about migration and remittances in Chapter 11, but for now, it should suffice to say that this has changed things in a very big way for Nepal's economy.

Understanding the Nepali Economy

When we are trying to reimagine Nepal, it becomes paramount to understand the way the Nepali economy has transformed since it was liberalized in 1990.

Nepal's economy has always been unique. Whenever I am asked to provide a perspective on Nepal to potential clients, I argue that talking about the GDP or the per capita income as indicators does not provide the real picture of the Nepali economy. This is because two major economic activities in Nepal do not feature in the GDP computation: remittances and activities around capital transfer related to land and assets.

Further, the economy is driven by consumption, and the government has been happy to tax consumption, making Nepal the country with the highest tax-to-GDP ratio in South Asia.[29] The government has also found different ways to increase taxes on consumption. Nepalis pay high import duties on vehicles, comparable to Singapore, as we discussed in the previous chapter. When the government saw that many Nepalis were frequently travelling—both domestically and internationally—they started to impose a 13 per cent value-added tax (VAT) on air tickets.[30] There are withholding taxes for any international firm providing education, consulting, or other services, which adds to the cost of services.[31] The bottom line has been to find an easy way—wherever there is spending, tax the spending! These are impediments in creating economic opportunities through reforms. Economic reforms are necessary to attract investments and create more revenues through the creation of jobs and an increase in business volumes.

Despite the fact that the GDP calculation isn't comprehensive, if one were to look at it as an indicator, Nepal's GDP has grown at a pace similar to other countries in South Asia. From a GDP of US$508 million in 1960,[32] when we began to record statistics, it staggered to US$4 billion in 1990, when multiparty democracy was restored, and crossed US$10 billion in 2006, when the Shah regime ended. Thereafter, the economy grew to US$44 billion in 2024, a fourfold jump in eighteen years. The Vision 2030 document projects Nepal's GDP at US$100 billion, and the Vision 2043 document of the government estimates that Nepal will be a US$423-billion economy with a per capita of US$12,100.[33]

I project that, given the current trends, by 2043, about 7 to 8 million Nepalis will be living outside Nepal, and the chances of formal and informal remittances crossing the US$100 billion mark are very high. Capital transfers will continue to grow, along with consumption. Higher literacy rates, better access to education and healthcare, and the shrinking of the world through innovation in communication and technology will all further increase the mobility of Nepalis, who will pursue 'higration' towards greener pastures.

When one dissects the Nepali economy, one discovers four distinct traits, particularly when it comes to consumer and spending behaviour. First, it is a rent-seeking populace and is slowly moving towards becoming an entrepreneurial one too. An expatriate consultant working with us was amazed to see the cafés filled with young Nepalis. We went to one of them, and he figured out that the prices were on par with cafés in the US. He was asking me how people can afford this; he had been reading reports about how Nepal is a poor country. I explained to him, as I do to many: that most Nepalis who spend the money do not have to earn it. Many of them receive remittances and therefore have the luxury to spend it the way they want. Four out of five households in Nepal have someone sending them remittances from abroad.[34]

Second, many of them also earn rent from inherited properties or properties they have built after selling inherited land. With 81 per cent of Nepalis living in their own homes, building a property for one's own use and renting it out is very popular.[35] When we at beed management worked on the remittances study in 2023, we realized that they amounted to nearly US$10 billion, or, in other words, a quarter of Nepal's GDP. We were also startled to discover that there was an equal amount of informal remittances as well. This means the total remittance is US$20 billion! For every dollar of remittances that come through formal channels like banking and money transfer agencies, there is an equal dollar that does not reach Nepal. This money is either retained in the country where it is earned or it gets to Nepal through informal channels like *hundi* or gold, electronics, and other goods.

Third, we were quite taken aback when we realized that social spending on festivities, events and lifestyle augmentation does not change during any crisis. Weddings and social functions continued undeterred in the aftermath of the earthquake, the blockade or the COVID-19 pandemic.[36] An intern from the UK, who was working with us, happened to be in Nepal during the unprecedented floods in his neighbourhood in October 2024. He was shocked that the damage caused by the floods did not deter his landlord or the neighbourhood from going ahead with the festivities.

Fourth, compared to other regional markets, peer pressure from family and friends seem to drive decision making rather than individual judgement. Ujaya Shakya, an advertising professional and author of *Brandsutra*, has been telling companies that the Nepali consumer is different. He explains that the youth, even in smaller towns and not just in Kathmandu, are more conscious of their lifestyle. They want better things in life.[37]

People running educational consulting businesses often share stories of students arriving in droves and making decisions based purely on peer pressure. Similarly, in our work with clients in the automobile sector, we at beed management have observed—backed by research—that decisions on which vehicle to purchase are more influenced by peer dynamics than by research. Our studies show that automobile companies resort to selling to social influencers and pushing their message through word of mouth.

Lastly, there is a large informal economy. A study by the Central Department of Economics and the Nepal Rastra Bank in 2024 puts the size of the informal economy at 38.6 per cent. The study also reveals that 99 per cent of real estate transactions happen in the informal space. Further, the study corroborates the existence of the well-known informal trade across the 1770 kilometre border with India.[38] There is a lot of potential

Private Sector-Led Economic Transformation

The private sector has been the engine of growth in Nepal since the economy was liberalized in 1990. It accounts for 80 per cent of economic activity and contributes 81 per cent to the GDP.[39] In 1990, there were four government-owned banks and two in the private sector. Private sector financial institutions started to grow, and the bulk of deposits and credit are with these 107 private sector institutions. By 2007, deposits had grown to NPR 367 billion and credit to NPR 330 billion.[40] In 2023, these figures had increased to NPR 5361 trillion in deposits and NPR 4.844 trillion in credits.[41]

Similarly, from just three insurance companies with a combined premium of US$40 million in 2000,[42] by 2024, forty life and non-life insurance companies were operating, with a total premium of US$1.1 billion. Beyond traditional sectors like carpets and handicrafts, activities in the information communication and technology (ICT) sector, which began only in 2000, now contribute 37 per cent of Nepal's exports[43] and have even crossed the US$1 billion mark in 2024.

The opening of private education in 1996 proved to be a game-changer. By 2023, out of 7.8 million students, 3.3 million were enrolled in private schools.[44] That same year, 1,00,000 students went abroad to study. Many of these students used educational consulting services, and the private educational consulting industry—non-existent in 1990—has now become a significant sector.

In healthcare, private hospitals that began emerging in the early 1990s have since proliferated across Nepal. Tourism has evolved from being international-centric to a mix of both international and domestic. From a quarter million tourists spending US$40 million in 1990,[45] the number rose to over a million international tourists spending US$464 million in 2023.[46] Domestic tourism now contributes twice as much revenue as international tourism. A nuclear family structure, improved connectivity and the rise of social media have all contributed to the growing number of Nepalis travelling within the country. In September 2023, during a day trip to Pokhara, I was astonished to learn that on their best day, airlines operated forty-nine flights between Pokhara and Kathmandu, carrying over 3500 passengers, compared to just two flights a day in 1990 using nineteen-seater Twin Otter aircraft!

The story of electricity production and consumption is mind-boggling. Nepal consumed just 176 MW of electricity in 1990, and the revenue of the Nepal Electricity Authority stood at US$24 million.[47] As consumption grew in the 1990s and 2000s, Nepal experienced scheduled load-shedding (blackouts) from 2007 to 2017. In 2023, consumption was nearing 10,000 GWh, with utility revenue crossing the NPR 100 billion mark, or US$751 million. At its peak, 657 MW was exported to India in 2023. By 2035,[48] Nepal plans to generate between 25,000 and 30,000 MW of electricity, as domestic demand is projected to reach 12,000 MW. India, through a cabinet decision in May 2023, has agreed to purchase 10,000 MW, which is expected to yield an additional US$5 billion in revenues.

The future growth of Nepal will be driven by the export of electricity, building of power-intensive industries, growth of tourism, service exports and rising demand and consumption fuelled by higher remittances and capital transfer gains. Societal structures will also evolve, and the idea of saving for the next seven generations will become a nostalgic tale that grandfathers tell their grandchildren. This story of economic transformation must be told as we reintroduce Nepal.

LDC Graduation 2026: From Development Aid to Trade and Investments

In Nepal's economic development, foreign aid has played a significant role. Bilateral support from India, China, the UK, the US and other countries has helped Nepal build much-needed infrastructure. Multilateral agencies such as UN bodies, the World Bank and the Asian Development Bank (ADB) have provided direct project support and budgetary support to the government. Foreign aid—barring the controversy surrounding the US Millennium Challenge Corporation (MCC) grant—is not looked at with suspicion.[49] Development partners receive considerable attention from politicians and government bureaucrats, as much of their foreign travel and constituency funding depends on such support. Jobs in development agencies are highly coveted and are often the first choice for young Nepalis over private sector opportunities. Nepalis have also made significant inroads into bilateral and multilateral development agencies around the world. Recently, it was heartening to hear stories of a farewell function in Nairobi for a Nepali working in the UN, where more than a hundred Nepali expatriates from various agencies gathered to wish him well.

However, the role of these agencies is set to change as Nepal graduates from LDC status to that of a middle-income country in 2026. Moreover, the closure of the US aid agency in January 2025, and the subsequent ripple effect of prioritizing aid for areas of strategic interest, will also reduce foreign assistance. The pace of conversion of international interest from aid to trade and investments will shape the future of Nepal.

This transition also calls for reforms to ensure that Nepal can sustain its progress. In this context, following its graduation, Nepal is expected to attract international investors and businesses through which it can maintain strong socio-economic ties. In this regard, it will face challenges on three major fronts. First, there will be an impact on the competitiveness of certain exports, as they will lose the preferential duties reserved for LDCs. Second, much of the current policy work is funded by bilateral and multilateral agencies—a situation that is likely to change. Third, there will be a reduction in development assistance flowing into the country. In other words, free money will dry up.

Despite these challenges, I firmly believe that LDC graduation will pave the way for a faster pace of economic growth driven by international investment. This inflow of capital will readily offset the current flow of free money through aid, grants and interest-free loans.

Integrating to Regional Blocs—BBIN and Beyond

The trade war between China and the US that began in January 2018 and the border skirmishes between China and India in May 2020 have altered the future of geopolitics for Nepal. Remaining neutral is becoming increasingly difficult, and this will only become more challenging in the future. Regional blocs have undergone multiple transformations, with the US pushing a new Indo–Pacific strategy to counter China's Belt and Road Initiative (BRI). Nepal played an instrumental role in the establishment of the South Asian Association for Regional Cooperation (SAARC) in 1985, with its headquarters located in Kathmandu. However, since the last summit in November 2014 in Kathmandu, SAARC has remained dormant, primarily due to the conflict between two member nations: India and Pakistan.

But it is not the end of the road for Nepal. The SAARC debacle has led to the formation of an informal group called BBIN (Bangladesh, Bhutan, India and Nepal) in 2014. This platform offers hope for regional connectivity, enabling Nepal to increase the movement of people, goods and services across the other three countries. Its multi-modal transport agreement has the potential to boost regional trade and tourism as well. Energy trade between hydro-based electricity suppliers in Bhutan and Nepal, and buyers in Bangladesh and India, will help advance the clean energy agenda. Drawing on the success of initiatives such as the East Africa Cooperation (EAC), the evolution of this platform will determine the pace of Nepal's regional integration. I have been personally involved in the BBIN framework on behalf of institutions in Nepal. Progress is slow, but we all recognize that this is the only way forward.

In January 2024, in an op-ed that I co-authored with Nilanjan Ghosh of Observer Research Foundation, India, we introduced a new concept: The Nepal–India–Bangladesh (NIB) Economic Corridor. By 2026, we should have a framework for this as the intentions behind Viksit Bharat 2047, Nepal 2043 and Digital Bangladesh will converge.

Conclusion

Keeping all of this in mind, the question in front of Nepal is not whether it has the potential to graduate to a high-income country by 2043. There is little doubt that the potential exists. The real question is whether all the stakeholders are willing to see this potential and walk the talk to make Nepal 2043 an actual reality.

Chapter 2

Advantage Location

Every five years, in my ancestral temple in Patan, 127 Dipankara Buddhas are brought out and placed in the large courtyard of Nagbaha, one of the sixteen '*bahas*'[1] or courtyards in the city of Patan. The beautifully carved deities have postures resembling the different Hindu deities of South India, yet are clad in Chinese silk fineries adorned with Mongoloid motifs. I often reflect that this may be the perfect symbol of our deep and simultaneous historical and cultural ties with both China and India.

The people living in the high mountains of northern Nepal have food, clothing and culture that resemble those of the TAR of China. This is in addition to strong social and marital ties to the region. Similarly, the people living in the southern plains of Nepal share the same—in fact, deeper—ties with the bordering Indian states. The question is how Nepal can leverage these relationships to its advantage in the run-up to 2043.

In this chapter, I look at Nepal and its relationship with its two key neighbours. I begin by contextualizing historical perspectives on Nepal and its neighbours. I then explore how globalization is being redefined, how global alignments are shifting and how the world's focus is turning towards Asia, particularly China and India. Finally, within this new world order, I discuss where Nepal stands vis-à-vis its relations with the world and its two neighbours, and how Nepal can leverage the opportunity of being the precious piece of real estate between China and India.

The Neighbours

While no ruler in Nepal ever seemed to have ties with Tibet in the North apart from the marriage of Princess Bhrikuti to the King of Tibet, most of the royal families that ruled Nepal, after the Kirat rulers, had deep ties with India. The Lichhavi and Malla dynasty that ruled until the Shah dynasty took over comprised kings who came from India. Even the Shah kings belonged to a branch of the Rajput family in Chittaur in the current state of Rajasthan in India. The Shahs and Ranas that ruled between 1776 to 2006, therefore, also had deep marital and social ties with India.

These relationships have continued well into the present, albeit in different forms. Nepal's relationship with the two countries has always been governed by special treaties and arrangements. The India–Nepal Treaty of Peace and Friendship, signed in 1950, grants special privileges to Nepali citizens residing in India and Indian citizens residing in Nepal. This includes visa-free access; individuals can also seek employment or set up businesses as they would in their own countries.[2] A transit treaty gives Nepal access to Indian ports, and a preferential trade agreement offers benefits to both countries in conducting business across boundaries.[3] Indian-licensed vehicles can enter Nepal by obtaining a permit at the border and paying a daily fee.[4] Similarly, Nepali licence plate vehicles can enter India through a permit issued by the Embassy of India in Kathmandu[5]. Nepali goods also receive special treatment in the Indian market. For instance, products made in Nepal using at least 30 per cent Nepali raw materials or labour are exempt from import duties in India.[6] This favourable arrangement has encouraged India-based multinational companies such as Unilever and Dabur to establish operations in Nepal.[7] The Nepali rupee is pegged to the Indian Rupee at a fixed exchange rate. Most credit and debit cards, as well as digital payment platforms issued in one country, function seamlessly in the other.

Similarly, with China too, Nepal has signed a Sino-Nepalese Treaty of Peace and Friendship in 1960. This was prompted after Tibet became a part of China in 1959. The Trade and Payment Agreement was signed only in 1981. A transit and transport agreement signed in 2016 freed Nepal from being dependent solely on Indian ports. Just as Nepal gets duty-free access to Indian markets in some cases, 8000 items enjoy the privilege of duty-free access to China.[8] Nepalis living within 30 kilometres of the border are allowed to cross the border based on their citizenship cards. They can not only undertake day journeys for trade but also obtain work permits and work. Chinese licence plate vehicles are allowed to enter Nepal, like Indian licence plate vehicles, by taking a permit at the border and paying a daily fee.[9] Access for Nepali licence plate vehicles into China, however, is complicated, as multiple procedures need to be completed. The Chinese yuan exchange rate is linked to the US dollar, and no separate fixed exchange rate exists. Chinese payment platforms like UnionPay are well accepted in Nepal, and many of the Chinese digital payments, such as Alipay and WeChat Pay, work well in Nepal.

After 1950 and all the way up to the 2000s, most of the political, business, and social elite in Nepal went to pursue their higher studies in India. In 2024, out of the hundred thousand students who went to study outside Nepal, thirteen thousand went to India.[10] While it has been rare for Nepali students to go to China to study, in 2023, nearly three thousand students chose China for their further studies. Aneka Rebecca Rajbhandari, Co-founder of The Araniko Project, a student who did her undergraduate studies in China and went back for her graduate studies, told me why more and more Nepali students are opting to study in China these days. 'Unlike in the past when Nepali students would venture into China to study medicine and engineering, in recent years, non-science subjects like economics, business, and the Chinese language are also becoming popular,' she says. 'Many Nepali students studying in China are driven by the full-scholarship opportunities that colleges offer, regardless of the subject. This also means that they are even motivated to pursue a Chinese-taught degree. Then there are career/business prospects in or with China, and the advantage of geographical proximity to Nepal, that have become other factors that draw students to China.'

Let's now look at some other statistics pertaining to employment and work. As per the World Development Report of 2023, produced by the World Bank, Nepali workers who go to India to work send back US$1.5 billion each year, and Indian workers working in Nepal send home US1.5 billion each year.[11] Overall, Nepal's relationship with the world has undergone a major transformation, and this is because Nepalis, who used to travel to India for education, in search of jobs, medical treatment, and pilgrimage, are now finding newer destinations.

As for China, in 2023, there were around 3500 Nepalis in mainland China and around 30,000 in Hong Kong. Around 7500 Chinese workers obtained work permits to work in Nepal in 2023, compared to a mere 1316 Nepalis who obtained work permits for China.[12] In fact, the relationship with China was barely existent until Nepalis took up the Hong Kong identity card and became Chinese nationals in 1997. I continue to maintain, as in my previous writings, that Nepal started looking up to China and conversely, China's interest in Nepal grew only after the Indian blockade of 2015.

In effect, the point I'm trying to make is this: Nepal will need to maintain, grow, and carefully balance its relationship with India and China, and here's why. In 2043, China and India's GDP will be US$48 trillion and US$28 trillion respectively.[13] These two countries will be two of the largest economies in the world by 2050.[14] In other words, in 2043, Nepal will be land-linked to close to 3 billion people—1.344 billion in China and 1.633 billion in India.[15] For Nepal's future, it is only natural that it takes maximum advantage of the meteoric rise of its neighbours. How? Well, before I answer that question, let's first understand the big picture on how the world is changing, where the opportunities lie, and how China and India are likely to transform themselves.

Global Megatrends and a Changing World

Today, the global order is changing, with Western dominance waning in the economy, trade, commerce, and services. When President Trump returned to power in 2025, he signed a series of executive orders that surprised the world. The US pulled out of the climate agreement and the World Health Organisation. USAID, the US development aid agency that provided nearly 42 per cent[16] of global humanitarian assistance, was shut down. The actions of the US will see multilateral agencies weakening, especially the availability of funds for work on climate change, diversity and health. Other countries in Europe are prioritizing their spending towards security, thereby also cutting the funds available for aid. The US dominance in influencing global work around strengthening democracy, promoting human rights, and building an inclusive society will be highly impacted, and time will only tell what the long-term impact of the series of decisions the US administration under President Trump made in the first two months of its second term will be.

Elsewhere, there are calls for some of the world's oldest institutions to transform themselves. For instance, on 1 July 2024, the Bretton Woods Institutions celebrated their 80th anniversary. This prompted deep reflections on how times have changed in the past eighty years and how serious reforms are necessary to ensure that these institutions keep up with the changing times.[17] The helplessness of the United Nations in the Gaza carnage that began in October 2023 has also raised eyebrows at the UN's efficacy as a peace-keeping body.

Geo-politically, in the first quarter of the twenty-first century, we have seen some major fault lines emerging. There is the war in Ukraine, the carnage in Gaza, and the cold war between China and the US. The United Kingdom is figuring out the post-Brexit world, and Europe is seeing the rise of right-wing politicians. After the victory of President Trump in the November 2024 US elections, there is a fear of the rise of right-wing powers in Europe.[18] Meanwhile, amidst all of this chaos, countries in Africa, Central and South America, along with Southeast Asia, are trying to make their presence felt. The global order is slowly transforming itself.

While the world is shrinking, thanks to better communication systems, transport connectivity, and the Internet, it is also being subjected to newer challenges like cybersecurity, health hazards and the impact of climate change. The proliferation of artificial intelligence can be both a boon and a bane, and how countries are going to negotiate their relationship with AI remains to be seen.

Amidst all of this, therefore, newer definitions of globalization are emerging. Ngozi Okonjo-Iweala, the director-general of the World Trade Organization (WTO), has been propagating the concept of re-globalization. At the World Economic Forum (WEF) in Davos in 2024, she said, 'We need to think of globalization not in the way it was done before, but differently. And we need to make sure that those who did not benefit during the first round benefit this time. Gobalization got a bad name because poor people from rich countries were left out, and poor countries or developing countries were at the margin. In the new paradigm, we don't want to repeat the same story.'[19] Indian Foreign Minister S. Jaishankar reiterated this call for re-globalization, calling for a more diversified version with more democratic globalization, where the global South will equally benefit.[20]

Now, in this context of the changing world, I look at four major factors that, in my opinion, will impact how business, trade, economy, and movement of people will happen globally and how they can potentially fuel this re-globalization.

First, companies in the private sector today are very large, and they are the ones who influence policies, the legislative framework, and which governments come to power. If Apple or Microsoft[21] were a country, it would be the sixth largest in the world, with a market capitalization of about US$3 trillion, equal to the GDP of the United Kingdom.[22] Gautam Adani, the business tycoon of India, at his peak in 2022, was worth US$144 billion, which is equivalent to the GDP of the tenth-largest state in India.[23] In Nepal alone, Forbes billionaire businessman Binod Chaudhary's wealth is more than the GDP of the province of Karnali.[24] Business tycoons and their companies are set to become larger than countries and their constituent provinces or states. How these businessmen shape their businesses will also shape the future of their countries.

Businesses are also taking a personality-led approach rather than a corporate one, and this too is shaping political discourse. Elon Musk, the richest person in the US in 2024, according to the *Forbes* list,[25] has been able to influence politics deeply, including buying the social media company Twitter, rebranding it as X and creating rules of his own. Musk has also created ripples after being nominated by President Trump in January 2025 as the chief of the Department of Government Efficiency (DOGE) to regulate government spending.[26] His wealth soared from US$260 billion[27] before the elections, and he became the first person to cross the US$400 billion wealth mark.[28] At the presidential inauguration, everyone watched as billionaires got priority seating.

Similarly, in India, the largest business groups owned by Mukesh Ambani and Gautam Adani own the majority of the media houses and have been successful in defining the overarching narrative. This narrative is generally pro-government and pounds back at the opposition, thereby challenging pluralism.[29] We do not see this trend reversing in the immediate future. In fact, we will see the normalization of the business-politics relationship as the new normal. In Nepal, this may prompt Nepali businesspeople, who once questioned Nepali dollar billionaire Binod Chaudhary's winning elections to become a parliamentarian, to emerge with greater political aspirations.

The second factor that I think we should consider is the rise of China as a competing force to the United States. China has been at the forefront of providing aid and lending to countries, especially in Africa. A Boston University study concluded that, at $170.08 billion, China's estimated total lending between 2000 and 2022 is 64 per cent of the World Bank's US$264.15 billion and almost five times the African Development Bank's (AfDB) US$36.85 billion in sovereign loans to Africa.[30] China, unlike multilateral development organizations, enters a country as an aid provider, lender, and investor. It is now the economy that competes with the United States in the business of wielding power and influence over other countries. The third factor is that there are fewer countries today that continue to receive aid, and by 2043, there will be even fewer countries left in the low-income category,[31] which means that the current aid architecture of mixing development assistance and humanitarian aid could potentially become irrelevant. With the shutting down of USAID, newer ways of humanitarian assistance and support during crises will have to be devised, especially for places like Gaza or Sudan.

Development aid has been substituted by trade and investments in many parts of the world, which means countries will also have to compete to attract investments and international attention. Economic growth will hinge on leveraging foreign investment, technology transfer and firms going global. Countries will invest in other countries to leverage their own growth; revenue from returns on investments abroad will be as important as exports were in the twentieth century.

In the twentieth century, Western countries went to other nations with aid, first as donors and later as development partners, and they shaped the discourse around human rights, governance, democracy and other values. However, investors and global firms have a different approach to these issues nowadays, as they are mostly business-oriented and may not care about many areas that state actors tend to be interested in. The fourth factor is that the future of economic growth and development will be led by Asia. Kishore Mahbubani, a thought leader from Singapore, argues that for the past two thousand years, apart from the last two hundred, Asian countries have dominated the world, and it is quite natural that this will repeat.[32] Parag Khanna, the author of the book *The Future Is Asian*, has simple facts to back his argument: 'Half of the world lives in Asia, and with GDP calculated under the PPP method, Asia's GDP is 54% of the world.' [33] Countries within Asia are doing business with each other like never before. ASEAN has displaced the US as China's leading business partner and China has dislodged the US as India's leading business partner.[34]

New Platforms, New Groupings

After the two World Wars, the world witnessed two major groupings based on military alliances: North Atlantic Treaty Organization (NATO) and the Warsaw Pact. However, over the years, the nature of groupings has changed dramatically. They have largely been driven by trade, economics, and financial control. For instance, over the years, the WEF, founded on 24 January 1971 by German engineer Klaus Schwab, has become an influential platform. Year after year, global business and country leaders compete to find a spot to speak or present at the annual conference held in Davos, Switzerland. A former colleague working at the WEF told me that a mere 2500 delegates get access to all the important meeting venues. The rest, 7500, have to be satisfied with attending ancillary events. In 2025, Mongolia was there as a 'showcase country' to attract global attention and investment. Sponsorships are not cheap, as an all-access elite badge to the event in 2025 was CHF 27,000 (US$30,000)![35]

I tend to agree with former Brookings expert William Burke-White, when he writes: 'Economic and corporate leadership on global governance challenges is so urgently needed today for two reasons: First, political leadership around the world is stalled or gridlocked, preventing progress; and second, the global challenges we face—from climate emergency to the perils of populist nationalism, from the regulation of cyberspace and the ownership of data to the dangers and opportunities of mass human movements—cannot be solved without action by wealth-holders and decision-makers of the corporate community.'[36]

The departure of the US from multilateral platforms starting in 2025 will push countries to think of newer platforms, and there are plenty to consider. US billionaire Michael Bloomberg-owned Bloomberg New Economy Forum is fast becoming a platform that attracts diverse ideas that shape the world. India, through its Observer Research Foundation, has developed the Raisina Dialogues to extend their own idea of multilateralism and national interest. The China Center for Globalization (CCG) has set up its own platform to define its own version of globalization and multilateralism by hosting the China and Globalization Forum. Their emphasis is on 'Global Vision for China, Chinese Wisdom for the World'.[37]

Trade blocs are the new tools of cooperation. That the Eurozone opted for a single currency, the Euro, demonstrates how far regional groupings can go. A meeting of the Regional Comprehensive Economic Partnership (RCEP), Asia Pacific Economic Cooperation (APEC), or the Association of Southeast Asian Nations (ASEAN) is considered equally important, or more important, than the annual talk show at the General Assembly of the United Nations. Working in Africa, I have personally witnessed the rise of the East Africa Cooperation (EAC) as a futuristic platform. With global divisions on issues like the war in Ukraine or the conflict in Gaza, members of the United Nations are divided, and the right to veto diminishes the possibility of a consensus.

The disregard towards multilateral institutions by President Trump that started during his four-year rule from 2016 to 2020 provided impetus to other leaders with nationalistic and authoritarian streaks to follow suit. Further, China, emerging with the Belt and Road Initiative (BRI) as its own structure for globalization and President Xi Jinping projecting China as a messiah of globalization in his speech at Davos in 2019, have also further changed equations around global integration.

Then there is the unique case of BRICS.

Building BRICS

China and India together formed this informal alliance with Brazil, Russia, and South Africa in 2009, and six more countries were inducted in 2024. Like the search for an alternative to tackle Cold War challenges through the Non-Aligned Movement, BRICS offers hope of a new order. This explains why many countries are applying for membership in this group. The GDP of BRICS in 2023 is 36 per cent of the global GDP, and the population of its members will be 47 per cent of the world's population by 2050.[38] The GDP, by PPP method, has already crossed the total size of the GDP of the G7 countries.[39]

But it needs to be remembered that BRICS emerged out of an economic compulsion. Neither does it provide military or security support to its various member countries, nor is it a group involved in policing nations or providing peacekeepers.

I see that BRICS will evolve to become a platform that offers a combined currency to challenge the US dollar for the position of the dominant global currency. In January 2025, India and Indonesia, two BRICS members, signed a historic trade agreement to settle transactions in Indian Rupees or Indonesian Rupiah and not US Dollars. Indonesian media outlet *Jakarta Globe* had an eye-catching headline, 'De-Dollarization: Indonesia, India Look Forward to Local Currency Trade'.[40] We have seen the demise of travellers' cheques and people carrying authorised currency equivalent to dollar bills. With digital platforms making inroads into many countries, digital currency is clearly the future. Both India and China have made great progress in this field; they are far ahead of the U.S. and Europe when it comes to digital platforms for money. During the 16th BRICS Summit in Kazan, Russia held in October 2024, BRICS Pay, as an alternative payment settlement mechanism to SWIFT, gained further momentum.[41] The declaration at the end of the Summit called for 'strengthening of correspondent banking networks within BRICS and enabling settlements in local currencies in line with the BRICS Cross-Border Payments Initiative (BCBPI)'.[42]

India and China's interests in the long run converge; their short-term challenges will not deter this convergence, in my opinion. Freedom from the US dollar is a significant reason for this convergence.[43] The pace of growth and the influence of BRICS will depend on the extent to which China and India cooperate on economic matters, putting aside their political and geopolitical differences. The question is whether they can actually pull it off. I continue to believe that they will, in fact, do so. In October 2024, China and India agreed to disengage militarily and move towards border settlement.[44] A visit by National Security Advisor Ajit Doval to China in December 2024 was followed by the travel of the Indian foreign secretary to China in January 2025. Whether it is border dispute settlement, the resumption of direct flights between the two countries, the opening up of tourism and pilgrimage, or other forms of cooperation, in the changing world order, both countries, in my opinion, see more benefit in working together than being at loggerheads.

Now, let's take a look at how India and China are perceived and are behaving on the global stage.

India's Assertion on the Global Stage

When India hosted the summit of G20 countries in September 2023 and invited the African Union to join, it was touted as a 'coming of age' party.[45] Prime Minister Narendra Modi projected it as India's declaration, an attempt to push for a seat at the UN Security Council.[46] India joined the grouping of Quad, formed in 2007, referring to the diplomatic network of four countries—Australia, India, Japan and the US—to counter China's influence in the region both militarily and diplomatically. There have been more groupings in recent years. I2U2 is a partnership between India, Israel, the UAE and the US that's working to tackle global challenges and advance economic opportunities.[47] India has been invited to the G7 group meeting, a group of the largest industrialised democracies. Apart from BRICS, India is also a member of the Shanghai Cooperation Organization (SCO), established jointly by China and Russia in 2001. So, India's participation in non-Western groupings such as BRICS and SCO compensates for its growing presence in the Western-dominated Quad and G7.

In a guest column for *The Economist* in November 2023, the foreign minister of India, S. Jaishankar, wrote that the 'country is more confident, capable and responsive than ever before'. He went on to add, 'India demonstrated during 2023 how to navigate the east-west polarisation around Ukraine and bridge the north-south developmental divide. The impact of skewed globalisation, Covid damage, conflict in Ukraine, big-power competition, climate events, and now violence in the Middle East have certainly made the world far more volatile and unpredictable. To rise in such challenging circumstances requires nimble and "multi-vector" Indian diplomacy.'[48] Prime Minister Narendra Modi, after getting elected for the third time in 2024, decided to go to Russia in July 2024. This was his first foreign visit in his new term, and it was seen as an attempt to send a very clear message on how India is pursuing this multi-vector diplomacy.[49]

Overall, India seeks a multipolar world—a multi-polar world where it deals independently with China, Russia and the US.[50] It wants to send a clear message to the world that it is a rising global political power that will, at one point, compete and collaborate directly with these countries.

India has even launched its Vision for 2047 by when it is to graduate to a high-income country. Viksit Bharat or a Developed India was a vision launched in December 2023 that declares that the country is about to take a 'quantum leap'.[51]

If this is India's plan, China isn't too far away.

China Challenging US Domination

In June 2023, China surprised the world by brokering a deal between Iran and Saudi Arabia, countries that were constantly under tension. This is the sort of deal that we previously saw the US and Western countries brokering. China, by 2049, aims to 'build a modern socialist country that is prosperous, strong, democratic, culturally advanced and harmonious'.[52] While the developed nations of the West look at developing nations with a donor-recipient mindset, China looks at them as fellow travellers, as China was also a poor country until 1980. Michael Shuman at the Atlantic Council writes that 'China claims to sympathize with those societies in Africa, Asia, Latin America and the Middle East, which also had their destinies altered by European imperialism and continue to face frustrations with persistent poverty and a lack of influence in a world still dominated by their former rulers'.[53] Along with Russia, China has promoted the SCO, a Eurasian grouping where Nepal has been elevated from a dialogue partner to an observer country.

China's ambitious tool, however, is the Belt and Road Initiative (BRI). Also referred to as the New Silk Road, it is an ambitious infrastructure project that began in 2013 just after a year of President Xi Jinping becoming China's President. There is a dedicated 'Belt and Road Portal'[54] that provides updates on the different BRI projects, and a segment is dedicated to 'Xi Jinping[55] that is full of updates on BRI and its agreements and projects with different countries. The Green Finance and Development Center quoting the website portal states: 'In February 2025, the number of countries that have joined the Belt and Road Initiative (BRI) by signing a Memorandum of Understanding (MoU) with China and have not exited the BRI is 149.'[56]

China's challenge to the US has not come out of military power but through establishing economic power. The *New York*

Times in January 2025 carried a piece with the headline, 'China's Trade Surplus Reaches a Record of Nearly $1 Trillion.'[57] This surprised many, as the general impression was that China was hit hard by COVID-19. China's major trading partner is the ASEAN trading bloc, with trade of over US$1 trillion in 2024,[58] followed closely by Europe at US$975 billion,[59] and in 2022, with the US at US$758 billion.[60] China sees itself as the biggest global trader, and now its ambitions are fixed on pushing its own currency, the yuan, into the world. In July 2023, the Renminbi overtook the US dollar as the major currency of trade with China.[61] China first allowed trade payments to be settled in yuan in 2009. This included settlements for freight, services and current account transfers, as well as capital transaction settlements, including for stocks and bonds. China's opening of its capital markets and a push away from the dollar in trade have been key factors in the shift toward the yuan. India, which has been one of the biggest buyers of Russian oil after the Ukraine conflict, has been making payments in Yuan.[62]

As Singaporean diplomat Kishore Mahbubani said in a conversation with me in January 2024, The Chinese global economic model of cooperation is to focus on mutually beneficial economic projects, while staying away from interfering in the internal affairs of any country or engaging in military alliances.

The Opportunity of the Yam

In *Unleashing the Vajra*, which I wrote before the skirmish between India and China in 2020, I argued that the interests of the two countries would converge in the long run. I continue to maintain that opinion. With China becoming India's largest trading partner in 2024,[63] the opportunities that both countries see in aligning their interests will only bring them closer. Tanvi Madan of the Brookings Institution argues that there will be a China-India deal soon, as 'New Delhi does not want another escalation at the border, where the four-year-old military standoff continues. Conflict could disrupt India's economic growth and other objectives and would have an uncertain outcome given the Sino-Indian capabilities gap.'[64] A friend of mine, who manufactures electronic products in India, with large parts of input components coming from China, said that it is important to realize that, as is the case for many components like cobalt, China has a global monopoly. Further, given the potential of tourism and travel between the two countries and their large populations, I continue to believe there will be a reconciliation. At its peak in 2019, there were 539 weekly direct flights between the two countries. Why would the two countries squander such opportunities? I believe the rapprochement has begun with the end of the military standoff, the initiation of people-to-people connections and a future of cooperation.

In a worst-case scenario, if relations between China and India sour, Nepal's location will become important. Singapore and Thailand would not have grown if there had been no Vietnam War. The UAE's growth has hinged on the sanctions against Iran, the wars in Iraq and Afghanistan. Like Indian tea reaching Pakistan after being packaged in Dubai, we will see Indian products heading to China but packaged in Nepal, and Chinese goods assembled in Nepal before they head to the Indian market. Let us not forget that Nepal's economy in the seventies and eighties, before Indian liberalization flourished on smuggling foreign-made goods into India. Now, it will be done formally.

How Can Nepal Leverage India's Growth

Nepal's growth has been tied to India, as much of the macroeconomic stability in Nepal largely comes from India being stable. With a currency fixed to the Indian rupee, Nepal has been able to stem waves of potential devaluation of its currency, inflationary trends, and shocks that come with changes in global economic trends.

I have been writing on India and Nepal for many years, and in addition to many issues I have written about in my past books and columns, here are the five key areas I like to emphasize when it comes to Nepal–India relations. These are the areas in which Nepal needs to work with India for mutual economic benefits, and if these work, the geopolitical issues will sort themselves out.

Leveraging water and energy: When India agreed to purchase 10,000 MW of power from Nepal in June 2023, it felt like, finally, energy would move from PowerPoint presentations to actual power lines. There is also the export of power from Nepal to Bangladesh through India. The key thing to do will be to get these agreements implemented and the quantum of exports increased. This would also require efforts to ensure that environmental guidelines are adhered to and the long-term impact of large-scale projects is considered as well. An India dependent on Nepal's power for its peak demand and a fair share of the downstream benefits of water means Nepal will be able to negotiate other terms with India on an equitable basis. There are already Indian investments across seven projects totalling 3491 MW.[65] This needs to grow.

Border economic zones: I always enjoy my trips to Eastern Nepal, driving from the plains to the hills with soothing views of the tea gardens. Once you cross the border into India from Pashupatinagar into the Darjeeling district, the landscape and views do not change. I have done this trip many times since my childhood. One can spend hours wondering where a country starts and ends. You encounter signage at a tourist spot, popularly called *simana*, that says: *Nepal border 0 km*. This spot is actually in India, and Indian tourists tend to think it is in Nepal! Here, one can take a break and eat at eateries in makeshift shacks that sell popular food items, including instant noodles packaged in India as well as in Nepal. They accept currencies of both countries. When you are paying digitally by QR code, you actually don't know what currency your payment must have been made in. Borders exist in maps, but in reality, they are very difficult to sketch. There is seamless movement of similar people and cultures.

There is an incredible opportunity here to better manage open borders in order to maximize trade, commerce, investment, and tourism that are mutually beneficial to both countries. In 2017, I presented a paper at the Institute for Defence Studies and Analysis (IDSA), New Delhi, on the concept of Border Economic Zones (BEZ), akin to Special Economic Zones (SEZ). I continue to argue that a BEZ could be a win-win model to ensure economic growth and the development of the border areas. We should not forget that these border areas are laggards in terms of economic growth and development in both countries.

Facilitating easier movements: Similarly, in many parts of the Terai, the southern plains of Nepal that border the Indian states of Bihar and Uttar Pradesh, it is very common for students from either side of the border to attend school on the other side. Similarly, people go to work on the other side of the border and return the same day. There are cross-border marital relationships too, and it is common to see weddings between two parties, one from each side of the border. Then there are village fairs on either side of the border, popularly called *haats*, attended by people from both nations.

The relationship is deep, and so are the numbers. While 60 per cent of Nepal's population lives in the southern parts of the country, close to two hundred million of India's population are within three hours' drive from the border. The potential for economic gains through easier movement is enormous. Crossing the border is seen as a task, with security, customs and other officials always acting as controllers rather than facilitators of the movement of people.

Facilitation can be carried out without compromising national security on either side. The movement of people, goods and services should be regulated well through digital platforms but at the same time made easy. There are global models from the European Union, East African Community and others that serve as examples. With better roads and infrastructure, we should see more movement on both sides. It is common to spot many Indian licence-plate vehicles in Nepal during peak tourist seasons, and with the increase in religious tourism, more vehicles are moving across both sides of the border. For instance, obtaining online permits to cross borders, such as online visas, would increase such movements multifold.

Air and water connectivity: Air and water connectivity are critical too for both countries, as it is important to look at this connectivity from the lens of economic potential rather than issues relating to geopolitics or security alone. For instance, more people flying between the newly opened airport in Bhairawa and New Delhi or Kolkata to the international airport in Pokhara would benefit both countries. Similarly, the use of inland waterways, agreed upon by the two countries, should be put into action. The same is true of the railways.

The relationship between people across the two countries can be strengthened too. Reels and videos about 'A Day on the Other Side of the Border' often flood the Internet. This momentum can be built up to help the youth on both sides of the border learn and appreciate each other's culture and country, thereby reducing the chances of heightened nationalism.

Young Indians coming to Nepal realize there is no Chinese influence in Nepal, unlike what they see in misinformation campaigns on social media. Likewise, young Nepalis discover the entrepreneurial and hardworking spirit of the Indian people. Whenever my team members, who travel to India for the first time in their lives and return, share their stories, they talk about how markets in India stay open late at night, how hard people work, how much time they spend commuting to work, and how conscious they are about finances. It is very common to see Nepali artists participate in reality shows in India, too. Menuka Poudel, a visually impaired singer, made it big on the reality show *Indian Idol* and provided a playback voice for a superhit film. Singers from Sikkim, India, who won awards on reality shows in Nepal, receive great recognition back home. Similarly, more sportspeople are engaging in teams across the border. Such exchanges would form the foundation of future relationships.

Working together on climate change: Nepal needs to make India understand that the full impact of climate change—natural calamities and changing weather patterns in the Himalayas—will affect India as well. With unpredictable changes in weather, there have been unprecedented floods and landslides in areas where it is very difficult to segregate political boundaries. A Glacial Lake Outburst Flood (GLOF) in Nepal would have repercussions in India. In 1985, when the term GLOF was little known, the bursting of Dig Tso, a glacial lake in the Khumbu region of Nepal, had an impact hundreds of kilometres downstream at the Namche Hydel plant in Sikkim, India. Therefore, it is important to tackle the climate crisis together.

More joint research projects and the building of shared knowledge repositories are the way forward. It would also be important to share data on river flows to ensure that unusual river activity can be analysed and understood. Both countries should jointly address issues related to natural resource extraction and ensure strict adherence to environmental guidelines.

China—Understanding the Opportunities

While looking at the future of Nepal's opportunities with China, it is important to understand the key difference between India and China. Contrary to the densely populated areas on both sides of the India–Nepal border, there are very few people living on either the Nepal side or in the TAR. The entire population of TAR—an area nearly eight times the size of Nepal—is just three and a half million. Kyirong, the largest town near Nepal's border, has fewer than 20,000 people, and Zhangmu (Khasa) has a population of under 5000. Similarly, the hill districts of Nepal bordering China are also sparsely populated. For instance, Mustang—though the fifth largest district by area among Nepal's seventy-seven districts—has fewer than 15000 residents. Therefore, the scale of trade, commerce and exchange of services in the north will not be comparable to that at the India–Nepal border.

When one travels to the Korala border point on the Nepal side in Mustang district, one wonders why the Chinese side has invested in such large infrastructure for customs and immigration. Clearly, it is not to cater to trade at the border itself but rather to facilitate bilateral trade and to prepare for potential future trade with India via Nepal. For instance, a significant share of electric vehicles imported into Nepal has come overland through the Tatopani and Rasuwa border points with China. On a visit to the Tatopani border in February 2025, we observed hundreds of electric vehicles waiting at the inland port for transportation to Kathmandu and other cities.

Economics will always determine the future of connectivity with China. A feasibility study is underway for a railway project in TAR to connect to Kathmandu. However, the billions of dollars required for such an investment are unlikely to materialize unless it is confirmed that the railway will also link with the Indian rail network, reaching Kathmandu. Therefore, Nepal's opportunity with China must be evaluated through the lens of economic feasibility.

When it comes to trade and investment, Nepal's relationship with China is typically discussed only when issues arise with India. Even now, it is not viewed as an independent relationship that must be cultivated in its own right. For example, Nepal began to actively pursue a transit treaty with China only after India imposed a blockade. Nepal must understand China's strategic priorities, particularly as China positions itself to become the world's largest economy by 2050. Nepal should also assess how China perceives its relationship with Nepal.

Nepal's geographic location could become significantly important if discussions around trilateral[66] economic cooperation—among Nepal, China and India—gain momentum. Nepal can serve as a link state from where goods, services, electricity, communication lines and the movement of people can flow. While there is a lot of research and analysis regarding India–Nepal trade, investment and economic opportunities, there is very little scholarship when it comes to understanding the Nepal–China economic relationship. Most of the writing is either interest-driven, propagandist or flawed due to the geo-political lenses through which it is written. There is a need to start with the fundamentals.

Here are four key areas I would like to focus on with regard to Nepal's economic relationship with China.

First, what could trade with China look like? What can we buy, and what can we sell? These are long-term considerations.

It will be important to determine the value Nepal can add to goods before trading them with other countries. If China demands processed agricultural products, Nepal must develop processing facilities capable of handling local produce or imported goods from India before re-exporting them to China.

One of the much-talked-about exports from Nepal to China is *yarsagumba*, a medicinal fungus found in the high Himalayas in its raw form. Once processed, the final product fetches multiple times the price of the raw product in Nepal.[67] There is also an opportunity here to establish a processing plant with Chinese technology that would ensure Nepal captures this value addition. Similarly, if there are products that have a market in India, Nepal must consider how to import, add value and then export goods to India, taking into account the geo-political issues as well. With many components, materials and parts made in China now restricted in India, Nepal could assemble and manufacture products for the Indian market using these Chinese components.

Second, the biggest economic potential with China lies in tourism. One is likely to see increased travel from China overland from TAR to Nepal. Once, when I was at a restaurant in Kathmandu, I parked next to a Chinese licence plate vehicle—a rare sight in the city. I chatted with the owner and discovered that he had driven from Lhasa in Tibet with his family. He said this was his fourth overland trip to Nepal. He then spoke about the growing interest among Chinese travellers who want to drive along the picturesque Himalayas on either side of the border. We have also witnessed increased air connectivity between China and Nepal. During the Chinese New Year holidays, Nepal has begun to attract single women travellers from China, choosing Nepal as their holiday destination. This is a specific, distinct and growing segment of the travelling population.

Extrapolating from the current trends in China's outbound tourism market of 155 million annual visitors,[68] it is estimated that the number of Chinese travelling outside China would reach 350 million by 2043. Therefore, just a one per cent share for Nepal would mean 3.5 million tourists. Nature, culture and Buddhism will be the biggest attractions for the Chinese tourist, and it will be important to develop products and services that would cater to this tourist. The Chinese market is unique. Fifty-four per cent of their outbound travellers are women, and most of the travellers are in the age group of thirty to forty-nine years, very different from Western segments. They are also very tech-savvy and want everything to happen online.[69] I have chatted with Chinese tourists and learnt how they book their lodging, food and all services online. They get very nervous when they have to leave the online world and engage in offline transactions like paying a cab or settling the bill at a restaurant.

Third, Nepal will need to make better use of innovations that are happening in China. In 2024, Chinese electric vehicle manufacturer BYD became the largest pure EV to be sold in the world, surpassing Tesla from the US.[70] That's not all. China's large-scale high-speed railway networks have become a point of global envy. Similarly, many innovations in the field of technology, digitization, digitalization and communications are happening in China as it continues to push for self-reliance. In February 2024, Chinese Open AI, DeepSeek, created ripples around the world when it launched its large language machine (LLM), DeepSeek R1. US AI company Nvidia lost US$600 billion in a single day.[71] By 2024, as per the World Intellectual Property Organization (WIPO), 'China had the highest number of patents in force at 5 million'.[72] The *Guardian* reported that 'China has overtaken the US to become the biggest contributor to nature-science journals, in a sign of the country's growing influence in the world of academic research.'[73] In 2024, we have also noticed how Chinese electric vehicles have dominated Nepali markets, with 85 per cent of new vehicle sales being electric vehicles.[74] After Norway, which boasts 89 per cent EV sales,[75] Nepal has emerged as the country that has the highest share of electric vehicle sales. Nepal would be building an ecosystem for these electric vehicles and therefore what this means is that it could also emerge as the interpretation hub for such technology.

Fourth, China has moved towards sustainable practices in the development of infrastructure; it has managed to reduce air pollution and mend its ways towards managing the costs of economic growth. For instance, in China, no brick can be manufactured from fresh soil—it must be made from recycled materials. Similarly, there has been innovation in waste management—it has been channelled towards energy generation. Infrastructure development in China, especially in mountainous regions, has become a global marvel. They are pursuing the 'Two Mountains' concept—'aqua-clear water and green mountains' as the country's valuable assets.[76] Nepal will need to work with China on technology transfer to ensure it also rapidly builds its infrastructure based on need and efficiency, with minimal environmental costs.

Nepali Assertion

Nepal's future relationship with both China and India has to be based on how Nepal wants to see itself between the two biggest economies in 2050. The biggest opportunity and challenge for Nepal will be to continue to keep the interest of both countries alive for mutual economic growth and benefit. This means Nepal will have to learn to be assertive. Nepal's diplomatic and bilateral efforts have always been short term and reactive rather than proactive and rooted in a long-term perspective.

This must change, and here are the three critical issues that we need to deal with.

First, we need to understand our neighbours well. We need dedicated centres that will study the two countries. These centres will be warehouses of data and provide continuous research and analysis. Since there is a lot of propaganda material that floats around and, often, even analysis that tends to have a geopolitical tint, it will be important to approach both countries after careful research.

At the Nepal Economic Forum, we have started a two-year study to understand the future potential between China and Nepal. We are calling the project 'Can Nepal BET on China,' using BET as an acronym for Business, Energy and Tourism. The study aims to understand the present situation and look at future pointers for collaboration between China and Nepal. Similarly, in collaboration with the Observer Research Foundation, India, we are exploring how to further the economic relationship between Nepal and India. The efforts are to build on the ORF report on Nepal titled 'Leap to the Himalayas[77]: Exploring Nepal's Growth through Indian Collaboration.' It is important to have more unbiased and futuristic analyses to understand the potential, but the onus of pushing these studies remains with Nepal. Nepal needs this more than its neighbours.

If there are policy announcements being made in China or India, and if they impact Nepal, then we need to talk about it and let concerned people and institutions know. The annual budget of India, at times, impacts Nepali businesses and trade in a big way, but we seldom have institutions study it. Government and non-government institutions must be equipped to work in these areas.

Second, the neighbourhood's history, geography and other critical issues need to be taught to students at school. If India is completing road construction at a phenomenal speed or China is building profitable high-speed railway networks, then students should know about these developments. They will not only grow up with aspirations and ambitions but will also be well-informed about the neighbourhood. This kind of awareness does not exist currently. China has initiated many scholarship programmes that take Nepali students to see the developments in China and learn about them. These learnings need to be institutionalized and implemented. Nepalis also need to develop pride in their neighbours; a successful, rich neighbour is always better than a failed, poor neighbour. The Nepali narrative of belonging to the future of the world must be one where we co-exist with pride with the two largest economies in the world.

Third, while Nepali government agencies need to develop a more robust internal structure to manage their relationships in the neighbourhood, it will be critical to ensure that all bilateral official structures are in place and regular meetings of the counterparts take place. When you are neighbours, you are bound to have issues, so it is important that they are handled through dialogue. In the past, when government-to-government dialogues became challenging, it was the track-two initiatives that helped resolve issues. We need to ensure there are adequate track-two mechanisms that continuously meet and discuss challenges, so as to help the government work on solutions. If there had been good track-two mechanisms, the 2015 blockade would not have taken place with India. Further, President Xi Jinping's visit to Nepal in 2019 would have resulted in more mutual benefits.

Learning from Other Nations

It will be important for Nepal to also learn from other countries as to how they handle global relationships and engage with different countries. In a special report produced after a roundtable on Nepal and the World, co-hosted by the National University of Singapore and the NEF, we used Singapore as a model to look at the role of the small South Asian States in the Global Re(order).[78] In the report, which I co-authored with Wini Fred Gurung and Amit Ranjan, we wrote, 'Singapore is a small city-state in Southeast Asia with a population of only around 3.5 million, excluding permanent residents and employment pass holders. The city-state has no natural resources and is highly dependent on imports for its sustenance. Despite this, it is one of the leading global economies and a politically significant country not just in Southeast Asia but also worldwide. In its foreign policy, Singapore has managed to avoid the strategy of pitting one country against another by maintaining a strong security partnership with the US and a comprehensive economic partnership with China. Singapore's management of the US-China dynamics presents a model for the small countries in South Asia on engagement with the major powers.'[79]

Bangladesh has been able to balance geopolitics well and foster growth. It took up the challenge of managing the border dispute with India and resolved it. There is more Chinese, Indian, Japanese and US investment in Bangladesh than ever before. The balance is brought about by using the contractor from one country for a project in another country. This has accelerated the growth of infrastructure and enhanced the country's ability to work with multilateral agencies, taking exports of ready-made garments to US$47 billion, second only to China.

My personal experience of watching Rwanda since we began our work there in 2012 has been fascinating. It is a landlocked country the size of two-thirds of Bhutan with 13 million people and surrounded by large countries. They have literally taken Singapore as their playbook and have asserted themselves to be the voice of Africa. They have hosted global events like the Commonwealth Summit in 2022, consolidated the African Union during their presidency and reached the ambition of becoming the hub airport for Africa by selling their stake in the airline to Qatar Airways and their airport to Hamad International Airport, Doha. Rwanda continues to attract global attention for good reasons, whether it is introducing new high-end tourism products, innovating tools on sustainable finance, or building up a financial centre. Rwanda also talks about providing African solutions to African problems.[80] There are lessons for Nepal to learn from Rwanda.

Switzerland is another example. Nepal can learn how to assert its position when you are surrounded by big countries. During my trip in January 2025, when I asked what Nepal can learn from Switzerland, Jörg Frieden, the former ambassador of Switzerland to Nepal, told me, 'You have to learn to not only live in harmony with your large neighbours but also learn to grow leveraging your neighbours.' After the trip, I wrote a reflective blog, where I talked about lessons Nepal can learn from Switzerland. I wrote, 'The first is to be able to respect diversity – be it of language or culture. When one travels in trains across the country, the announcements turn from French to Swiss-German to Italian, depending on which part of the country you are going to. On the cultural side, the local self-governance models of cantons have been able to manage this diversity. This is also the hope for Nepal post-federalism, where we are realizing how diverse Nepal is and how we have evolved with this diversity.'[81]

The Buffer State Narrative

Over the past two decades, I have been continuously arguing that Nepal needs to reposition itself as a country that China and India need more, rather than the other way around. The opportunities of the 3Ts—transit, tourism and transmission (power and communication)—remain, but it will be important how Nepal plays out its narrative by putting its interest first.

India and China share a border of 3488 kilometres. The land border between India and Nepal is 1752 kilometres, and between China and Nepal, 1389 kilometres. Both India and China are aware of the cost of managing their borders between the two countries. In 2022, the Government of India announced a budget of US$2 billion to build 2088 kilometres of road in the border areas with China.[82] Nepal's annual budget for road construction that year was US$1 billion. India is building fences on its border with Myanmar that will cost a whopping US$3.1 billion.[83] China is spending similar amounts of money to build infrastructure, especially roads near the border. For both countries, the spending is to ensure better planning and execution of the movement and support of forces. For the border with Nepal, there are hardly such expenses. On the Indian side, it is not even the Indian Army at the border; it is left to a border guarding force—Sashastra Seema Bal (SSB), which means Armed Border Force—to do the job. Interestingly, this force is under the administrative control of the Ministry of Home Affairs (MHA) and not part of the Indian Army.

One of the ways to really make Nepal's importance felt to both of its neighbours is to highlight its role as a buffer state. Nepal needs to make it clear to India what the cost would be of deploying troops at the Nepal-China border. Similarly, this needs to be highlighted to the Chinese authorities also—i.e. the savings in cost of having a buffer country in between. It is about how you change the narrative and sell it; Nepal needs to do so in a proactive fashion. We need to continuously tell both the neighbours that they are saving money by having Nepal as a buffer zone!

With China and India becoming the two largest economies in the world in the next two decades, I always say that Nepal is the most valuable piece of real estate in the world. When your house is between two big rich neighbours, you benefit. If both of them put bright streetlights, you do not have to invest in one; the bright light from both the neighbours' would illuminate your compound! Singapore, UAE, Switzerland, Panama and other countries figured out their strategic importance in their neighbourhood, became proactive and raced to build strong economies that provide jobs and better lives for their citizens. Similarly, Nepal needs to leverage its location and assert itself. If we draw a line on a map between the financial capitals of China and India—Shanghai and Mumbai—the line passes through Kathmandu. This visual has to be ingrained in every Nepali. Geographies can never be changed. We suffered when our neighbours were poor for a few centuries, but we need to remember that in the sixteenth–seventeenth century, China and India were the two formidable economies of the world, and they will return to take that position. Nepal benefitted then, and now, history will repeat!

Chapter 3

Federalism and Further

When I was growing up, my cousins in the eastern city of Dharan used to say they're 'going to Nepal' when they meant they were visiting Kathmandu. Nepal was Kathmandu and Kathmandu was Nepal back then. This wasn't surprising because of the kind of centralized and unitary leadership structure that the Rana rulers had built back then. King Mahendra even had to issue a notification on 2 February 1959 through the Home Secretary to use the word 'Nepal' to mean the entire country and not just Kathmandu.[1]

Nepal's experimentation with devolution of power began in 1962 when the then constitution proposed four tiers of government but even then, did not bring decentralization.[2] It created 4000 local units (*gaun sabhas*) but they were directly under the king. After the interim constitution was promulgated in 1990, there were attempts to push the agenda of devolution of power again with a specific mention in Part 17 on 'Local Self-Governance'.[3] The nomenclature changed from village panchayat to village development committees and from district panchayat to district development committees, but even here, the decentralization of power did not quite happen. It took another nine years for the 'intention' behind the provision to be converted into action.

The Local Self Governance Act was finally promulgated in 1999 'to make provisions conducive to the enjoyment of the fruits of democracy through the utmost participation of the sovereign people in the process of governance by way of decentralization'.[4] There was a wave of excitement. Local elections were held and dynamic men and women started to take up positions in the government. I was working at the Soaltee Group, one of the largest business groups in Nepal at that time. I was leading the business development function there and we worked out a public-private partnership programme with the government to leverage this legislation and have the private sector work with local governments. We started with the district of Kavre, adjacent to the Kathmandu Valley, and began exploring the different ways in which we could work together for infrastructure and entrepreneurship development along with creating jobs. However, these efforts were short-lived as Prime Minister Sher Bahadur Deuba decided to dissolve all local governments in 2002 as King Gyanendra became the monarch. It took another sixteen years for a local election to take place again.

It was the Nepal Constitution in 2015 that finally brought a semblance of decentralization. This constitution specified three layers of government: federal, provincial and local. Seven provinces were carved out of Nepal after a lot of discussions, and it took quite a few years to name each one of them. From east to west, they are Koshi, Madhes, Bagmati, Gandaki, Lumbini, Karnali and Sudhurpaschim.

Earlier, the country was divided into fourteen zones. However, the seventy-five administrative districts provided one with an identity rather than the zones. One would say one is from Jhapa or Dang rather than the zone that Jhapa or Dang belongs to. This trend continued and the provincial government, like zones, was just seen as another layer of government between the federal and local governments. The fact that many provincial ministers and assembly members ran for the mayoral elections in 2022 speaks a lot about how that perception has changed today.[5]

Today, the local governments, be it municipalities or village municipalities, definitely have more authority than their provincial counterpart. After the 2017 elections, the Local Government Operation Act came into effect in line with the Nepal Constitution of 2015. This has paved the way for a strong legal foundation towards institutionalizing legislative, executive and quasi-judiciary practices of newly formed local governments in Nepal. The envisaged devolution of power is more prominent today than ever before—753 local empowered bodies have unprecedented power compared to the previous structures of local units. A World Bank report of 2022 said, 'Under Nepal's 2015 Constitution, the country embarked on a historic transition to a federal democratic form of government. State restructuring on this scale was unchartered territory.'[6]

Does this mean that decentralization is a reality today in Nepal? Not really. The federal government continues to resist the devolution of power. The future of Nepal, especially the journey to 2043, will depend a lot on how quickly this attitude changes and how quickly Nepal realizes that a decentralized structure of governance is the only way forward.

Community Forestry

It is not like Nepal has not seen successful manifestations of federalism in its history. One of Nepal's globally recognized successes has been making community forestry work. Nepal's forest cover increased from 26.2 per cent in 1992 to 46.08 per cent in 2022. A *New York Times* article in May 2022 drew global attention when it had an eye-catching headline: 'How Nepal

Grew Back Its Forests' and explained how 'an effort decades in the making is showing results in Nepal, a rare success story in a world of cascading climate disasters and despair'.[7] The article further stated: 'Over the years, large swathes of national forest land have been handed to local communities, and millions of volunteers have been recruited to protect and renew their local forests, an effort that has earned praise from environmentalists around the world.'[8]

I had the honour of interacting with the late Elinor Ostrom, an American political scientist who won the Nobel Prize in 2009 for her work in Nepal on the study of the commons. She talked about self-governance and how, in Nepal, communities of farmers set aside their individual interests to manage their single most precious resource—their forests—without any outside management at all. When the planning and decision-making shifts to the community, it is always more effective than centrally driven plans and actions. Similarly, community-driven healthcare and educational institutions have delivered better results too. The award-winning Dhulikhel Hospital and Kathmandu University, also located 30 kilometres from Kathmandu in Dhulikhel, are both examples of how local-level governments and communities can push for large-scale transformations. A supportive local government was willing to provide public land for building hospitals and universities. The community was supportive by providing contributions through free labour and donations. The development partners and private sector came forward to help build the infrastructure and operate these institutions. There were dedicated leaders who led these initiatives. This was thus a clear example of what I call a 'bottom-up' approach, where decisions and initiatives started at the bottom and successfully travelled all the way to the top. A similar approach within the government has not been easy or welcomed.

The Power of Local

One of the objectives of the insurgency led by the Communist Party of Nepal (Maoist) between 1996 and 2006 was to provide local people with more power. The Madhes people in the southern plains, who have always felt discriminated against, were the major backers of the insurgency. My friends from the community keep telling me about the discrimination they face in Kathmandu and other parts of hilly Nepal due to their dark skin and the fact that they speak Nepali with a southern accent. When members of the Constituent Assembly were elected and the process of writing the constitution began, federalism was no longer an option, but a necessity. The question was how to figure out the model of federalism that we should adopt. In fact, Nepal had already declared itself a 'Federal Democratic Republic' in 2008 when the King abdicated the throne and left the palace.

The State Restructuring Committee originally proposed to demarcate provinces using five kinds of identity—ethnic, linguistic, cultural, geographical and historical—and four bases of capability—economic inter-relationship and capability, infrastructure development and potential, availability of natural resources and administrative accessibility. These were later overlooked, however. The discussion became more focused on the names and numbers of provinces rather than the above-mentioned criteria.[9] Between 2022 and 2024, each time the federal government changed, the provincial government also changed, frustrating the people even more. A concerted effort has to be made to ensure the provincial layers of government actually work by themselves. The Nepal Law Society, in their publication, wrote that 'provinces have formulated many laws in the past seven years—each province has formulated over 60 laws. But many of them could not be implemented because of various reasons such as conflict with the federal level, problems on constitutionality and other technical matters'.[10] For instance, the constitution assigns provinces the exclusive right to exercise police powers, but this has not been allowed in practice. The question, therefore, is how to find a way out of these challenges.

One of the questions I'm often asked by visiting international mission members is whether there will be a constitutional amendment to do away with the current structure of three tiers of government. I always explain to them that federalism is here to stay. Nepal will not return to a unitary system of government. There are two reasons for this. First, and very simply, local leaders and people who have tasted the devolution of power will not want to go back to the earlier arrangements. As a ward chair said to me recently, 'Do you think thirty-eight thousand local leaders who have tasted power will let it go?'

Second, it is what the people want. The Asia Foundation surveyed Nepali people in 2022,[11] according to which 70.4 per cent of Nepalis see their local areas improving if local governments are more empowered. A growing awareness of the high quality of services pertaining to healthcare, taxation and education provided by local governments is a testament to their popularity among the public. The respondents to the survey also named local governments as the most responsive actors during the COVID-19 pandemic, and the overall satisfaction with local government services stood at 57.2 per cent. These surveys tend to support the general logic that local governments, being closer to their constituents, are more responsive to their concerns.

Travelling across Nepal, I realize that ground observations corroborate what the different studies have to say. In 2023, a study by the International Institute for Democracy and Electoral Assistance (International IDEA) had concluded that—across health, education and infrastructure sectors, considerable progress has been made in achieving a form of federal system in Nepal. However, in many aspects of service delivery in these sectors, federalism in Nepal is at an early stage. This is especially when it comes to fulfilling the promise of the new Constitution—when it comes to functioning as a devolved system guided by collaborative federalism.

A great example of the success of the federal structure is the proliferation of trail bridges over rivers that connect villages, giving them access to markets and aiding tourism. From ten trail bridges in 1970, Nepal has built ten thousand trail bridges in forty-five years. The pace of construction accelerated once local governments were given the responsibility of supervising new bridge constructions.[12] Similarly, in 2024, records from the Department of Roads state that there are 38,000 kilometres of blacktopped roads in Nepal. If you add the roads built by local governments, the total exceeds 1,00,000 kilometres. This is significant, considering 80,000 kilometres of roads were reported in 2015.[13] Local roads are growing at more than ten per cent per annum.

The implementation of the new constitution has also resulted in increased political participation and the inclusion and empowerment of previously excluded groups, such as women and marginalized communities. This too will play a huge role in Nepal's journey towards embracing federalism.

No Turning Back

A transition to federalism takes time and involves significant initial costs, but over time, the benefits far outweigh the incurred costs. No transition is perfect, and issues naturally get resolved over time. So far, there have been two elections to the local governments; financial mechanisms and more acts are being promulgated to facilitate the devolution of power as prescribed by the constitution. Reversing all of this would be a nightmare! There are always voices against the prevailing system in every country; in any democracy, divergent views should exist. Furthermore, Nepalis and the world cannot forget that the ten-year insurgency between 1996 and 2006 was against a unitary central rule, and any attempts to reverse federalism could lead to another phase of political disturbance, which Nepal cannot afford economically. Federalism also holds immense relevance in a country with such heterogeneity in ethnicities, cultures, and social behaviour, making it ideally suited to Nepal. The journey to 2043, therefore, must ensure that federalism is made to work, with coordinated efforts from politicians, government, and bureaucrats. In this regard, here are a few points to consider:

Understand it is a long-term process: Let's begin with the understanding that federalism is a long-term process and short-term wins are rare. Therefore, it is important to ensure that federalism works in the long run. Politicians and development partners cannot afford to be in a hurry. Patience is the real virtue here. In India, the competition between states for investments led to some states accelerating their economic growth compared to others. However, there are always issues that arise regarding the extent of the powers of the state. The only way these issues get resolved is through mechanisms established in the constitution. There is much we can learn from what has worked or not worked in India. Globally, too, there are lessons to be learned. In Yugoslavia, federalism failed, the states broke up, and many lives were lost in the process. Bizuneh Yimenu, a lecturer of Comparative Politics at Queen's University Belfast, writes: 'In Africa, there are lessons to learn, both of successes and failures. Federalism has helped reduce conflict in South Africa but not in Nigeria and Ethiopia. Federalism enabled South Africa and Nigeria to preserve their diversity by reducing identity-based exclusion and improving diverse groups' access to power. In Ethiopia, it facilitated cultural and linguistic plurality but was unsuccessful in reducing exclusion and improving groups' equal access to power. Africa, therefore, illustrates that federalism fails to manage conflict unless incumbents embrace democracy, curtail centralism, and are loyal to the idea'.[14]

Bottom-up approach: Federalism requires a bottom-up approach. One must understand local needs and issues rather than assume what the local government needs. During our work on the development of the Local Economic Development Index, bureaucrats from Kathmandu continued to dictate what they thought the locals needed, and we continued to push back based on our findings from the ground. For instance, we felt entrepreneurial development is best supervised by the local government through various programmes, but federal government officials were keen to have contests and awards, where they would judge the entrepreneurs. These mindset transformations will take time, but continuously pushing back on these ideas will be important.

Building fiscal federalism: The Nepal Fiscal Federalism Update in June 2023 by the World Bank identifies key reforms to help Nepal improve fiscal federalism outcomes. It recommends 'developing a fiscal federalism roadmap to guide and monitor the reforms in this area, reinforcing the Inter-Governmental Fiscal Transfer system, and establishing a consolidated Public Financial Management (PFM) performance database at the subnational level'.[15] The 2024 Update continued its call for reforms and states, 'Progress on the regulatory framework for fiscal federalism and institutional development has been slow, and urgent action is needed on reinforcing expenditure and revenue assignments, as well as upgrading the Inter-Governmental Fiscal Transfers System.'[16] In our visits to different local government units, the major complaints remain about the way the federal government tends to decide what the local government should do, rather than the other way around. Development partners are supporting this massive transition to fiscal federalism, and it is important that there is will from politicians and bureaucrats to make this happen.

Initiating a dashboard: There must be a communication platform between the different local governments, where, through a co-created dashboard, they can each monitor how the different units are functioning. In one of the meetings at a municipality, I demonstrated how these dashboards would work. The dashboard could show progress on different projects and programmes of the local governments and also be used to monitor them. There must also be ways in which we can share learnings between the different governments. Here, we can take a leaf out of Estonia, where the government dashboard provides much-needed information on multiple variables that helps not only to bring transparency to operations but also to increase trust in the government systems.

Implementation of the local economic development index (LEDI): This will foster a competitive spirit among the local governments to attract investment, grants and other resources. Better performance means more investment, which will result in more job creation, more enterprises, and, in turn, push economic growth. In India, the States of India Index and State Competitiveness Report have been able to provide critical comparative data. Competition between the provinces and local governments will be the way forward in making the federal structure work for Nepal. When an international investor would like to invest, or a development partner would like to decide where to build their partnerships, these indices could help them decide.

Building local economic development strategy: It would be important to work on a local economic development strategy.

Through the Nepal Economic Forum in September 2022, I was involved in producing a framework for a similar strategy based on the values of investment, entrepreneurship and employment. Our framework aims to promote sustainable and productive local self-reliance, the ability to adapt to the local environment using local resources and making meaningful collaboration with community cooperatives and the private sector to ensure equitable distribution of benefits. In our interactions with different locally elected leaders and bureaucrats at various levels of local government, the conclusions were homogenous. They seemed to have shunned political rhetoric and the idea of 'isms'; the focus is on the economy. They collectively believe economic growth revolves around job creation and the augmentation of quality of life through better income, education, healthcare and social security.

Ensuring access to resources: There must be more access to resources for the local governments, whether through the issuance of municipal or other bonds for financial resources or programmes in partnership with global organizations to attract the best talent to their respective institutions. The success of Dhulikhel Hospital in the district of Kavre has been its ability to raise both financial resources and attract global talent, supported by international institutions. Global companies are willing to collaborate with governments. During the Himalayan Consensus Summit, which we hosted between 2014 and 2019, a Hong Kong-based reinsurance company was keen to work with local governments to issue municipal bonds for disaster risk management. For a small, subsidized insurance premium, local governments would be able to get the initial cash needed to disburse in times of natural calamities like earthquakes, floods and landslides.

Constitutional amendments: Finally, follow the Constitution; amendments should be made based on practical challenges that need to be overcome. The Constitution is not a document set in stone. The aim should be to continuously push for the devolution of functions and resources to the provincial and local governments. Political and bureaucratic power is very difficult to let go. In Kathmandu Metropolitan City in May 2024, when the sidewalks were expanded, the federal and local governments went into loggerheads. The Department of Roads under the federal government went and stopped the sidewalk expansion. The matter went to court, and the Patan High Court ordered the right of the local government to determine the expansion of sidewalks. Similar challenges can emerge in determining the jurisdiction of different tiers of government for various government services. In a federal structure, it is important that the mindset changes and each challenge is looked at from a win-win perspective. It will also be important to push transparency and an inclusive nature of governance to ensure that the accountability of any tier of government is not compromised.

I believe, therefore, that the transformation of the future of politics in Nepal will be a result of the strong foundation of grassroots politics and the federal structure that is being built. Though the process has been frustrating, we cannot turn our back on federalism for the reasons discussed above. But, as I have said before, a key element in making all of this happen is the will of our leaders. How willing will our politicians be in embracing federalism? What does the political landscape in Nepal look like? Let's dive in.

Nepal's Political Spectrum

Many surprises emerge in every nation's history, and events can rarely be predicted during their course; people cannot say what change may happen in the next two to three years. If we think of 1988 or 1989, who would have thought that the people of Nepal would challenge the monarchy and its party-less panchayat system and move to a constitutional monarchy? Similarly, when we think of 2004 or 2005, who would have believed that a monarchy that had ruled for 240 years would see an end? Whenever we feel we have lost hope, whether during the insurgency, an economic crisis or a natural calamity, we spring back; we manage to spring surprises, and then another trajectory emerges.

The biggest events of 2022 were two elections—local elections were held in May and the federal election in November. In the local elections held in May 2022, 81 per cent of the candidates elected were new faces.[17] It was a strong anti-incumbent vote. In Dharan in eastern Nepal, Harka Rai Sampang, a lone campaigner who did not belong to any political party, became the mayor. The fact that he campaigned with a small budget and support proved that money is not the only ingredient necessary to win elections. Moreover, the success of such candidates in the local elections prompted more people to run as independent candidates in the subsequent federal election.

In 2022, a group of candidates who were to fight the elections as independents formed a new party, the Rastriya Swatantra Party (RSP) and became the fourth-largest force in Parliament. There was a strong #NoNotAgain campaign against the old, male politicians across established parties who have been dominant for the past three decades. Many of them lost the re-election. Fifty per cent of those elected were parliamentarians for the first time. I wrote for the Indian media outlet *The Hindu* that 'New faces in Nepal's politics, a phase of change' has begun. 'With changes in Nepal's Parliament, India and the rest of the international community will have to be recalibrating their ways of dealing with Kathmandu.'[18]

Popular wisdom has always dictated that to win elections, one had to either spend money or pay for a ticket from a major political party. It was about getting campaigners to campaign for you. It was believed that the grassroots workers of the political parties delivered the wins. So feed them, get them swimming in booze, dispense money for gasoline, meet their demands and you win! This time, there were thousands who joined the fray with few resources or connections. And they actually won with a decent number of votes. This has changed the game and will ensure that more people become encouraged to contest the next elections.

In the by-elections of 2023 to the Tanahu-1 parliamentary constituency, made vacant by Ram Chandra Paudel being elected President, a Nepali Congress (NC) member, Swarnim Wagle, left to join the RSP and won with a thumping majority. A Harvard-educated development professional with global experience of working in international organizations, his journey from leaving NC to joining RSP, contesting the elections, and winning was undertaken in twenty-five days! In other words, there is change happening, and it is happening at a rapid pace.

To understand this new political context and what a refreshing change this is from the old order, it is important to gain an understanding of the political actors that have emerged and been around since the restoration of democracy in 1990 and after Nepal became a republic in 2006. We will also examine which of these actors we can bank on and who will have the political will to accelerate economic growth towards 2043.

Understanding Nepali Politics

Political parties in Nepal are not very different from each other when it comes to ideology, economics, or development agenda. Even when parties split, it is not because of differences in ideology or the model of political or economic development structure that they are proposing, but often because of personal differences with the leadership. There are five key forces in Nepali politics, and we will look at what the future of these parties looks like in their own journey to 2043.

First, NC, established in Calcutta in 1946 by people who fought as freedom fighters in India, brought the Gandhian model of grassroots democracy and the Nehruvian model of economic development, generally referred to as a mixed economy, to Nepal. Matrika Prasad Koirala was one of the founders of the NC, and he and his two younger brothers both served as prime ministers. One of the brothers, B.P. Koirala, is still regarded as the most popular political leader. He was later removed by Mahendra and jailed in 1960. The youngest, Girija Prasad Koirala, became one of the key figures in the Nepali Congress post-1990. BP Koirala's nephew, Sushil Koirala, too became prime minister, and BP's son, Shashank, continues to fight for party leadership. In 2024, Shekhar Koirala, another family member, continues to position himself as a potential next leader of the NC. Onlinekhabar, a Nepali language news portal, ran a story on how the fourth generation of this family is distancing itself from politics.[19]

The NC is thus dynastic, like many other major South Asian political parties. It was only when Sher Bahadur Deuba (elected PM six times) challenged the domination of the Koirala clan that things began to change. He split the party in 2001 when he was not given space in the party and returned to be the President of the party in 2016 after the demise of Sushil Koirala, another member of the Koirala clan. However, after leading the Nepali Congress for a few years, he too started to override the democratic system within the party to establish an autocratic rule, with his wife and family members playing critical roles, just like the Koiralas. In July 2024, his wife, Arzu Rana Deuba, was appointed the foreign minister of Nepal in the coalition government. Deuba is also not interested in holding the National Convention of the party, which was last held in 2021.

Gagan Thapa, a mascot for young political leaders in Nepal, was seen as the hope when he was elected to the Constituent Assembly at the age of 32 in 2008. He was elected as General Secretary in 2021 and, as of 2025, is nearing fifty years old. He remains the 'lone challenger to Deuba', as *Himalayan Times* declared in its headline.[20] But there has been another challenger for many years: Ram Chandra Paudel, who was made President in March 2023 as per a power-sharing deal.

In the 2022 parliament, the Nepali Congress introduced new faces in the parliament, but just two parliamentarians were under fifty years of age. Many of them are Deuba loyalists, as it was he who decided who would receive party tickets in the elections. The party continues to be under the strong grip of Deuba,[21] and he is turning eighty in 2026. He would like to see his wife, Arzu Rana Deuba, succeed him.[22] The youngest parliamentarian, Yogesh Gauchan Thakali, from Mustang, whose father and uncle have both been parliamentarians, explains to me that it is tough for the NC to hand over the mantle to young leaders, but it must do so to make itself relevant. Further, the NC also needs to examine its socialist and distributive economic policies to push for reforms that create jobs and attract investments.

The second key player is the Communist faction. This comprises parties of various kinds and sizes, each with its own story of multiple splits and reunions. The first Communist Party of Nepal was, like the NC, established in Calcutta in 1949 along the lines of the communist parties in India. This was unlike the communist parties of China, where communism flourished. I have been writing about the personality-driven splits that have seen many leaders come and go, but none of these Communist parties or leaders have been able to make any transformative impact in Nepal.[23] By 2024, only three major sub-groups were remaining within the communist parties in Nepal. There is the Communist Party of Nepal (United Maoist Leninist)—popularly called UML currently the largest. The party is led by K.P. Oli, who likes to mimic the larger-than-life image of leaders in the neighbourhood. His charisma and oratory skills have made him very popular. He became prime minister in 2015 during the Indian blockade and led the united communist parties to win a two-thirds majority in parliament. However, splits within the party brought him down. He tried to save his prime minister's chair twice by dissolving the parliament unsuccessfully with the help of his close friend and former party colleague, Bidya Devi Bhandari, who was then the President.[24] The President, as per the constitution, can dissolve the parliament. He managed to become prime minister again in July 2024 with the support of the NC, a party he fought against in the 2022 elections. He is now the prime minister with the support of both the NC and the Maoists. Looking ahead, this party will most probably face challenges similar to those of the Communist parties in India, which have dwindled in importance after the demise of their popular leaders. While the party commands strong grassroots support and has created grassroots-level structures, it has been seen as a party led by a strongman who does not tolerate opposition. While major heavyweights like former Prime Ministers Madhav Nepal, Jhalnath Khanal and Pushpa Kamal Dahal are no longer part of the UML, in December 2025, the party expelled then Vice President Bhim Rawal and suspended two other critics of Oli: Binda Pande and Usha Kiran Timilsina.[25] The UML is undoubtedly the largest among the communists, but how they will continue to attract the youth of Nepal and convince them to vote for them remains to be seen.

The Nepal Communist Party (United Socialist) was formed after a faction broke away from the Nepal Communist

Party (UML). This party has two former prime ministers, Madhav Nepal and Jhalnath Khanal, as key leaders. They split with CPN UML citing the high-handedness of leadership, however, they are not people who would like to bring in democratic governance within their party. When it came to their own party convention in July 2024, they could not manage to elect office bearers by consensus. Instead, they resorted to the appointment by President, a system that they resented and split from UML for.[26]

The Communist Party of Nepal–Maoist also went through multiple splits and mergers. It made itself popular and powerful when it led an insurgency in which more than 13,000 people lost their lives between 1996 and 2006.[27] The political settlement of 2008 and the delay in the delivery of justice by the Truth and Reconciliation Commission meant that the party got away with the crimes committed during the insurgency.[28] After coming to power, they too were no different from the other political parties they were fighting against. They were accused of promoting crony capitalism and personality-based political systems. The first family of Pushpa Kamal Dahal 'Prachanda' has proliferated the same dynastic politics as the Koiralas. His ally during the insurgency and competitor for leadership, Baburam Bhattarai, who also became prime minister, left the party in 2015,[29] paving the way for Dahal to become the undisputed leader. Veteran columnist Deepak Thapa writes about the 'Dahal, Dahal, Dahal' world, where he lists the ten close family members in the Dahal family and says, 'gifted folks who happen to be related to Prachanda were as follows'.[30] Dahal is projecting his daughter Renu Dahal, who won the mayoral elections in 2022 in Chitwan, as his successor.[31] Whether this party will still hold on to power on its own over time will be the big question. The *Kathmandu Post* in 2024 reported, 'Leaders say a "serious soul-searching" is underway in the Maoist Centre, which emerged as the single largest party from the first Constituent Assembly election in August 2008 but has been consistently downsized in successive elections.'[32]

The third group comprises the turncoats who have joined every cabinet, irrespective of whether it is led by royalists or republicans. This group includes many parties—more than twenty—that claim to fight for the cause of the lowland—Madhes people. Among them are those who have even gone on to join royalist parties in the hope of staying relevant.[33] For instance, Sharat Singh Bhandari, in July 2024, became a minister for the twentieth time. He served as a minister under different factions during the Panchayat era and now, he has become a minister in practically every cabinet, changing parties multiple times. Such groups will continue to exist until society stops believing that there is nothing wrong with political opportunism.

The fourth group comprises the royalists who use the revival of the monarchy and, moreover, the revival of the Hindu kingdom as their agenda. However, the irony is that they have been in governments led by staunch republicans as well. They have also leveraged anti-incumbency votes well, winning 5 per cent of the popular vote and emerging as the sixth-largest party in parliament. With the strong Hindutva movement in India, these political leaders see the use of the religious card as a good strategy to make inroads. However, the results of the Indian elections in 2024, which put the brakes on the Hindutva wave, have started to affect them. The party just won 404 votes in a by-election held for the Ilam constituency in May 2024.[34] In April 2025, there were attempts for major demonstrations for the return of a constitutional monarch that received global attention, but it faded as the demonstrations turned violent and the support group started to split.

Further, when we think of the future, playing the religion card too aggressively will impact Nepal, which has a unique history of Buddhism and Hinduism co-existing. I strongly feel that if this fabric is disrupted, Nepal will face serious challenges from some ethnic groups who, while respecting the Hindu pantheon of deities, consider their practices to be Buddhist or non-Hindu. We have already seen indications of this in recent protests by the Tamang community, who regard themselves as Buddhists.[35] There may be occasional revivalist movements, but given the youth's global connectivity and their aspirations for a brighter future through education and migration, such movements are unlikely to capture their attention for long.

The fifth group comprises the emerging breed of new politicians, including those who have formed the Rastriya Swatantra Party (RSP–Independent Party) and independent candidates such as Kathmandu Mayor Balendra Shah. The RSP was formed in June 2022 by Rabi Lamichhane, just six months before the federal elections. He had returned from the United States in 2017, renounced his US citizenship, joined a television channel as an anchor and hosted a popular show that was projected as a voice for the voiceless. Many independent candidates came together under the RSP banner with Rabi as Chairman. From climate scientists to education campaigners and management specialists, they brought international education and experience alongside a passion to transform Nepal. They managed to win thirteen seats directly and, by securing 12.19 per cent of the vote, gained seven seats through proportional representation.[36] This party became a symbol of hope for Nepalis who sought an alternative to the quarrelling, inefficient, ageing male leaders of the traditional parties. For their part, the older parties see a threat from these new parties and are trying newer ways to impede their progress. For example, Rabi Lamichhane, the RSP president, was remanded to eighty-four days' custody in connection with an alleged cooperative scam. However, many viewed this as a political vendetta.³⁷ He was again arrested on April 5, 2025 and continues to be in custody.³⁸ Whether through the RSP or other independent groups, I believe these new leaders will be the big challengers to the existing big three political parties—NC, UML and Maoist—in the 2027 elections.

Transforming Politics for the Future

There are four key lessons from the elections of 2022 that will have a bearing in the future in Nepal's journey towards 2043. Firstly, the way the people voted has disrupted the status quo. They voted for independents, looking at the candidates' competencies rather than their allegiances. Many senior party leaders had to swallow the bitter pill of their party's candidate losing in the wards where they voted. It could be voter frustration against the party leaders who have been doing little but fighting within the party and against other parties, not on ideological or significant issues, but on petty matters. In a country where 70 per cent of the population is below the age of forty, old male leaders have been given a wake-up call and a clear message that they should hang up their hats. It is going to be important to watch how the traditional parties respond to this.

Secondly, the 2022 election indeed demonstrated the power of social media. Gone are the days when candidates and parties relied on speeches, dinners and parties to woo voters. Things have taken a different turn with social media platforms entering people's lives. Your messages and causes should be understood by people. Balen Shah, the young Mayor of Kathmandu, has 2.3 million followers on Facebook, 6,40,000 on Instagram and a strong presence on YouTube. The Facebook page Routine of Nepal Banda, which had 4.4 million followers as of February 2025, has become a source of news and was instrumental in pushing Balen's agenda during the elections. Moreover, political actors can no longer depend on false data or bluster to mislead voters. Accountability has moved to an entirely new level. Every individual with a smartphone is now a potential source of news, capable of capturing and sharing videos or expressing opinions that can go viral within minutes. The 2024 Indian elections of 2024 have demonstrated the power of social media, wherein a handful of people with followers on social media have challenged financially dominant traditional media platforms.

Third, it is all about managing expectations. A 2021 study on local economic development conducted by beed management revealed that people wanted local governments to prioritize economic transformation, be it the creation of jobs, providing access to markets for their produce, helping them in their entrepreneurial journey or seeing some major projects come to their neighbourhood. The prevailing mood was one of disillusionment with the older political parties. Many respondents strongly criticized how these parties transformed their behaviour during elections—suddenly becoming accessible and attentive, only to disappear once votes had been cast. This pattern was particularly disliked by younger people and women. Several surprise-winning candidates likely recognized this disconnect and addressed it effectively during their campaigns.

Finally, all eyes are on Kathmandu. Much attention is focused on how a candidate like Balen Shah will perform. He has his work carved out, but in terms of basics—cleanliness, waste management, misuse of building permits and the removal of shabby structures—his success in Kathmandu could set a precedent for cities across Nepal. He has given hope to many young Nepalis that one can fight an election and win it if with the right strategy. They also perhaps understand that one does not need to have affiliations with any party.

Going forward, the focus will be on the 2027 elections. The RSP has already begun campaigning to topple the old parties in both the federal and local elections. It has launched an ambitious countrywide drive to recruit members and build party structures in preparation for 2027. Similarly, the CPN–UML has undertaken a nationwide membership campaign. A party with a strong local presence and a genuine understanding of the changing political landscape may well find success, while many prominent leaders and established parties could face significant setbacks.

Corruption is also becoming a central issue, with newer parties actively working to expose corrupt, older-generation politicians. In 2023 and 2024, several major scams came to light—not because corruption was previously absent, but due to a heightened demand for accountability in recent times. Many old cases have been revisited, and senior leaders of parties sent to jail.[39] This trend is likely to persist, as emerging leaders recognize that political success increasingly hinges on integrity and a clean track record. Those with strong values and a commitment to honest governance are now better positioned to challenge seasoned politicians. Moreover, as Nepal integrates further into global financial systems and complies with anti-money laundering and related protocols, it will become increasingly difficult to sustain corrupt practices.

From 2024 to 2043, Nepal will witness four more rounds of federal and local elections. Many of the key leaders currently at the helm may have passed away or withdrawn from active politics. Even Gagan Thapa, the youth mascot of the Nepali Congress, will have turned sixty-six by then, as will several other prominent leaders of today's major parties.

In South Asia, politics has become a hereditary profession, but I think it is only a matter of time before voters begin to reject such non-democratic conduct within parties. Merit and performance will increasingly matter, as governments that deliver jobs, economic growth and development will be rewarded. Social media ensures greater accountability. Fake news rarely endures, and achievements must be substantiated by evidence. Citizens are becoming more inclined to verify data and statements. Nepalis are searching for inspiration. They seek integration with the global economy, bringing about clean and efficient government, promoting digitalization and easy public service delivery. People are looking for inspiration to go out and return to Nepal with better education and skills.

I continue to argue that one of the greatest benefits of federalism has been the emergence of capable local leaders and the opportunity for more people to enter politics at the local level rather than attempting to begin their careers at the federal level. This would also mean more competition at the local levels as many people from each party will have to compete for party tickets. Organizational structures of political parties will move in line with the three governmental branches. We must remember that before becoming prime minister of India, Narendra Modi served two terms as chief minister of Gujarat. Similarly, Chinese President Xi Jinping spent fifteen years in regional roles and five years as vice president before assuming the presidency. Nepal's political landscape in 2043 will depend on the pace at which young people enter politics, the extent of internal reform within political parties to make them more democratic and the nation's overall commitment to federalism.

Chapter 4

Thriving in Chaos

In April 2015, after the Gorkha earthquake of 7.8 magnitude, Nepal witnessed a barrage of international support. Volunteers from across the world arrived through various agencies. Our office too supported several initiatives; we diverted all our resources to assist rescue efforts and coordinate the delivery of food and essentials. I was also asked to brief and help coordinate with many international groups arriving in droves.

One such group, comprising twenty volunteers, set off for Sindhupalchok, one of the districts most severely affected by the earthquake. Their first visit was a reconnaissance trip—an approximately three-hour drive to the district, a few hours on the ground and then a return to Kathmandu. They carried some relief materials and food supplies for survivors and had packed sandwiches for themselves from their hotel.

I met them that evening for a briefing to plan the next few days. When I arrived at the hotel lobby, I noticed that several members of the group were in tears. Concerned, I asked what had happened. They began to recount their day. One of them asked how people could be so kind when they were going through so much pain. Apparently, the households they had visited were cooking lunch in the open and were offering food to the volunteers who had come to help them. The group told me they were overwhelmed and unsure how to respond to such generosity. They had expected to find people crying, helpless and desperately waiting for aid. I explained that this is the essence of Nepali resilience—it is to move on and focus on what lies ahead.

In Nepal, we have learnt to thrive despite the chaos. This is our hallmark. We confront multiple challenges each day and overcome them by looking forward and continuing onward. It is this very idea—of thriving in chaos—that I wish to explore more deeply in this chapter, for I believe it will be a key force in propelling Nepal towards its goals by 2043.

Resilient Nepalis

When we speak of Nepali resilience, we often refer to the fact that people in this country have learnt to manage their lives in difficult terrains and face natural and human-induced adversities with a lot of strength. Often, when I travel through the rugged terrain in the remote areas of the country, I wonder how people keep up with their day-to-day lives. In September 2023, I undertook a six-hour-long, scary journey by road in a jeep to Jomsom, the gateway to Mustang district, located 160 kilometres west of the tourist city of Pokhara. The alternative was no better: a four-day walk. As the local hotel owner said, 'We have no choice but to go through these hardships; we live in hope that the roads will get better someday.' A documentary titled *Most Dangerous Way to School in Nepal*, posted on the Free Documentary Official Facebook page in May 2024,[1] garnered 8.6 million views in a year. It documented the daily journey of students crossing the river in an area not very far from the capital city of Kathmandu. People walk miles to reach a health post; students undertake dangerous journeys crossing rivers in all sorts of contraptions—in all these cases, people take up the challenge as long as they get what they are looking for. The weather can play havoc, from droughts to floods and landslides, earthquakes keep coming back at regular intervals, and extreme weather keeps taking a toll on people's lives and livelihoods. However, as tough as it all sounds, we must go on.

Absorption, Adaptive and Transformative Capacities

Oxfam is a global organization that fights inequality to end poverty and injustice. After the earthquake, at the Nepal Economic Forum, we worked with Oxfam on an impact assessment of the earthquake on small and medium enterprises. I came across some key literature in that process. Oxfam lists three capabilities as necessary ingredients to resilience: 'First, Absorption capacities, the ability of social actors to cope with and overcome all kinds of adversities. Second, adaptive capacities—their ability to learn from past experiences and adjust themselves to future challenges in their everyday lives. Third, transformative capacities—their ability to craft sets of institutions that foster individual welfare and sustainable societal robustness towards future crises.'[2] Nepalis have developed these capacities to build their resilience. Strong social structures across communities have helped people cope with adversities for thousands of years. Even Nepalis who migrate know they can rely on these social structures and bonds outside the country amongst the diaspora.

In the Kathmandu Valley, the concept of Guthi[3] or community trusts has been able to provide much-needed social service delivery in times of need. For instance, a friend is actively involved in Morang Samaj Kathmandu, a group with members from the Morang District in Kathmandu, responsible for taking care of the needs of people from the district, whether helping with administrative procedures in government offices, facilitating the admission of children in colleges, providing legal counsel support, or offering monetary assistance in times of medical or other emergencies. Similar groups based on ethnicity or geographical locations can be found outside Nepal too. It is not surprising, therefore, to find over one hundred such groups in the Washington, DC area alone.

Many such groups are also formed to provide the last-mile support at the time of a loved one's death in the family. In Hinduism and Buddhism, death is seen as only a part of one's journey from a past life to the next. Therefore, rituals and processes become very important. In the Newa community across Nepal, there are different guthis or *samaj* (community trusts) that help people arrange a respectable farewell from the earth. These communities also provide continuous support to the bereaved family, especially when the deceased was the breadwinner.

Such social structures also get activated during disasters. For instance, after the 2015 earthquake, case studies from the Newa town of Khokhana revealed how culture and social structures have built resilience. A paper by Venkat Rao Pulla and Sandesh Dhakal titled 'Culture and Resilience to Earthquake Trauma: Nepal Newari Community' illustrates 'the cultural competencies and a unique form of Newari community organization "Guthi" that provides strong emotional and moral support to its members and plays a detrimental role in conducting their daily lives'. In the aftermath of the earthquake,[4] the study revealed that the community commenced group cooking, pooled in-house resources remaining within the community, initiated cleaning debris around their habitat, and began collective living in tents. Many of the houses were reconstructed even before government initiatives. In fact, the people of Khokana were able to bounce back to their normal lives earlier than people from adjacent areas. 'In this phenomenological study, the narratives reveal a strong adherence to traditional lifestyle;

obedience to the moral sense of responsibility, loyalty to their independence, unquestionable faith in God, and responsive emotional and moral support from membership as being vital to their resilience. Our conclusions corroborate the connection between spirituality and resilience, and that pain, suffering, and failure are but normal components of life that assist people's capacity to respond to trauma,'[5] the authors wrote.

After the 2015 earthquake, many such studies were conducted around Nepali resilience. For instance, a study was conducted to quantify resilience by building frameworks and indices to be able to explain this in numbers.[6] However, resilience is qualitative as it has multiple qualitative components that cannot be quantified. With Nepalis having very little faith in the state and low expectations from their government, societal and other structures like the ones discussed above have had to remain robust to build resilience against natural or man-made disasters and challenges.

Another big earthquake struck Western Nepal on 3 November 2023, with the epicentre in Ramidanda, Jajarkot, around 525 kilometres west of Kathmandu. The earthquake, with a magnitude of 6.4, killed at least 153 people and destroyed 62,000 houses in eleven districts of western Nepal.[7] The *Nepali Times* reported on how the 'survivors were showing collective resilience'.[8] It was again people fending for themselves. 'Familiar with [the] slow delivery of government services, most surviving families have taken matters into their own hands to get through the bitter winter and to rebuild their lives and livelihoods.'[9]

The incessant rains between September 26 to 28 in 2024 cut off Kathmandu from Eastern Nepal, with some sections of the B.P. Highway heavily damaged. The *Rising Nepal* reported that fifty-seven roads across the country remained blocked.[10] A few days later, I was in Dhulikhel, the entry point to the nearest point in the East, 30 kilometres away from Kathmandu, as the festive break had started. I was chatting with people who had just taken the arduous journey to Kathmandu. They narrated how local lodge and eatery owners were involved in helping open the road, even if it was just one way and temporarily. They shared the stories of locals setting up community kitchens, not only for themselves, but for the people who operated bulldozers and excavators belonging to the government and some local contractors.

After the April 2015 earthquake, Blair Glencorse and I wrote an op-ed for the *New York Times*, where we talked about how 'the earthquakes have generated an unprecedented sense of collective responsibility for the future'.[11] We saw the spontaneous volunteerism and wrote, 'This is not to suggest that Nepali society has suddenly been transformed, but there is a volunteerism, community spirit and social consciousness that is new and very different from before. This can be harnessed in positive ways well beyond post-disaster relief work.'[12]

We need to build on this social character. The improvement in governance and better service delivery at all levels of government, along with a reduction in corruption and predictability of government policies, laws and institutional frameworks, will only drive Nepali human and economic development. Together, these would complement the existing structures of Nepali resilience. For instance, if youth groups who work in relief measures after disasters can coordinate with the government, it will have a multiplier effect in efficacy and speed of providing relief. If local politicians co-opt different local groups rather than thinking of them as political rivals, there would be more synergy.

Political Uncertainty

On 14 July 2014, the French newspaper *Le Monde* carried a piece with the headline: 'Nepal, the world champion of political instability'.[13] It further stated, 'In the political instability Olympic Games, Nepal continues to claim the top spot on the podium.' Nepalis, in the past seventy-four years after the end of the Rana regime in 1950, have seen 22 prime ministers in forty years between 1950 and 1990. Thereafter, there have been twenty-seven prime ministers in thirty-four years from 1990 to 2024. Between December 2022 and March 2024, the cabinet has been reshuffled 16 times, and the same prime minister has led four different coalitions. Nepal has seen the permutation and combination of different ideologies and, strangely, also seen people with divergent views in the same government, but with no significant change in governance. Apart from those whose lives and fates are directly linked to the politicians, others simply take this kind of political turmoil as a constant—that it is something we have to live with and move on.

However, in this same period, Nepali GDP has grown from US$7 billion in 2004 to US$44 billion in 2024. This is a six-fold jump, despite all the political challenges. I always argue that you can have political certainty—like Robert Mugabe's thirty-seven-year rule in Zimbabwe—but it will not necessarily deliver economic growth. In a conversation with the former Foreign Secretary of India, Shiv Shankar Menon, in Kathmandu during the Himalayan Future Forum, he explained that firm majoritarian rule may not deliver in South Asia and argued that political parties need to make constant adjustments to form different coalitions and work with friends and foes alike.

Nepal has also made commendable progress in reducing extreme poverty and hunger during the Millennium Development Goals (MDG) period (2000–15). Extreme poverty dropped from 33.5 per cent of the population in 1990 to 16.4 per cent in 2013, thereby achieving the target of halving the poverty rate by 2015.[14] Nepal is one of only a few countries on track to achieve the Millennium Development Goals for maternal health, infant mortality, and universal education. I keep imagining what the results could be with better politics and governance.

Political uncertainty has had an obvious impact on governance and the efficient functioning of bureaucracy and the state. Any country needs strong institutions that can provide certainty in policy-building and the day-to-day functioning of the state. Even the World Bank, in its evaluation report for 2014–23, admitted that 'The World Bank's programme made little progress in building stronger institutions with the capacity to implement policy and deliver services.'[15] In my column in the *Kathmandu Post*, I argued that 'If the greater politics is to change, the focus will have to shift to building institutions, and the people leading institutions have to sacrifice their greed of wanting to be the centrepiece at the cost of the organisation.'[16]

Learning from the Past

While there is a tendency to blame all our problems on politicians, we need to also be aware that we have been through trying circumstances in the past and yet, somehow managed to carve a path out of them towards a better life. It is important to look back and learn from the past.

Let's look at Nepal's history, particularly the insurgency and the royal massacre, for instance.

The country reeled through ten years of insurgency from 1996 to 2006 that led to over 14,000 deaths, thousands of incapacitations and injuries, and hundreds of thousands of people being displaced. The country's infrastructure was destroyed, and travelling from one part of Nepal to another became a humongous challenge. People were caught between insurgents engaged in extortion and killings and the state that was also engaged in indiscriminate arrests, killings, and disappearances. The economy and development suffered. However, Nepalis still managed to find a way out. I shudder to think what could have happened had things been even worse. What if the King and his government had decided not to give in? What if the political parties and the Maoist insurgents had not agreed to move ahead together? What if the Maoists had not wanted to give up violence?

While working on a Vision 2030 document for the Nepal Army Welfare Fund, I asked a general as to whether he could spot the soldiers that were integrated from the insurgent army and the original recruits of the Nepal Army, he said he could not.

Former Assistant Secretary-General of the UN Kul Chandra Gautam wrote, 'Following protracted and contentious negotiations, the integration and rehabilitation of the Maoist combatants happened in a relatively peaceful manner with a generous "golden handshake" offered to most combatants.'[17] Pushpa Kamal Dahal, the person who led the insurgency, became prime minister with his party, the CPN Maoist, winning the highest number of seats in the elections to the first Constituent Assembly. In an op-ed he wrote for the *Kathmandu Post* in November 2021, coinciding with the completion of fifteen years of peace agreement, he said that 'one reason why Nepal's peace process has been successful is that it has adopted a home-grown model.'[18] The home-grown model emphasised a solution that was not mediated by international actors but developed by Nepalis through the trial-and-error method. He went on to emphasize, 'Significantly, there has been no relapse of large-scale violence throughout Nepal's peace process, unlike what many other post-conflict countries experienced. Clearly, Nepal's peace process has laid the foundation for sustainable peace for all Nepalis.'[19]

Five years into the insurgency, another event changed the future course of Nepali history. On the fateful day of 1 June 2001, a maverick crown prince killed his father, mother and fourteen other members of the family before killing himself. Given the century-old tradition, he was still declared King before his death, and consequently Gyanendra, the brother of the slain King, became the new King. Nepalis wept, said adieu to the members of the royal family who were killed and even accepted the new King. There were no coups, there were no political challenges, there was no rebellion. Unlike in Rwanda in 1994, where the death of a President in an air crash resulted in the horrible genocide that took away a million lives, just in neighbouring India, when Prime Minister Indira Gandhi was killed by her Sikh bodyguard in 1984, angry mobs went on a rampage, killing Sikhs, and thousands were killed across the country.

In contrast, the transition from one king to another was peaceful in Nepal, contrary to many reports that were being filed by international media. While international media outlets like the *Guardian* wrote, 'Tension on streets as people demand to know the truth behind royal bloodbath,' in reality, the transition was peaceful. The article went on to say, 'As the curfew began in Kathmandu last night, Nepal's deeply spiritual people remained shaken to the core by the murder of their monarch, a man they regarded as an incarnation of god.'[20] Yes, Nepalis were shaken, but they put the past behind and moved on like they always do. Nepalis have always learned to find peaceful ways out of challenging situations.

The King who was crowned in 2001 became ambitious, and there was a popular uprising against King Gyanendra in April 2006. He agreed to relent and end direct rule, reinstating the parliament he had dissolved fourteen months ago.[21] The 240-year-old monarchy came to an end after the first constituent assembly formally abolished the monarchy on 28 May 2008.[22] Gyanendra did not resist. 'He swept out of the sprawling Narayanhiti complex in the heart of the capital in a black limousine, driving behind an armed police pick-up, past thousands of onlookers and hundreds of riot police,' said a news report.[23] Peaceful transitions have been a hallmark of Nepal's tumultuous political journey, and perhaps there is merit in studying why Nepalis always choose peace in the wake of a crisis.

The Belief in Hope

Generally, Nepalis are used to taking things lying down, and perhaps this also needs to change. On the one hand, some of these issues speak volumes about the average Nepali's patience and perhaps optimism that things will change in the long run. On the other hand, one is also forced to wonder how much longer they will be able to put up with unfavourable conditions if things don't change. Let's look at a few more examples.

Darkness to light: Nepalis started experiencing planned power outages, popularly known as load-shedding, from 2008 onwards. It lasted all the way until 2018. At its peak in 2016, it was twenty hours a day. Citizens made adjustments by installing solar panels, relying on inverters, managing schedules based on the published timetable, and using generators to generate their own power. People switched their wedding reception dates based on the power schedule in the area where they lived, and functions were held according to the schedule. The monsoons were better, but when winter hit and the rivers, the source of hydropower, started to dry up, people anxiously waited for the schedule to be published. Students adjusted their reading time, and social functions were managed accordingly. There were no protests by citizens. People made jokes about the schedules and challenges; life just moved on. An article in the *Nepali Times* said, 'In 2016, Nepalis got a pleasant surprise. As soon as the NEA had a new chief, Kul Man Ghising, they started getting

24 hours of power supply.'[24] The power cuts were happening 'not just because of undersupply but because of structural corruption'.[25] Even after this news came out, we did not see citizen protests.

Fuel crises come and go: When I was taking a friend who was visiting from the US to a neighbourhood restaurant in Kathmandu, he and I saw a long serpentine queue of motorcycles leading to the neighbourhood fuel station. My friend wondered whether there was an audition for a reality show going on. Many visitors are surprised at the orderly, yet serpentine queues at fuel stations that do not lead to brawls or fist fights. Nepal is dependent on India for its fuel, and many times, due to different reasons—from supply to pricing issues—fuel supply gets impacted. Queues become the norm. People use their networks to source fuel, and hoarding becomes standard. At one time, we had ten cooking gas cylinders at home just to be able to tide through all crises. Perhaps, when electric vehicles started to become easily available, people rushed to change their vehicles to electric ones. The memories of serpentine queues force us to think differently. No mass demonstration, no public outcry. Price does not matter as long as there is supply. To a large extent, this challenge has been solved. Now, fuel moves from India to Nepal via pipelines. With the adoption of electric vehicles, it is becoming rarer to see fuel crises.

Withstanding banda or closures: Only a few years ago, nationwide strikes or closures declared by various political, business, or civil society groups used to cripple the country. Nepalis did not complain; they just decided to find ways to manage their lives by walking to offices, stocking up on food, and planning their days depending on the days of closure announced. General strikes were happening frequently in Nepal and had become so common that the United Nations Department of Safety and Security (UNDSS), Nepal Office recorded 1205 general strikes in 2010 alone. A public website, nepalbandh.com, became a popular go-to tool. It recorded 100 separate actions across the country in one month, and up to nine in one day. This page then became a Facebook page, 'Routine of Nepal Banda', which became so popular (4.3 million followers on Facebook in March 2025) that now, as RONB, it competes with media outlets. Referred to as 'Rootiney' in Nepali, hundreds of pages have emerged with similar names. One could argue that perhaps Nepalis knew these strikes were part of a transient phase and would die down, because today, bandas have really gone away. The last attempted closure was in February 2021 during the pandemic.[26] No attempts towards countrywide shutdowns have been made since then.

Apart from the crises fuelled by Nepal's domestic politics, there are also other issues that are a result of geopolitics, particularly the fact that Nepal is a landlocked country, and the stability of its currency is dependent on its neighbour. While there have been great advantages to riding India's growth wave, Nepal has also suffered from challenges whenever the Indian rupee depreciates or there is a major disruption in the Indian economy.

Surviving blockades: As a landlocked country that was, until 2017, completely dependent on India for its supplies and transit, Nepal had learnt to withstand both formal and informal blockades imposed by India. Since 1950, apart from different forms of challenges to transit at provincial and border levels, such as regulations on testing of products and bans on imports to and exports from Nepal, there have been three major blockades: 1970, 1989 and the most recent one in 2015. The 2015 blockade, which began in September, was just five months after

Nepal was hit by a big earthquake. People paid five times more for cooking gas, bought fuel on the black market, paid high prices for goods due to increased prices and supply restrictions, but the country moved on. I believe that a country smaller than its neighbour tends to build up resistance over time. We see this in landlocked countries like Switzerland, surrounded by large neighbours. It is like when one has a small house and has to put up with the antics of neighbours who own a palatial mansion. When big parties happen at the mansion, your driveway gets blocked, and you know you can do little about it. Blockades are always at the back of a Nepali's mind. One is prepared for the blockades of highways and supply chains due to natural calamities, but it takes a slightly longer time to adjust when blockades are imposed by neighbours.

Unpredictable inflation: Many communists who come to Nepal on visits from India are surprised that price hikes are not resisted or protested. In the early 1990s, we saw some protests that were violent, but people now just accept the fact that prices can only go up, and if they do not go up by a long shot, it is okay. Take a look at the average shopper or the traveller during festivals, paying multiple times the normal price, or the person in remote parts of the country, just accepting the price that the trader charges. I attribute it to the economy that is greatly influenced by trade and arbitrage opportunities. Since everybody is working on high margins and pricing models with high profits, Nepalis have come to accept inflation as a way of life. Some of my economist friends attribute this to being highly import-dependent and the acceptance of not having control over the pricing of products and services. In my writings, I have continuously described the Nepali consumer as someone who 'is not adamant about getting their money's worth'.[27]

So why do Nepalis thrive despite chaos? I have always asked how Nepalis can manage to go through natural calamities, political uncertainties, and multiple events that impact their day-to-day lives and yet remain optimistic. I tend to attribute this to economic security that comes with the ownership of land and houses, the open border, and mobility across the world. This, complemented with unique and strong social structures, the sense of needing to resolve your own problems and wanting to move on, putting the past behind, helps them thrive despite chaos.

From India to the world—a shock absorber: The open border with India has historically been a shock absorber. Nepalis have worked in the British and Indian armies under government-to-government arrangements. With airline connectivity and easy passport issuance, global education destinations and job markets are becoming a big insurance that helps to build resilience. In the 1850s, when the Rana autocracy made landholding by common people difficult, people moved to the fertile plains of Gangetic India. In fact, their movement can be traced right up to present-day Malaysia. When I tell people in Africa that a child can just cross the border to get back home from India during their school holidays or that I could just go to India to work, they ask me about the legalities of such easy travel across borders. I tell them we have a special treaty with India that allows free movement within the two countries. During difficult times in Nepal, people went to India for seasonal as well as long-term work. Now global job markets are absorbing Nepalis at a phenomenal pace. The existence of such alternatives helps build one's resilience, as one is not dependent on the opportunities and structures of one's own country but can think of options beyond. During the insurgency years (1996–2006), hundreds of thousands of Nepalis crossed the border to go to India to work.[28] When one travels to India, one can travel to anywhere in the world through India as long as you have a visa. Imagine for countries like Mauritius, the Maldives or Fiji, how difficult it is to get to a connecting point. Being land-linked to a large nation helps one find an alternative during chaos.

You have to fend for yourself: In the US, if there is a crisis at home, the first thing you do is dial 911, a very effective public safety system that responds. This is a government-operated, efficient system that offers an immediate response to problems, and even if one lives alone, has no family members, or does not know who their neighbours are, one can feel safe during any emergencies, as there is a government system to take care of them. This is also true in many other countries. However, in Nepal, while there are police hotlines, the immediate impulse of people is to look for friends and family, members of the ethnic group or the geography one belongs to. So, the general belief is that you should fend for yourself. There are very few interfaces with the government—getting birth and death registered, getting land, house deeds, or vehicles registered, getting citizenship, driving licences or passports, getting approvals for studies abroad etc. Common citizens generally do not have to deal with the government on a regular basis. Public transportation is privately owned, and education and healthcare are dominated by private players. People have perceptions of the government rather than interactions with the government offices. Ameet Dhakal, editor of Setopati, quoting a survey conducted by Sharecast in January 2025,[29] wrote on the perception of corruption. '85 percent of people said they had never had to pay a bribe to an employee or middleman when receiving a public service. But 80 percent of them said corruption was widespread.'[30]

If there are medical emergencies, if one can afford it, it is the private hospitals to which one would rush their near and dear ones, not government hospitals. In Ghunsa, a village in the Kanchenjunga area in Eastern Nepal, when I saw a helicopter landing, I was told by the lodge owner that it had come to fetch their daughter-in-law, who would be going to a private hospital in Kathmandu to deliver her child. No risks were taken with the local health post, and the nearest town, Taplejung, is a three-day walk away. They have built up cash reserves to be able to pay for such emergencies. The helicopter service cost him NPR 5,00,000 (US$4000). I am not sure how many countries see people of low or lower-middle income thinking of using helicopters for medical purposes, putting a good part of their savings into just one trip. When I visited the newly built Mediciti hospital in Lalitpur, the district next to Kathmandu, the manager showing us around told us they built a helipad in the hospital thinking of emergency evacuation for tourists and expatriates, but they told us that 90 per cent of the patients arriving by chopper were from different parts of Nepal. You trust in yourself, your savings, and your network of friends and family. That is what gets one through chaos. One of the biggest tests for Nepalis who thrive in chaos came during the COVID-19 pandemic, and it overcame it with the least impact. Perhaps lives could have been saved, better management would have resulted in less anxiety and ease for citizens, but given what happened around the world, we need to be grateful that we managed to get over it better than many of us expected to. We will examine what worked and what did not.

Pandemic Strikes

In February 2020, during my trip to Boston, people were looking at Chinese and Asian-looking people and referring to them as 'virus'. This was happening across the world, where governments and people were busier mocking China and Chinese people rather than thinking about what would happen if the world were impacted by the pandemic as it did. I took the last flight from Bangkok to Kathmandu before the world started to shut down. I had just come from Singapore to Bangkok. I saw an empty Changi Airport in Singapore and a frighteningly empty Don Muang Airport in Bangkok, both typically super busy airports. When I reached my hotel in downtown Bangkok in less than an hour and a half from landing and saw serpentine queues for masks, I felt something unreal was happening. It was slowly starting to sink in.

I had travelled in and out of East Africa during the Ebola[31] outbreak in 2013 and in East Asia during severe acute respiratory syndrome (SARS)[32] in 2003, but this time it looked different. Back home, I called our daughter, who was enjoying her spring break from her college near New Delhi. We pushed her to take the next flight back home. My wife and I look back at what prompted us to be so insistent, but if we had not, she would have been stuck at the college for months! She went back to college after two years. We heard the plight of many parents trying to connect with their children studying abroad, and some of the stories of people not being able to see their loved ones were heartbreaking. You could have the money to travel, but you couldn't actually go. You were stuck where you were.

The sense of preparedness comes perhaps from your own experiences. Perhaps, if I had not seen how Singapore was preparing and heard from our local team in Rwanda about how Rwanda was preparing, we would not have taken this so seriously. At work, we started doing our drills for complete remote work as we knew that it wasn't whether lockdown would happen or not, but only when. We had about ten days more than others to plan. Like knowing where the emergency exit is on one's flight or the hotel one is staying in, it is really important to learn and prepare. Perhaps, that is one of the biggest lessons the pandemic taught us. One day can mean a lot during these times.

The pandemic also taught us how to have empathy and the importance of two words: precaution and prevention. Across the world, whenever political, religious or societal rhetoric fought these two words, they suffered. We will examine the positive attributes that led to the containment of the pandemic and the rollout of vaccinations.

Obedient Nepalis

Nepalis were very obedient when the lockdown was imposed a couple of days before India imposed its lockdown. People were surprised at themselves, that they were being obedient and compared themselves with people in other neighbouring and far-off countries where they were not. Innovations of various kinds began as social distancing became the keyword. Neighbourhood shops started to have different precautionary measures—from glass to plastic sheets to the use of tongs and different forms of clips to avoid human touch. Places of worship were shut with only basic rituals being undertaken. Masks became something that people started to use in common family spaces. Medical professionals were extremely disciplined as they worked hard as professionals and not because of government encouragement or incentives. There was a sort of order and discipline that prevented the numbers of people infected from remaining low in the first wave. Only 25 per cent of the 8,133 deaths caused by the pandemic occurred during the first wave.[33]

Spontaneous Citizen's Support

There were volunteer groups taking care of people crossing the border from India—providing food and shelter. CNN Hero of the Year 2015, Maggie Doyne, grabbed global headlines as she managed a quarantine centre for herself, her biological child, and other children.[34] Other stories of volunteerism also caught global attention.[35] Publications like *Altruistic Traveler* began spreading the news of various voluntary organizations that needed volunteers.[36] Studies showed that, despite the challenges and risks to their lives, 90 per cent of medical staff were willing to volunteer during the pandemic, which helped different corners of Nepal find willing volunteers.[37] There were also groups working to feed not only humans but stray animals[38] who were going without food.[39] Feed The Hungry Nepal[40] was providing similar services, prompting us to raise support for the organization.

Local Governments Structure Helped

Nepal had just implemented the new federal structure in the Nepal Constitution 2015, and the local governments were elected for the first time in 2018. The roles and responsibilities of these local governments—especially if they were in charge during such a pandemic—were unclear. Rather than waiting for the federal government to decide what to do and how to do it, the local governments began taking proactive steps, whether creating quarantine centres, undertaking tests, or later administering vaccines. As I discussed in the previous chapter, when the second dose of vaccination was being rolled out, I was taken aback when an official from my ward office sent me messages reminding me to get my shot. When I did not respond to the messages, the official called me, and we went to get our second dose, which happened in a jiffy.

Impact on the Economy Was Not Big

The COVID-19 pandemic also taught us which parts of the economy were impacted and which were not. Nepalis who rely on their social network of living in the dwellings they own, family support, and help from social organisations were able to manage the basic challenges the pandemic posed, such as food. They were only challenged when they were infected. Unlike in neighbouring countries and countries in Africa, people in the villages did not have to forgo much in terms of food.

Our team in Rwanda shared that during the pandemic, they had to cut down on their meals. They told me they had become 'vegetarians' like me! One of the key reasons the Nepali economy stayed afloat was that Nepal was also fortunate that remittances did not shrink. Contrary to popular belief that overseas workers lost jobs, studies by the Nepal Economic Forum showed that this was not true, and people were receiving their salaries as they waited to return to their jobs. Countries like the UAE, in 2022, allowed visitors with visas to work, and suddenly, 65,000 Nepalis took a visitor visa to the UAE.[41] In the US and other countries where people receive social benefits, they began sending that money back to their families and relatives. During my visit to the US, I heard stories of Nepalis who received support from New York due to the loss of salaries during the pandemic. Not only did they send some of the money back to Nepal to support family and relatives, but they also went on to invest in the local stock market.

Social and religious spending is one of the key drivers of consumption in Nepal. While it took a hit during the initial months, people began returning to their normal routines and habits. Weddings, social and religious events started taking place despite infections. People underwent social and religious rituals. The former King decided to take a dip in the rivers in Haridwar, India and returned infected.[42] People clashed with the police to allow a chariot festival to take place,[43] and while celebrations were delayed, they were not drastically cut down. In a country where social spending is a significant part of consumption that keeps the economy afloat, it suffered an initial dent but recovered in the long run.

The pandemic largely hit international tourism. Later, with high flight prices and tardy guidelines, people were not inclined to travel much internationally. The trekking, mountaineering, vehicle rental and companies specializing in international tourist management suffered. Hotels faced challenges filling rooms, but due to the banqueting business from local clients and room sales to domestic tourists, the recovery was faster. By 2024, more than a million people will have visited Nepal, bringing the numbers back to the pre-pandemic levels.

Corruption Proliferates

If there was a significant negative impact of the pandemic, it was the proliferation of corruption. Government spending took a hit as development projects were affected. Instead, government contracts that emerged because of the pandemic saw the same set of politically connected businesses receiving contracts. From the procurement of medical supplies to vaccines, there were controversies as politicians worked with individuals who could provide kickbacks.[44] On 6 June 2020, a frustrated young Nepali started a Facebook page entitled 'Enough Is Enough'. His frustrations were with government apathy towards the COVID-19 pandemic, continuous political wrangling, nationalistic jingoism in the form of redrawing maps, and corruption in government finances. The group quickly grew in numbers.[45] Private sector groups were also not behind in taking advantage of the situation, as we saw Nepali arbitrage minds working overtime. Businesspeople were caught sneaking thermal guns in privileged blue number-plate vehicles,[46] and there were individuals trying to get their cut on vaccine imports.[47] It was a field day for journalists who became busy working on investigative stories. The challenge of procurement corruption was not limited to Nepal. The Anti-Corruption Resource Centre states, 'Between December 2020 and October 2022, there was a wave of COVID-related corruption incidents across service delivery; health financing; governance and leadership; medical products, vaccines, and technologies; health management information systems; and human resources.'[48] This prompted us at the NEF to host an event—Neftalk—to discuss procurement and the pandemic.[49] We learnt that it was not only in Nepal, but in countries like the UK, there were widespread allegations of corruption during the pandemic. Peter Trepte, Member of the Public Procurement Research Group at the University of Nottingham, who was invited to be part of the panel, shared how in the UK and other countries, in the absence of procurement guidelines for emergencies, there is always room for manoeuvring..[50] We learnt that, like the pandemic, challenges of corruption can be global in these trying times.

What Needs to Be Done—Lessons for the Future

We cannot, of course, be satisfied with the fact that Nepalis can thrive in chaos. Governments and institutions cannot escape their responsibilities. Instead, we need to push for better governance, better service delivery and accountability. Here are some of the lessons we have learnt from handling the pandemic. I believe these are equally applicable when Nepal faces a natural or human-induced disaster in the future.

Constitutional clarity: During the COVID-19 pandemic, even the most powerful governments found themselves helpless. For situations like aggression against a country or a compromise in security, there are well-laid-out chains of command and structures. Similar frameworks must be developed to handle disasters, whether natural, health-related, or arising from a breakdown in communication networks, or other areas that could pose a threat in the decades to come. Therefore, it is important to develop constitutional clarity on how a calamity of this magnitude—perhaps even bigger than this one—should ideally be managed. What would be the role of the federal, provincial, and local governments?

With whom will decision-making lie? How can governments incorporate people through lateral entry as advisors or even in key decision-making positions? Which ministry should be responsible, or should it be shifted directly to the Prime Minister's Office and run by a team of competent people based on merit, irrespective of party background, ethnicity, age, or other usual parameters? What would be the role of parliamentarians? Following this, we need to establish special laws, regulations, and institutional structures. The role of the court will also need to be clearly defined.

Developing emergency response system and protocol: Hollywood movies, series, and other productions have made the number 911 known globally as the emergency number to dial in case of an emergency. The entire US operates on this model of emergency response systems. Many countries have replicated it, but not all have done so successfully. In Nepal, when we dial the traffic control room of Nepal Police on 103, the response has been, until now, not bad at all. We need to design and implement a nationwide emergency response system where people can dial a number to get help. Unlike in the US, where people are completely dependent on the state, in Nepal, it must be a system where those manning the emergency numbers at the local unit level can also leverage different volunteer groups within their own sphere of influence. Just as we do not depend on the blood bank during an emergency need for blood but activate different volunteer groups and networks, this must be replicated in a more structured way. In this regard, the usage of the Nagarik (Citizen) App[51] can also be explored.

Procurement protocols: One of the biggest challenges the world faced during the pandemic was that government procurements or procurements at private hospitals or institutions had to be managed without following the normal procedure. At a micro level, when a branch of a bank needed sanitisers and gloves, there was no time to write memos to the head office and get approvals—they had to just do it. At the federal government level, it was about millions of dollars' worth of procurement for medical supplies or vaccines. Just as there are procurement procedures during security threats, there must be established protocols for such times, and imagining the scale of the problems will be key. Furthermore, since wars, pandemics, or disasters often become tools for profiteering due to the suspension of such protocols, there must also be strong provisions to punish those convicted of financial fraud or corruption.

Volunteering codes: Whether in natural disasters or pandemics, millions of volunteers are mobilised, and there must be codes to regulate them from the perspective of facilitating their work rather than creating control mechanisms. Simple matters need attention. If volunteers are willing to travel to Nepal, their visa approvals must happen instantaneously, like how airline crew members can enter a country. Similarly, mechanisms must be put in place to prevent the misuse of privileges granted during emergencies. If doctors are willing to help, we should not ask them to get an equivalence certificate from the Nepal Medical Association but allow them to begin their work immediately. This does not require much legal or regulatory process but demands a mindset of openness towards the movement of people, the authority they can have, the issues they can address, and the manner in which they can tackle these issues.

Open spaces for quarantining facilities and disasters: Natural disasters like floods, earthquakes, and landslides, as well as pandemics like COVID-19, teach us the importance of open spaces. In Kathmandu Valley, when the second wave started infecting many people, the big question was where quarantine facilities would be located if the situation worsened. Urban centres in Nepal tend to consume all open spaces, as the general mindset among Nepalis is that building is a sign of development, while open spaces are not. Therefore, existing green spaces and open areas must be preserved. If schools have open grounds, there should be a legislative blanket ban on leasing such spaces and constructing buildings on them. Similarly, the Nepal Army, which controls the largest amount of open spaces, needs to share those spaces with civilians.

Border protocols to help citizens: The borders have always been viewed from a security perspective, whether it concerns the movement of unwanted people, smuggling, or illegal activities like human trafficking. However, the pandemic exposed a new type of problem. There was no way to completely close the border, as you had to allow your citizens in and foreigners out, but there was also the humanitarian aspect of not preventing people from moving for basic needs such as food, health, or family issues. In a paper for the Observer Research Foundation, just over five months after the pandemic broke out, I suggested two critical action points.[52] First, it is necessary to establish a joint disaster management border team with representatives from both countries to ensure they can discuss and decide on border openings, timings, provision of essential services, rules related to quarantining and self-isolation, testing, and other protocols. Further, joint teams should undertake patrol measures to ensure porous areas are protected. Second, emergency crisis centres: Since the pandemic is border-agnostic, efforts should be made to establish emergency crisis centres on both sides. These facilities could provide primary health services, testing and spaces for quarantine and self-isolation. Such facilities can be of immense help when access to major towns and cities is hindered. When direct flights from Kathmandu to Delhi or Kolkata were non-existent, we used the land borders to travel across to deal with family and medical emergencies. When Sikkim was cut off from the rest of India during the October 2023 floods, the road link from eastern Nepal, if it had been open, would have helped to build alternative supply chains. We need to use borders as facilitation points.

Change of mindset—from control to facilitation: Government and its apparatus, including people, have been designed for control functions, and it is very difficult to switch to a facilitation mode. This applies to many service-oriented private sector firms as well. It is hard to understand that unnatural situations require different and creative responses! This can only come from training. While disaster preparedness training is typically centred around equipment and materials—since it comes from development partner budgets that have to be spent—the human element is often overlooked. The Army is well-trained to change its mindset from normal times to emergencies; a response to an injury during combat is dealt with differently from an injury during normal times. These adaptations are built into the training system. We need this preparation to proliferate across the country.

Nepal's growth potential and the path toward graduating to a high-income country by 2043 can be derailed by major natural disasters or something as incomprehensible as the pandemic. We need to look back at history and learn from it. We must continuously assess potential causes of disruption of great magnitude and scale. Will a software glitch shut down communication, which in turn will shut down power lines and impact every element of our lives? Will a cyberattack paralyse a nation, and if so, what needs to be done? As more innovations emerge, we will need to continue to extrapolate the risks—be it from blockchain technology, artificial intelligence, or other innovations that will emerge in the years to come. Yes, we have learnt to thrive in chaos, but that can only take us so far in the future. What we need is to complement our existing efforts with collective proactive action.

Chapter 5

Climate Change

'Places that were safe for centuries will no longer be safe in the coming years,' climate scientist Arnico Panday said at a gathering of the steering committee of the Himalayan University Consortium in May 2024.[1] He added that 'even if the world miraculously manages to stabilize the global average temperature at 1.5 degrees above preindustrial levels, we will still face an onslaught of climate change-driven changes, the likes of which we have only had small glimpses of so far'.[2] That's not all.

'Retreating glaciers will create fast-growing glacial lakes, many of which will burst their dams and flood the valleys below,' he continued. 'Many of our glaciers will disappear completely, taking with them our dry-season water supply. Places high above the tree line that used to only get snow will get rain instead, triggering debris flows into the valleys below. Cloudbursts and other extreme weather events will increase, taking out our infrastructure and inundating our lowlands. Low-lying areas will face more and more life-threatening heat waves.'[3] And lastly: 'We will also see increasing numbers of cascading disasters, such as what the Melamchi Valley[4] in Nepal faced in 2021, or what took out the Chungthang dam in Sikkim[5] in 2023.[6]

Extreme weather and rising temperatures are among the easiest ways in which we can see that climate change isn't an abstract concept but something that is impacting our day-to-day lives. The harsh truth is that Nepal will be among the countries that will be worse off and terribly impacted as the years go by. The signs are already evident. In September 2024, the Kathmandu Valley saw an unprecedented 600 mm of rain in two days. This was half of the valley's annual average rainfall![7] Conversely, in the winter of 2024, there was no rainfall at all, impacting the plantation of wheat and barley. Senior watershed expert, Madhukar Upadhya warns that 'the other extreme of no precipitation is even more concerning. The months with record low precipitation were 38 percent more common in 2024 relative to the 1995-2005 baseline period'.[8] He explains why this is important: although winter precipitation is only about 20 per cent of the total annual precipitation, 'winter precipitation is vital in our water budget to support winter crops, maintain grasslands, contain wildfires, and, most importantly, deposit snow in the high mountains. Heavy monsoon rains followed by a dry spell leads to forest wildfire that has created havoc in many years in the past.'[9]

Additionally, air pollution has become a big issue in Nepal with pollution from Bangladesh and India impacting the country. This is apart from the pollution created by fossil fuel vehicles and industries in Nepal. Bad air does not see political boundaries. Therefore, what one needs are cross-boundary efforts to understand and manage the impact of climate change.

While historically, Nepal has been at the forefront of different kinds of affirmative climate action and has benefitted tremendously from being proactive, there is a lot more that needs to be done to make sure the impact of climate change is mitigated. Further, the growth towards 2043 has to be sustainable and achieved with the least impact on the environment, natural habitats and people. This to me is non-negotiable.

In this chapter, we will look at how Nepal has historically been at the helm of discussions around climate change, how the journey has been so far and the lessons we have learnt. We will also look at the commitments Nepal has made in the global discourse around climate change. We will then take a look at some social, cultural and future trends. Finally, since Nepal will be among the countries that will be affected the most, we will discuss why leadership in this field is something Nepal should aspire towards.

A Seat at the Table

Globally, the discourse around climate change first began in the seventies when environmental activists started to make this a political issue. The Intergovernmental Panel on Climate Change (IPCC) was established as a scientific body in 1988 by the World Meteorological Organization (WMO) and the United Nations Environment Programme (UNEP). It was established 'with the objective of informing governments about the latest climate science and the impacts that climate change will bring in the coming decades'.[10] The IPCC presented the first assessment report in 1990, and the work to adopt a multilateral treaty began soon after. Finally, the United Nations Framework Convention on Climate Change (UNFCCC) was adopted in 1992, and till 2024, there are 198 parties to the convention. The focus of the first convention was 'to stabilize greenhouse gas concentrations at a level that would prevent dangerous anthropogenic (human-induced) interference with the climate system'.[11] Each year, member nations meet at the Conference of the Parties (COP), the formal UNFCCC meet on climate, which has, over the years, gained much visibility. In Nepal, we saw common citizens interested in climate change when newspapers started talking about who, from the country, was going to the Earth Summit in Rio de Janeiro in

Brazil in 1992. The then Prime Minister G.P. Koirala led a large entourage from Nepal. It was also perhaps the first time, after the ushering of multi-party democracy, that many Nepalis outside the government and the privileged sphere got to travel internationally. There was a sense of the citizens' participation in deciding the future of Nepal.

Nepal also became a signatory to a number of global agreements in the years that followed. The major agreements adopted are the Kyoto Protocol in 1997, which makes industrialized countries and economies in transition commit to limit and reduce greenhouse gases (GHG) emissions in accordance with agreed individual targets. The actual protocol was only adopted in 2005, and 192 countries, including Nepal, are signatories to this protocol. In 2015, the Paris Agreement was signed. The Paris Agreement is a legally binding international treaty on climate change. It was adopted by 196 Parties, including Nepal, at the UN Climate Change Conference (COP21) in Paris, France, on 12 December 2015. It entered into force on 4 November 2016. Its overarching goal is to hold 'the increase in the global average temperature to well below 2°C above pre-industrial levels' and pursue efforts 'to limit the temperature increase to 1.5°C above pre-industrial levels'.[12] The University of Oxford has initiated Oxford Net Zero as an interdisciplinary research initiative. Oxford Net Zero states that, 'it is international scientific consensus that, in order to prevent the worst climate damages, global net human-caused emissions of carbon dioxide (CO_2) need to fall by about 45 per cent from 2010 levels by 2030, reaching net zero around 2050. Global warming is proportional to cumulative CO2 emissions, which means that the planet will keep heating for as long as global emissions remain more than zero. This implies that climate damages, caused by global heating, will continue escalating for as long as emissions continue'.[13] When we ponder upon the numbers, it is difficult to really get a grip on the impact, but it does provide a comparative perspective to understand the gravity of the impact of climate change.

Despite being a country at the centre of the impact of climate change and a country that took serious interest in mitigation and adaptation early on, Nepal did not get a lot of space in the global discourse. Situated between two large nations, Nepal was considered a small country. Despite Nepal's leadership in issues around climate change, it took thirty-five years for a Nepali to be appointed to the Intergovernmental Panel on Climate Change (IPCC). In July 2024, Nepali atmospheric scientist Maheswar Rupakheti was elected to the thirty-four member bureau.[14] Nepal's work needs to be showcased, and the world needs to know the history of Nepali climate activism and what they have been able to achieve.

Early efforts

Nepal started working towards climate action very early. When the World Conservation Strategy was launched in 1980 by the International Union for Conservation of Nature and Natural Resources (IUCN) and World Wildlife Fund (WWF) for the United Nations Environment Program (UNEP), Nepal was already seven years into institutionalizing its conservation efforts at a national scale. The country's first national park—Royal National Chitwan Park—was created in 1973. In 1982, Nepal recognized the need to look at the impact of climate change and formed the King Mahendra Trust for Nature Conservation (now Nepal Trust for Nature Conservation [NTNC]). A special act was brought in to create the institution, and King Birendra's brother Gyanendra was made the chair. It was given a high profile. The Trust then embarked on creating conservation areas across the country, pioneering the concept of

Integrated Conservation and Development Projects that work closely with communities. Over the course of four decades, the Trust has come to control three major conservation areas—Annapurna, Gaurishankar and Makalu—that comprise 33 per cent of the protected areas in Nepal.[15] The trust has also implemented over three hundred projects and continues to be the nodal agency for conservation management in Nepal. With a corpus of NPR 1.7 billion (US$120 million), it has a long list of achievements as well as planned activities.[16] In 2023, it became one of the two institutions accredited to the Green Climate Fund (GCF).

I vividly remember the long treks to the Annapurna Area Conservation Project (ACAP) offices in the early days of my career to undertake an internal audit of these offices. I realized quickly that the ACAP, established in 1986, was a unique effort to integrate conservation and development with the involvement of the local people. From a few hundred trekkers at the start in the '80s, it has grown to over 2,50,000 tourists visiting the area in 2024. The initiative increases local employment opportunities and showcases a unique conservation-led tourism effort. Shailendra Thakali, who began his career at ACAP and rose to become Education and Information Director for the National Trust for Nature Conservation, explains the unique model in an interview with *ECS Magazine*: 'ACAP was the first protected area, at least in Nepal, to integrate conservation and development, and to involve locals in the decision-making process. At the time, those were very innovative ideas. Today, you find it in many other sectors, but during that time, protected areas were protected areas, and people were excluded from that system. Now, we know that if you really want to protect and sustain goals in the long term, you need to get local people involved in the decisions you are making.'[17]

In 1983, the International Centre for Integrated Mountain Development (ICIMOD), a regional inter-governmental organization was established with an office in Lalitpur, Nepal. The organization's mandate is the safekeeping of the Hindu Kush Himalaya (HKH) mountain range that spans eight countries and stretches 3,500 km across Asia. ICIMOD covers two billion people across Afghanistan, Bhutan, Bangladesh, China, India, Myanmar, Nepal and Pakistan. In its own words, the organization says its goal is to make the region 'greener, more inclusive and climate resilient'.[18] This institution, in its initial days, attracted some of the best minds in the world to Nepal and conducted various types of scientific research. It continues to be the neutral transboundary institution that operates in an environment with major geopolitical challenges between some of its member countries. In October 2022, Pema Gyamtsho, director general, in an interview with *Nepali Times*, marking the forty years of the institution, said, 'The advantage of ICIMOD is its status as a politically neutral organization. So, we are able to bring scientists from our member countries to sit at the same table and discuss climate change impact, about trans-boundary disasters.'[19]

In 1986, during the era of *panchayat raj*, when free press did not exist, the Nepal Forum of Environmental Journalists (NEFEJ) was started and became a prominent civil society voice. When multiparty democracy was restored, this group assumed leadership in matters relating to the environment and conservation. When I spoke to journalist Binod Bhattarai, who was an active member at that time, he recalled, 'NEFEJ was founded with the vision of creating a platform for journalists to focus on environmental issues, raise awareness, and advocate for sustainable development. Over the years, we have worked tirelessly to ensure that environmental journalism in Nepal is robust and impactful.' The institution continues to run the community radio established over three decades ago and publishes, especially in Nepali, on pertinent issues relating to building awareness on the environment.

The Himal Association was formed in 1987 and published the *Himal* magazine. This went on to become a prominent voice in the world of sustainable development and is still popular as *Himal Southasian*. My initial exposure to thought leadership in the Himalayas was through this institution when I got involved as a volunteer. The wealth of information and perspective is still archived at the Digital Himalaya at the University of Cambridge. For me, the *Himal* magazine provided a perspective on climate, sustainable development and the fragile Himalayas that I could not find in other publications of that time. I went on to chair the Southasia Trust, which published *Himal Southasian*, and that gave me an opportunity to also meet and learn from many thinkers and writers who were so concerned about the future of the planet. The association continues to host the Kathmandu International Mountain Film Festival (KIMFF).

When I spoke to climate activist and thought leader Ajaya Mani Dixit, he recalled the setting up of the Nepal Water Conservation Foundation (NWCF) and Nepal Water for Health (NEWAH) in the early 1990s. One of the issues close to his heart was practising and advocating for roof rainwater harvesting, a method that was largely unknown then. Since then, many others have started harvesting rain. Smart Paani, a new company, has even turned water harvesting solutions into a business.

Climate Activism

Environmental activism in the 1990s in Nepal led to many major decisions and projects being scrutinized. The Arun III, a potential World Bank-funded hydropower project, had to be retracted. There were also protests demanding the closure of factories around the Kathmandu Valley. A marble factory on the outskirts of the city was asked to close by the Supreme Court based on a petition by activist groups.[20] Similarly, a government cement factory was shut down due to local pressure. Ajaya Dixit, an international expert on issues of water, climate change, and disasters, told me: 'The changes in 1990 liberalized Nepal's political environment, creating space for contesting the mainstream water development model, mostly based on seeking loans, hiring foreign consultants and contractors with little opportunity for local capacity building. A majority of the debates during this period centred around the Arun III hydropower project, the Indo-Nepal Mahakali Treaty, the West Seti Hydropower Project, the awarding of the 10,800 MW Karnali Chisapani Project with sovereign guarantee to Enron, and the Melamchi Drinking Water Project.' It was not an easy journey for the activists, as they were taking on powerful politicians, development organizations and businesses.

Large development projects have serious environmental impacts that need to be mitigated, but investments for environmental protection increase project costs and are, therefore, often circumvented. Activism builds pressure to ensure proper environmental assessments are made. Public pressure seems to stop these projects, or one has to build them with environmental considerations, as in the case of the Arun III hydropower project. The project is now developed by the private sector with revised designs. In the past decade, the plan to build a new international airport in Nijgadh, eighty kilometres south of Kathmandu, continues to surface time and again. The building of this airport will destroy 40 square kilometres of pristine forests. Therefore, it has been accused of being a 'logging contract'.[21] The activists have been successful in taking the legal route and in getting the Supreme Court to order the halting of the construction in 2022.[22]

During the building of the Bhote Koshi Hydroelectric project, we had to work with the locals to ensure that the design of the tunnels made sure no sacred trees were cut down. There were also guidelines to ensure we put fifty thousand fish into the water every month to secure the fish habitat. In January 2025, when a cable car project began construction in Pathibhara in Eastern Nepal, citizens came together to protest since this was a sacred forest area. Since the private company had the state and security forces supporting the project, protesters ended up getting injured in police action.[23] The project is yet to be completed.

In the media, Nepal continuously gets global attention for its pathbreaking work in the area of climate change. In August 2024, the *Times* reported that drones were going to be used to airlift mountains of rubbish from Everest.[24] This would help manage trash as Everest gets crowded with climbers. A *New York Times* story about how protected Nepali shrublands are used in the making of Japanese currency notes surprised people.[25] It explained how a plant from the Himalayas is harvested under traditional systems and converted into paper that is used in Japanese banknotes.

The point I'm trying to make is this: Nepal started early on, both in terms of thought leadership and action. There have been many successes on multiple fronts. For instance, Senior Fellow at the Nepal Economic Forum, Bibek Kandel, who works in the field of renewable energy in Asia and Africa, shares the story of the success of electrical mini-grids. He says, 'Far from the spotlight, in the last three decades, Nepal built one of the world's most extensive networks of mini-grids, electrifying its remote villages in some of the most unforgiving terrains on Earth. Here's something that might surprise you: with over 3000 mini-grids, Nepal arguably leads globally in the share of its population connected to decentralized renewable grid mini-grids used for rural electrification.' Nepal has been able to adapt to climate change, and efforts to mitigate the impact have begun early on. As Martin Raiser, Vice President of the World Bank, said in September 2022, at an event I was involved with, 'The good news is that the country's notable successes in community forestry and hydropower investments are a strong foundation for future climate-smart growth.'[26]

The positive side has definitely been the addition of forests, energy sources becoming nearly one hundred per cent clean through hydro and solar, harnessing indigenous knowledge for adaptation and mitigation, and community-led efforts. Nepal adopted the Climate Change Policy in 2011 to ensure that there is an overarching national policy to ensure that 'the country is spared from the adverse impacts of climate change, by considering climate justice, through the pursuit of environmental conservation, human development, and sustainable development—all contributing toward a prosperous society.'[27] The key successes have been driven by 'local adaptation of the plan of action',[28] where the community has owned and driven the adaptation and mitigation efforts.

But there are lessons to learn for the future, too, in terms of what can be done better. The electric transport revolution through trolley buses ended without expansion. This needs revival through the use of electricity-based transportation systems, be it railway or long-distance electric buses. The Environmental Impact Assessment (EIA) reports have been criticized as just eyewash. Newspapers keep publishing news about EIA reports being prepared using the 'cut and paste'[29] method. Also, human capital enhancement is required to ensure that there are enough skilled inspectors to look at environmental issues. The lack of technically qualified personnel has hampered environmental monitoring.

Replicating Community Forestry Success

The *New York Times* story of how 'Nepal Grew its Forests Back'[30] is worthy of attention here. The story uses the reflection of Khadga Bahadur Karki from the Kankali Community Forest, located around 150 kilometres west of Kathmandu, on Nepal's growing back its forests. 'The old man moved gingerly, hill after hill, cutting dry shrubs until he was surrounded by trees that had grown from seedlings he had planted two decades ago. He pointed to a row of low peaks above the Kathmandu Valley that were covered with dense foliage. "You see that? They were barren mounds of red mud 15 years ago," said the man, Khadga Bahadur Karki, 70, tears of pride fogging up his glasses. "These trees are more than my children."'

Nepal has been able to grow back its forests with the ownership of action moving from the government to local communities and the support of international development partners. Further, these forests have transformed livelihoods by giving people access to firewood and the ability to commercially exploit the resources within set guidelines. However, Nepal now needs to move to the next phase of leveraging the success of community forests and ensuring that this resource is better utilized. Hemant Ojha, from the National University of Australia, advises using proven techniques that exist to facilitate forest regeneration after harvesting mature trees. In an opinion piece in *Nepali Times*, he says, 'Nepal's community forests are an important natural capital for locals. Forests make up nearly 45% of Nepal's land area and there are over 500 commercially tradable products, with 150 species already in trade. Across the country, over 22,000 forest user groups manage 34% of the total forest area. They can be brought into active management.'[31]

When I was visiting the Gisovu Tea Garden in Rwanda, I was amused to see that the factory was using firewood from the designated forest. Justin Lepcha, the manager, explained to me how the tea garden owns and leases government forests, and in a systematic way, trees are cut and replanted in a forty-year cycle. The cost of the fuel used in furnaces in the tea garden was nearly 15 per cent of the total cost of manufacturing tea. Rwandan tea has been able to reduce the costs of tea by using firewood instead. This can be a great example of how Nepal can think about using increased forest cover for commercial purposes, especially when it comes to substituting expensive imported fossil fuel. I continue to talk about the need for strong policies to ensure that we can leverage the forests we have been able to grow for productive use. For instance, for organized harvesting and production of timber that can substitute expensive aluminium doors and windows we import. Better technology around cooking stoves is making it energy efficient, and the technology around converting forest waste to energy through briquettes has started in a small way in Nepal and should be encouraged.

The Electric Vehicle Revolution

In October 2023, my wife and I attended the auto expo and were looking around for an electric vehicle (EV) that we could buy to replace her existing ICE (internal combustion engine) vehicle. We found the Chinese-made BYD to be the best buy in the price range we were looking for. There were many brands and models on display, and by 15 July 2024, when the Nepal financial year ended, no one would have comprehended that half of the passenger cars sold in Nepal were EVs. After Norway, Nepal is the second country in the world that has gone through rapid EV adoption. In a country where queuing for fuel is a memory that is hard to erase and the cost of rising fuel prices a nightmare, EVs have become popular on account of low operating costs. The Nepal Electricity Authority was quick to install a separate meter at our home, where a week's charge of less than a hundred rupees would substitute for fifteen hundred rupees of petrol. In a year, we spent Rs 6000 on electricity, whereas we spent Rs 60,000 on petrol and always worried when there would be a disruption in the supply. The adoption of EVs has also been made easier as lower duties on EVs meant one could buy the latest models at half the cost of ICE vehicles in the same segment. Further, there were lucrative financing schemes available as EV financing came under priority sector financing.

EV adoption in Nepal also accelerated with automobile dealers putting up charging stations across Nepal without waiting for the government to build networks. While the state utility NEA has been building charging stations, it is interesting to see charging stations mushrooming even in shacks outside teashops on the highways. When I talked to a driver of a microbus operating from Kathmandu to eastern Nepal, he told me he keeps ensuring his vehicle is charged when they have pit stops for tea or meals. Users find innovative ways to ensure their vehicles stay operational. If these microbuses that ran intercity stopped at fuel stations, now they stop at locations that can ensure the charging of vehicles. Teashops and highway eateries are competing to put up charging stations as they know that EVs are here to stay.

When I speak to experts about the reasons behind the faster adoption of EVs in Nepal compared to, say, India or Bangladesh, two major reasons emerge. First, the distances in Nepal are shorter, so a full charge can help people cover more hours and days. Second, many Nepalis who can afford four-wheelers live in their own homes, which means putting up charging stations is easier. When people live in apartments, putting up individual meters is a challenge. This would be a challenge that will be better managed in the future as innovative charging solutions develop.

While we have successes in managing climate change, I find the relationship between climate change, culture, and religion intriguing. I regard climate change as a concept that has emerged in the West. However, I look at the broader issues of the need for co-existence with the environment. In this regard, I find the proliferation of consumption in the name of culture and religion to be an equal threat, like climate change, that we have to manage.

Climate Change, Culture and Religion

In Buddhist monasteries, during ceremonies, it is not difficult to spot the thousands of packets of packaged food offered to the monasteries and monks. During alms-giving ceremonies, when devotees are offering packets of biscuits, instant noodles and other packaged food, I have questioned religious leaders why they allow devotees to indulge in these practices. Yes, it is convenient for devotees to make these offerings, but they also need to learn that they are doing more harm than good. Each one thinks it is just me and a few packets; but when thousands of devotees do that, they are creating excessive waste. When I was ordained as a temporary monk, I did not know what to do with the hundreds of packets of biscuits and instant noodles that came as my share.

The next time there is a religious function, just observe what is going on and what sort of wasteful consumption can be curtailed.

Somewhere, we have come to believe that opulence is doing more dharma. So, we end up consuming more and spending more than is required. With economic prosperity, of course, the number of days of religious functions is expanding, and so is consumption. There is more waste at such functions than ever before. In Dubai, there are campaigns that have started to reduce food waste during Ramadan,[32] which, as a festival of austerity and fasting, produces the biggest food waste as hotels and houses start to serve endless varieties of food that never get eaten. In Nepal, in recent years, Teej, a fasting ritual for Hindu women in certain castes and communities, has become widespread and pushed consumption along with food waste.

There is a perception that the demonstration of opulence is a matter of social pride. At family functions, we used to finish our plates without a morsel of food left, just as we were trained in our childhood. People would look at us in shock, as leaving food on your plate was seen as a sign of economic arrival and prosperity.

If that's on a personal level, on an institutional level too, perhaps it is time to take a look at what is happening. I have been continuously campaigning to reform religious institutions[33] amongst the Theravada Buddhist community in Nepal. The country is dotted with dilapidated religious structures of religious leaders who are dead and gone. In Kathmandu Valley itself, there are so many Tibetan Buddhist monasteries that have sprung up in the past fifty years. Every hill, if not covered by a view tower built by politicians, is covered by mammoth Buddhist monasteries. In my interactions with the monks, I ask them how right it is to keep building structures to teach the teachings of the Buddha, who actually teaches about detachment from the material world, frugality, and conscientious consumption.

I recall the big conference hosted in Nepal by the World Wildlife Fund in 2001, where leaders from all religions congregated in Kathmandu under the aegis of the World Wildlife Fund for an Alliance of Religions and Conservation (ARC) meeting. The ARC made a pledge on Sacred Gifts for a Living Planet:[34] 'The Gifts are ground-breaking actions pledged by the faiths to combat forest and marine destruction, climate change and a wide range of other environmental issues.'[35] The discussions involved promoting simple solutions, such as shifting from wood-based cremation to electric crematoriums, whether for Buddhists, Hindus, Sikhs or others who cremate bodies. There have to be similar small, scalable initiatives. But in the past twenty years, we have seen minimal impact from such pledges.

My research proposal to the Global Sustainability Institute at Anglia Ruskin University also highlighted that governments can do little to combat climate change without the support of their citizens, and if certain age-old traditions and beliefs are not recalibrated to reduce consumption and construction in the name of religion and culture. In Southeast Asian Buddhist countries, many studies are emerging to highlight such issues and the need to tackle them. In Thailand, brands use religion to push the consumption of luxury goods, resulting in conspicuous consumption.[36] A strong government in India is encouraging Hindu temples to go global, and huge Hindu temples are coming up around the world. And it seems there is never a dearth of funding for building colossal structures that could otherwise go into building much-needed schools and hospitals. The increasing acceptability of religious practice in China has fuelled interest in Buddhism and created an industry that, like other consumer brand products, links one's religiosity to consumption and materialism. This is a sensitive issue but building awareness of how consumption in the name of religion needs more scrutiny is becoming increasingly crucial.

At COP26, there were again voices raised by inter-faith groups and other campaigners looking at climate change through the lenses of religious leaders. In a world where religion and conservatism are seeing a revival, it could also be an opportunity to revisit and reform religious and social practices to push contentious consumption, eliminate opulence and make one's conduct in protecting the planet an act of compassion and merit-making (earning *punya*).

Nepal, too, has the opportunity to provide these new lenses to the climate change discourse. For instance, in the popular

Buddhist stupa of Boudha, environment campaigners have been trying to move away from the large volume of synthetic prayer flags that are used. They are pushing for prayer flags made out of organic cotton, bamboo fabric and recycled materials.[37] Such efforts that begin in Nepal can proliferate around the world and this in turn would help Nepal take on thought leadership in the discourse and lead by example.

Himalayas—the Fragile Third Pole

Atmospheric scientist Arnico Panday, in the policy brief for the United Nations Development Program (UNDP) *Melting Glaciers, Threatened Livelihoods: Confronting Climate Change to Save the Third Pole*, writes: 'The region of Asia containing contiguous ranges of high glaciated mountains is often referred to as the Third Pole.' According to *The Hindu Kush Himalaya Assessment* published by ICIMOD, even if the increase in global average temperature is capped at 1.5°C above pre-industrial levels, glaciers in the region will lose one-third of their ice volume by the year 2100. 'If current emission trends were to continue, the mountains would lose two-thirds of their ice volume by 2100. The region contains the world's third-largest storage of frozen water. Glaciers here provide a key source of dry-season water in the ten major river systems; loss of this water source affects agriculture, drinking water and hydroelectricity production. Over 240 million people live in the Himalaya and nearby mountains; 1.7 billion live in the river basins downstream, while food grown in these river basins reaches 3 billion.'[38]

This explains the fragility of Nepal, which lies at the centre of the Himalayas. Among the many recommended actions, the key is to keep the Third Pole snow and ice-covered, the skies blue, the lungs healthy and rainfall regular. The prime minister of Bhutan, Tshering Tobgay, speaking at the Himalayan Future Forum meet, emphasized that 'efforts at utilizing local resources and indigenous knowledge would create much-needed productive local opportunities while protecting the unique culture and traditions of the Himalayas.' There is a deep connection to be built by leveraging past knowledge for a better future.

For me personally, the key discourse in the future around climate change is how we connect individual awareness and behaviour with nature. This would range from basic transformation in how households manage their waste, how people in businesses become aware of the damage they are creating, the importance of taking environmental assessments for businesses and projects seriously, and the government taking a multi-stakeholder approach in policy formulation and transformation. This is the only way we can save the Third Pole. Ramesh Bhushal, South Asia coordinator for Earth Journalism Network, writes for *Purak Asia*: 'As a country, an individual and a community, we have a wealth of opportunities to change the way we think about prosperity and development. Governments and institutions could reframe and redesign what is currently in place. We can think of something small but could be an example to the world.'[39]

Nepal Cannot Act in Isolation

Every country is making commitments at the Conference of the Parties (COP) of the United Nations Framework Convention on Climate Change (UNFCCC) on how they would move towards zero emissions. At COP26, the government delegation committed that 'Nepal's goal is to achieve net zero emissions from 2020–2030 and, after a period of very low emissions, to full net zero by 2045.'[40] Apart from that, the other two commitments were to halt deforestation and increase forest cover to 45 per cent by 2030, and to ensure all vulnerable people are protected from climate change by 2030.

The world has been slow to respond to the commitments made at COP, especially the developed countries. On 4 November 2019, the US withdrew from the Paris Agreement. This was reversed by President Biden's executive order once he took office in January 2021. However, the US, after the installation of President Donald Trump in January 2025, again pulled out of the Paris Agreement,[41] reducing the much-needed financing and support to sustain global initiatives for mitigating climate change.

In a world where China and the USA are seen as two competing powers, China has taken the position of providing leadership in the discourse on adapting to and mitigating climate change. On 22 September 2020, President Xi Jinping spoke at the UN General Assembly (UNGA), announcing the so-called dual carbon targets—namely, that China will peak CO_2 emissions before 2030 and achieve carbon neutrality before 2060.[42] India's commitment at Glasgow, during COP26, of cutting the emissions intensity of India's GDP by 45 per cent, increasing the share of non-fossil fuels to 50 per cent by 2030, and achieving net zero by 2070 has remained its position at COP27 and COP28.

Young climate activist from Limi Valley, Humla, Tashi Lhazom, argues that 'communities that have contributed nothing to climate change have been hit the hardest'.[43] The fact is that Nepal's commitments are dependent on how seriously its neighbours take their own commitments. Nepal's air pollution and the resultant impact on climate change are affected by pollution in India. When farmers in the Indian states of Haryana and Punjab set fire to their fields to burn off the straw, the strong winds bring thick smoke across to Nepal, creating hazy skies. Similarly, Nepal's river systems can be disrupted by the actions China takes on rivers that flow to Nepal and then to India. For instance, construction activity has been observed on the northern side of the Mabja Zangbo River in Burang County, Tibet, since May 2021. The Mabja Zangbo flows into Nepal's Ghaghara or Karnali River before joining the Ganga in India.[44] There are multiple transboundary issues to be borne in mind, therefore.

Advisory Board member of the Himalayan Future Forum, Bangladeshi diplomat and thought leader Ambassador Tariq Karim says that 'the myriad local and national solutions that we are striving at can be given greater relevance through synergizing those activities in a collaborative manner, through cooperation across communities within the nation-states, and then enlarging and expanding them to collaboration between states in the region.'[45] He suggests that 'the new globalisation has to be a bottom-up, community-level fanning outwards, grassroots-spawned process'.[46]

Nepal continues to develop models that can be replicated in other countries. On 24 September 2021, I moderated a high-level session featuring the Government of Nepal and seventeen development partners in Kathmandu. It was at the end of this session that the Kathmandu Declaration[47] was signed, a document that would pave the way for Green Resilient Inclusive Development (GRID) through a strategic action plan. The GRID approach involves a fundamental shift in managing risk and development: from a simple reactive response mode to a deliberate, proactive recovery strategy for long-term green growth, climate action and sustainable development for all.[48]

In November 2023, another high-level meeting was held that I moderated, where a joint communique[49] was issued by the government and development partners. The biggest shift for me was that it was the government presenting the priorities and the action plan for the next ten years, which meant the government was taking on ownership. This initiative has support from the major development partners and, as Nepal graduates from the LDC category, development partners have to redraw their engagement strategy. What this means is that the GRID Action Plan emerges as the tool for development partners to collectively engage in Nepal. This framework can be used as a tool in other countries also.

Nepal's Opportunity to Lead Global Discourse

While Nepal was at the lead in the '80 and early '90 in the discourse on sustainable development and the impact of climate change, it did not keep pace as global geopolitics elevated the discourse, and there is also a lot of mistrust within the government. As scientist Maheshwar Rupakheti points out in an interview with Ramesh Bhushal for *Third Pole*, 'In general, all regions are politically divided, but the problem with the Himalayan region is that there is more mistrust among governments to collaborate in scientific research. Most of the science in the region has been done by actors outside governments, where individual scientists or organisations have collaborated to do science. The scientific community should keep this going and provide some crucial information from their research to the policymakers to help them make better decisions.'

As the Secretary General of the Himalayan Consensus Institute, Hong Kong, I hosted five Himalayan Consensus Summits in Kathmandu between 2014 and 2029, bringing together different people from the Himalayas to Nepal to discuss and take action on topical issues. As Prof. Mahendra P. Lama, advisory board member of the Himalayan Future Forum, said to me about the opportunity of the Forum, 'it is a great platform for China's Belt and Road Initiative (BRI) and India's "Look East" policy to converge'. However, while hosting the Summits, we realized that such platforms require government ownership and convening.

Prof. Mahendra P. Lama went on to present the idea of 'Sagarmatha Sambad' or (Sagarmatha Dialogue) to then Prime Minister K.P. Oli in 2019. Nepal hosted the inaugural Sagarmatha Sambad in May 2025. Prime Minister K.P. Oli, speaking at a meet to announce this event, emphasized the 'location Nepal offers'. He went on to say, 'If one sees the map, we are very much in the heart of Asia. While the center of economic gravity is shifting to Asia, our location has immense prospects to be a convening venue for global dialogues.'[50]

In 2022, along with scientist Arnico Panday, then an advisory member of the Nepal Economic Forum (NEF), we came up with the idea of the Himalayan Future Forum (HFF). Actually, Arnico was the one to provide the name for the platform, and we launched it as an incubation programme of NEF. In October 2023, the inaugural roundtable was held, and the first meeting took place in February 2024. The Himalayan Future Forum is an initiative to encourage multi-faceted dialogues on the Himalayas by bringing together stakeholders from different countries and sectors. The major themes of work revolve around three areas—climate, community and connectivity.

I have been discussing with Cecile Fruman, Director of Regional Integration, South Asia, at the World Bank, how to push for more integration in the region. At the Forum's inaugural address, she emphasized the high costs of thick borders on one hand and the considerable gains of regional cooperation on the other. I keep discussing with her how we can reduce the former and expand the latter.

I have always been a strong believer in the need to build more empowered regional institutions in Southasia and in the importance of regional forums and platforms to build consensus and take collective action forward. My passion for the Himalayas and the unknown fear of what the impact of climate change may bring to the region continues to push me to build platforms and collaborate.

One of the areas that interests me is bridging the knowledge gap through the Forum. I am also continuously seeking young minds to engage in dialogue with, because I feel they will have a higher stake in the future than my generation. As Prof. Mahendra Lama asks, how do we take the famous COP discussions to the Himalayan classroom? One of the areas where our interests converge is in managing 'the real challenge to make the scientific and technical literature on climate change—mostly written in foreign and alien languages—accessible and affordable to the public so that they could be read by schoolchildren, farmers, professionals, literary figures, media persons and housewives'.[51] He asks, 'Can young minds and communities be galvanised to these classrooms and laboratories to create platforms to share sustainable solutions?'[52]

Kunda Dixit, editor of *Nepali Times*, a weekly I wrote for over eleven years, also teaches at New York University, Abu Dhabi campus. He spends time talking to international student exchange visitors who come to Nepal for a few weeks to a semester to learn about the country. He says that the key takeaway for students is that climate change must be understood as a multifaceted challenge. The region should not impede action, but instead spur the development of a holistic approach to managing climate change.[53] In a conversation, he told me: 'Few places in the world are so suited as Nepal for international students to study the impact of climate breakdown, local adaptation measures, successful interventions like community forestry—and all this in a low GDP per capita setting.'

While we can become an international space to convene global discussions, it is important for Nepal to walk the talk in its own journey to 2043. The rapid economic growth that is envisaged must not come at the cost of the environment.

Balancing Development with Sustainability

A common sight across Nepal is the number of earthmoving equipment, bulldozers and people involved in the construction of roads. With the road-building agenda becoming an important one for local governments, we see a proliferation of roads along with construction on open spaces. The Nepali mindset of wanting to construct on every inch of space available stems from the high cost of land. Therefore, over the past thirty years, leasing private and public land for construction has also proliferated. I left the Rotary movement after a large-scale construction project for a commercial building began instead of a library in an open space in the heart of the city. The land was gifted by King Mahendra to the Rotary to build a public library.

In the landslide of September 2024, Roshi, in eastern Nepal, about 80 kilometres away from the capital, suffered major damage. The area has seen excessive extraction of sand and the building of roads with a thriving crusher industry. Locals blame collusion between contractors and municipality officials.[54] Earthquakes and natural disasters have made us realize the value of open spaces, but it seems we forget that quickly. In an event in Surkhet, when I talked about 'Bulldozer Terrorism',[55] a term I used to describe the rampant use of bulldozers to build roads, a village municipality head came to defend the need to build multiple roads to reach the same place because of the hilly terrain. My argument was that building roads that do not go through proper environmental assessments, especially using heavy equipment, do not last long. I used the examples of how, in Switzerland, they spend years planning a particular village road, and once it is built, it lasts for centuries. Further, the usage of technology, especially heavy equipment, in fragile environments can never be the best solution, as many studies have pointed out.

This is just an example of how we can prioritise sustainability and our future in the projects we undertake and in our daily lives. I echo what Ramesh Bhushal says in his blog for *Purak Asia*: 'Climate has become a concern of all. Climate has become a story of the century. Climate has become an agenda in diplomacy. It's everywhere, but in a divided and economy-dominated world, it's hard for anyone to take the lead and say we should think about ecology before the economy. Richer world has been thinking on how to build an economy that will eventually help protect ecology, but Nepal could think the other way round. How if we think about protecting ecology and the economy will be built around it as we have so much to show to the world.'[56]

Section 2

The Enablers

Chapter 6

The Himalayan Powerhouse

'We do not have to dig deep into the earth to find gold, it is flowing from our mountains,' a tea shop owner near the Arun 3 project office once told me. Arun 3 is a 900 MW hydroelectricity project in Diding, around 650 kilometres east of Kathmandu, which is being developed by the Indian public sector enterprise Sutlaj Jal Vidyut Limited. The electricity from this project will travel through 210 kilometres of transmission lines in Nepal and another hundred in India to the Muzaffarpur substation in Bihar, India.

For Nepal, hydropower is indeed white gold. It is not only about the money it generates; it can transform Nepal for the better. From hospitals running well to better-lit shopfronts and roads, from the mushrooming of eateries to small household businesses, from telecom towers and the proliferation of the Internet to cable car projects for tourism and cold storage facilities for agriculture; from data centres to technology companies, the power of white gold equals the power of water to transform villages and economies. Rivers that were just part of the landscape or impediments to cross have now become the lifeblood of Nepal's energy future. And this energy will be driving Nepal's growth in the future as well. Gold and coal transformed the United States. Oil transformed the Middle

East. Nepal's economic future will be transformed by this hydropower.

In September 2024, the Indian cabinet approved the purchase of 10,000 MW of electricity from Nepal over the course of ten years.[1] According to a report in the *Nepali Times*, two Indian state-owned companies, SVJN Ltd and NHPC Ltd, are currently involved in projects in Nepal and are dealing with a combined capacity of 4600 MW across Nepal.[2] Overall, Nepal has the potential to produce 43,000 MW of electricity commercially, and the government has made plans to produce and sell 28,500 MW of electricity by 2035.[3]

I got involved in this sector in 1996 when Nepal's electricity capacity was just 307 MW. It all began with the Bhote Koshi Power Company, the first US–Nepal joint venture hydropower company funded by international financial institutions led by the International Finance Corporation (IFC). I have vivid memories of the seventeen nights in December 1997 that I spent at the Soaltee Hotel, working on documents and coordinating with the legal and lender consortium sitting in Washington, DC. Finding funding for hydropower projects is not easy, as the people who finance these projects do not have much recourse if the project fails. They cannot take away 90 per cent of the items they paid for. After roads, hydropower projects are regarded as the most difficult ones to finance.

In the Sunaula Board Room of the Soaltee Hotel, we had set up a closing room with a snake pit of wires for multiple fax machines (email had just started to be used). Over conference calls that were super expensive (US$6 per minute), we spent hours sorting out the punch list items. This was my first big introduction to how a power project gets financed. It is non-recourse financing, where the repayment of the loans to the project is just securitized with the asset of the project itself and cannot be recovered from the project developer's other assets or personal assets.

I went on to get more involved in the company at the board level and eventually helped the Nepali partners I worked for to buy out the US shareholders. I took over as the president of the Bhote Koshi Power Company in 2006 and led the company until I left in September 2008. It was an interesting journey of twelve years—seeing the project move from a design on paper to reality, into the most profitable power company in Nepal.

With keen interest and experience in this sector, I will discuss in this chapter the history of the hydropower sector, how it has evolved and, finally, why I believe this sector will lead Nepal's transformation. It is also important to understand that in Nepal, where nearly all electricity in the national grid is generated through hydropower, there is a tendency to use the words hydropower and electricity at times as synonyms. I also argue that while Nepal's hydropower generation must be exported at the beginning, in the long run, only increasing domestic consumption will power Nepal's economic growth. We will also discuss the opportunity of leveraging green finance and the need to understand the impact of climate change seriously. We end the chapter by looking at how Nepal can pursue the dream of becoming a hydro leader.

Evolution and Transformation of Nepal's Hydropower

Even though Nepal built its first hydropower plant in Pharping in 1911, twenty-nine years after the first power plant in the world was built, the electrification process has been slow. In a blog written in June 2024, senior hydropower specialist Pravin Karki at the World Bank and Deepak Subedi, an energy consultant, provide their perspectives on a key development that took place in 1974 which led to the development of more hydropower projects in Nepal. This was the Kulekhani I project. 'When the World Bank appraised the Kulekhani I Project in 1974, Nepal had an installed capacity of only 40 MW,' they write. 'The population at the time was 13 million and total GDP stood at US$1.2 billion—just US$100 per capita. There were about 64,000 consumers of electricity, representing less than 3% cent of the total population. The Kulekhani I hydropower project became functional in 1983 and it had a transformational effect on Nepal's power sector, providing 60 MW of continuous power supply for all hours of the day.'

Nepal's challenge over the past several decades has been its inability to produce enough power to meet domestic demand—like a farmer unable to grow enough for home consumption. This led to Nepal reeling under scheduled power cuts called 'load-shedding' for many hours each day, with huge economic costs. Between 2008 and 2016, Nepal experienced structured power rationing that peaked at twenty hours of power cuts per day in 2011.[4] More hydropower projects were built by government utilities and the private sector to meet this deficit. In 2022, Nepal managed to add 500 MW of power[5]—equivalent to the country's total electricity production in 2005. As energy expert and columnist Bikash Pandey wrote in the *Nepali Times*, 'Nepal has had an impressive growth in hydropower development over the past decade, from 734 MW in 2014 to a combined capacity of 2,625 MW from solar and hydropower stations, with 95 percent of households connected to the grid.'[6] According to the Nepal Electricity Authority (NEA)'s 2024 annual report in 2024, the demand that year alone had crossed 4000 MWh. From US$35 billion in losses in 2018, the state utility has been able to increase accumulated profits to US$350 million in 2024.[7] Also, in 2024, the utility began construction of new projects that will produce another 8000 MW, and by 2030, production is expected to rise to 15,000 MW.[8]

Nepal has therefore moved from producing just 40 MW of power in 1974 to 3157 MW in 2024—a nearly eighty-fold increase in fifty years. From just 3 per cent of the country having access to electricity in 1974,[9] it is now nearly 100 per cent in 2024. The state utility Nepal Electricity Authority (NEA) reported 97 per cent of households connected to the NEA grid,[10] with multiple off-grid networks powered by solar and micro-hydro plants.

Now it is time for the next step in this transformation. Like a farmer whose produce only fed his family, to a farmer who now has surplus crops to sell to the market, Nepal's perspective on hydropower has to transform as well. We need a departure from the perspectives of the past, where the aim was to meet the gap between demand and supply. Now the challenge will be to find markets to sell the electricity. This can be done through exporting electricity and increasing sales through increasing domestic demand and consumption. Let's discuss how we can do that. First, let us talk about the export of power.

Exporting to Manage the Region's Peaking Power

Globally, electricity is generated from different sources—coal is the dominant source, followed by natural gas, nuclear and oil. The electricity generated from these sources must be consumed as it is being produced. In this context, hydropower is seen as a valuable source of power, as it is the only energy source that can be stored and thus manage peaking power. If you always light ten light bulbs, and at times up to twenty on special occasions, your base load is ten bulbs and you can use stored energy when you peak to light twenty. Hydropower is the only source that can be used to manage the difference in demand, and therefore, it is of tremendous value. Currently, hydroelectricity powers 15 per cent of global power requirements, with other renewable sources like wind, solar and biomass meeting 14 per cent[11] of demand.

Can Nepal's hydropower resource become important not only for itself but for the region?

In the first five months of the fiscal year 2024–25, the Nepal Electricity Authority (NEA) exported electricity worth NPR 13.04 billion (US$93 million).[12] When the energy secretaries of India and Nepal met in February 2025, the *Kathmandu Post* reported, 'Nepal and India plan to build at least five cross-border transmission lines in order to evacuate at least 16,000 megawatts of power by 2035.'[13] When the scale of projects grows in size, then the mindset must also transform—from a country producing power solely for domestic demand for decades to one producing power for export.

Currently, all domestic contracts for the sale of electricity are structured as power purchase agreements with the national utility, where price and volume are largely fixed. However, electricity must now be seen as a commodity to be traded in regional energy markets. Trading electricity is unlike trading other commodities—it is a product that cannot be stored, yet traded instantaneously. In his paper 'Regional Electricity Trade for Hydropower Development in South Asia', Govind Timilsina, Senior Research Economist at the World Bank, argues: 'If Nepal exports 3,608 TWh (or billion kWh) under the regional electricity trade scenario during the 2020–2040 period, it generates US$289 billion over that 20-year period at the 2018 price.'[14]

There is a *Nepal Energy Sector Vision 2050* prepared by the Water and Energy Commission Secretariat (WECS) in 2013, projecting 30,000 MW of installed capacity by 2050. Given the rapid pace of growth since 2013, I believe this number of 30,000 MW could be achieved by 2043. Even at the current dollar price and rates, this would mean annual revenue of US$20 billion for Nepal.

Nepal's hydropower will be critical in the region to manage this peaking power. Further, with the pressure on India and Bangladesh to move towards a sustainable mix of power, i.e.

to have a significant share of renewable energy, they will have to look up to Nepal for hydropower. Even if India exploits its hydropower potential of 1,50,000 MW[15] to the fullest, they will still need power from Nepal to ensure a necessary share of renewable energy in the sustainability mix.

Augment Exports with Increased Domestic Consumption

While exports are critical to selling surplus electricity, it is equally important to focus on boosting domestic sales in a country with one of the lowest per capita consumption rates in the world. Experts like Dipak Gyawali continue to argue that 'Policy makers have chosen to ignore a critical USAID study[16] in 2003 that showed that if Nepal exported electricity, it would earn only 6¢/kWh whereas if it used that electricity within Nepal itself for its commerce and industry, its value added would be 86¢/kWh.'[17] Therefore, there are greater long-term economic benefits for the country in pushing domestic demand and sales.

We will now discuss how to increase consumption and stimulate demand.

Pushing Consumption to Increase Demand

I have always disagreed with how the country's planners and utilities have projected electricity demand in Nepal. I believe this misjudgement is what led to the country reeling under hours of power cuts. It is important to develop a more nuanced understanding of what demand is likely to be when households that previously consumed less electricity begin to consume more due to improved supply. The same applies to commercial establishments, which will also drive demand.

Demand is likely to rise further as we shift energy sources—from liquefied petroleum gas (LPG) to electricity, or from furnace oil and other fossil fuels to electricity. Additionally, new demand will be generated by the charging of electric vehicles, the development of e-mobility solutions and the expansion of high-capacity transmission lines across the country. (Even if we cut petroleum imports of US$2 billion a year by 10 per cent, the country would save US$200 million annually.) Planners must consider all these factors when making projections.

It is also crucial to understand electricity demand trends as Nepal graduates to middle-income and then high-income status. Currently, Nepal ranks among the bottom sixth of countries in terms of per capita electricity consumption. At 250 kWh per annum, Nepal consumes one-tenth of the mean for middle-income countries. The current global average is 21,039 kWh per annum.[18] Nepal's consumption is thus just 1 per cent of the global average!

When comparing Nepal, with its 30 million population, to countries with similar populations, the contrasts are striking. Mozambique, with a similar population but half of Nepal's per capita income, consumes 60 per cent more electricity. Ghana, a similarly populated country in Africa with double of Nepal's per capita income consumes more than twice the electricity Nepal does. Malaysia, with 33 million people (just 10 per cent more than Nepal) and a per capita income ten times that of Nepal, consumes 4498 kWh per capita.

If Nepal were to reach Malaysia's per capita electricity consumption levels by 2043, then potentially 1,50,000 GWh would be consumed—produced by 34,000 MW of installed capacity. This shifts the perspective: Nepal must prioritise strategies to unlock domestic demand, rather than focusing disproportionately on finding export markets without addressing its own low consumption.

Suman Basnet, a senior fellow at the Nepal Economic Forum and Team Leader at the Nepal Renewable Energy

Programme (NREP), argues that 'Nepal has ambitions to utilize the immense benefits of rapidly harnessing its huge in-country electricity-generating potential. This can range from electric cooking to electric mobility, powering all industrial heating, cooling and motive power with electricity, and electrification of all agricultural-related energy needs.'

The math is very clear: more productive consumption will be necessary to utilize both the electricity currently being produced and the additional supply expected in the future. A study and analysis of latent demand would clearly produce the figures necessary to make investment in new projects commercially viable. I've outlined seven areas we should focus on to boost consumption.

Managing distribution: In the early 1990s, when fixed-line telephone connections were hard to obtain, demand remained low. However, as mobile phones proliferated and people could get handsets and SIM cards over the counter, demand exploded. Similarly, if electricity connections could be provided within twenty-four hours, giving the consumer the choice of different options and if payment for such electricity would be made easy, the offtake would suddenly increase. After we purchased our electric vehicle in December 2023, we were advised to take a separate electricity connection that would have a higher capacity, a different tariff structure and would be metered separately. However, the process took two weeks to complete. If the utility appointed firms to manage last-mile connections, consumers would gain easier access.

Similarly, when new commercial establishments are being planned, the electricity infrastructure must be integrated to the potential demand that is emerging from the area. This may mean enhancing the capacity of the sub-station, adding more substations and adding additional or new transmission lines to the sub-station. On paper, we may have achieved 100 per cent reach, but what matters is that this access is reliable and capacity augmentation happens without delay.

Differentiated Product and Pricing: Telecom companies have observed that their revenues increase substantially when they started selling differentiated products with varying tariffs. Manufacturing and commercial consumption tend to peak during the day and, in the evenings, domestic consumption picks up, but at night, the consumption drops. Therefore, there can be pricing incentives that will bring about a whole new dynamic when it comes to how people consume electricity in an environment of dynamic pricing. Further, how ISPs purchase bandwidth in bulk and resell it to different categories of consumers at varying rates, electricity can also be marketed the same way. If there are large laundromats running, they can choose which part of the twenty-four hours with the lowest tariffs. Bakeries can start running their dough-kneading machines or ovens during the most cost-effective periods. High electricity-consuming small and medium industries—where energy is a major cost—could begin planning their operational hours to align with more economical tariff slots.

In Rwanda, for example, in our rented home, we simply pay an amount online, receive a code and enter it into the meter. No meter reading, no batteries of meter readers, no queuing to pay bills and no paperwork generated. There is much innovation happening in electricity billing systems.

In Nepal, a meter reader still visits each house, reads the meter and issues a consolidated bill for the electricity used since the last reading. We then pay that amount online. In the future, electricity bills could resemble mobile phone bills—providing itemised usage breakdowns for large and small appliances, lighting and other devices. For instance, bills could show how much electricity the refrigerator and air conditioner consumed that month, and whether each appliance was more energy-efficient compared to the previous month. This allows consumers to understand more directly the details of appliance power consumption and energy-saving algorithms of appliances operation, thereby optimizing electricity consumption.[19]

Aggressive substitution of fossil fuel: There must be a planned and aggressive push to replace fossil fuel-based vehicles and equipment with electric alternatives. While campaigns such as the utility's 'Quit LPG Gas and Use Electricity' have been launched, adoption needs to accelerate significantly.

The 2021 census revealed that only 0.5 per cent of households used electricity for cooking.[20] A study examining the substitution of LPG with electricity indicated that by 2035, an additional 2635 MW of generation capacity would be required to substitute consumption of LPG.[21] LPG, as per 2021 census, accounts for only 44.3 per cent[22] of the source of energy sources. According to the same census, the potential for converting the remaining 55 per cent to electricity also exists. As of 2024, the utility's domestic electricity tariff for cooking or charging electric vehicles at home is capped at Rs 11 per kWh. In contrast, petrol costs Rs 18.50 per kWh and LPG Rs 9.83 per kWh. Although LPG appears cheaper due to government subsidies, its real cost—factoring in rural transportation and investment in cylinders—makes it less economically viable. To ensure electricity becomes genuinely competitive, fossil fuel and LPG subsidies must be withdrawn.

Like the telecom and LPG companies that were supply-driven and decided to open stores to provide new connections and service the connection, the utility needs to enter a new era where authorized stores or online portals would sell connections, provide service to make and maintain the connection and ensure customer service is provided 24x7. Commoditization of electricity is the biggest transformation that is needed.

Getting ready for future smart homes: Smart homes are rapidly becoming a reality, with appliances, security systems and entertainment platforms increasingly controlled through mobile apps. This growing integration means a constant need for reliable electricity and internet connectivity. Even electric vehicle charging can now be scheduled remotely through apps. Smart home-enabled devices, appliances, and systems are designed to communicate with each other. They integrate and analyse usage data. They are smart enough to then communicate with the homeowner to help them make informed decisions about their energy use.[23] Further, AI is transforming smart home automation. We see people buying smart washing machines and air fryers that are connected to Wi-Fi. This trend will only proliferate.

Pushing energy efficiency: The way cities are being designed, and distribution networks established, there is increasing emphasis on energy efficiency. Frédéric Vassort, CEO of Ampacimon, a company focused on energy efficiency, states: 'We must replace fossil fuels with clean electricity, but it is generally produced in places different from large power plants and in a much more dispersed manner, which modifies the topology of electrical flows and generates a significant phenomenon of congestion.'[24] He also highlights how 'connected sensors installed on high and medium voltage lines, can help network managers with a safe and secure way to collect data on the state of their infrastructures. Valuable information which, once processed by their software solutions, provides a snapshot of the state of the network, with a view to maximizing its use, but also to supervising its state, so as to detect and if possible, anticipate breakdowns potential, and act upstream.' Pushing energy efficiency in Nepal will require a combination of enabling policies, technological adoption, public awareness and institutional coordination. Policy recommendations could include incentives for firms adopting energy efficiency measures, stricter building codes and the enforcement of energy efficiency standards for electrical appliances.

E-mobility solutions are going to be big consumption drivers: The *Guardian* newspaper reported that 'more than 70% of four-wheeler passenger vehicles largely cars and minibuses imported into Nepal last year were electric, one of the highest rates in the world.'[25] In India, a 2030 Brookings study[26] states that if 100 per cent of vehicle sales were EVs by 2030, their electricity demand would reach approximately 100 Terawatt-hours (TWh), averaging less than 400 Megawatt-hours (MWh) per EV annually.

Nepal's Nationally Determined Contribution (NDC) Report from December 2020 states that, 'By 2030, increase sales of e-vehicles to cover 90% of all private passenger vehicle sales, including two-wheelers and 60% of all four-wheeler public passenger vehicle sales.'[27] By extrapolating the Indian consumption data, we are then looking at 10 TWh of electricity consumption by 2030. There would be more innovations powered by electricity that require minimal infrastructure investment. Pictures from China that flood our social media every day show newer energy-efficient, electricity-driven transport solutions, a trend that will only drive further electricity consumption. People have vivid memories of queuing up for fuel. After one year of operating electric vehicles, our calculations showed we spent NPR 5500 (US$40) on electricity bills, compared to NPR 60,000 (US$450) the previous year. There were no visits to fuel stations. Conversations with drivers of electrically powered vans, the dominant mode of transport between cities in Nepal, reveal that aside from low operating costs, freedom from visiting and queuing up at fuel stations and worrying about the uncertainty of supply were key reasons to switch. Nepal's swift adoption of EVs has surprised the world.

This momentum is likely to extend to more advanced transport modes such as driverless electric pods, transport drones, air vehicles and others. For a country historically dependent on fossil fuels, this transition is both necessary and transformative.

Promoting high electricity-consuming businesses: There must be a comprehensive study conducted to identify high energy-consuming businesses that could utilise large volumes of electricity. For example, is there potential for an electric vehicle assembly plant that could serve both Nepal and India? A well-established manufacturing plant producing millions of vehicles could give rise to a township housing 10,000 people. Globally, similar large-scale vehicle plants have led to the development of such townships, each becoming significant electricity consumers.

Kushal Gurung, a cleantech professional, argues that 'Nepal could also use surplus electricity to produce green hydrogen that can be further processed to produce chemical fertilizers like ammonia and urea.'[28] To offset Nepal's annual import of 8,00,000 metric tonnes of fertilizer a study by the Investment Board Nepal (IBN) concluded that 10,800 MWh of dedicated, uninterrupted electricity per day—equivalent to a 450 MW project—would be required to produce 7,00,000 metric tonnes of chemical fertilizer annually.[29]

There are other avenues worth exploring. One of the major natural resources of Nepal are forests and forest. Forest management is an area that needs to be commercialized wherein forests are commercially utilized, replenished and the withering away of trees through mismanagement is averted. One high electricity-consuming industry is wood processing for paper and related products. Stora Enso, a Swedish–Finnish company and the world's largest paper and pulp producer, is known for its sustainable practices and consumed 33 TWh of energy in 2021. This illustrates the scale of operations needed to meaningfully absorb large volumes of electricity. Increased domestic consumption of electricity can only push the demand to a certain extent, it is high consumption industries that will transform overall demand.

Cyber Gurkhas to unleash data center that consume a lot of power: In April 2025, Bhutan's national daily *Kuensel* reported that 'Bitdeer Jigmeling's 500MW mining centre to go full-scale in 2026.'[30] A bitcoin mining center that will consume 500 MW of electricity. Bhutan has been leveraging electricity to mine bitcoin and generate revenue. Ujjwal Deep Dahal, CEO of Druk Holdings and Investment, was quoted by *The World* as saying, 'So theoretically, you could be generating bitcoin in the summer which can hedge your energy security during winter, it is a foreign currency reserve for us.'[31] I started thinking about large-scale energy usage for data centers in Nepal since beed management was hired to work on the Vision 2030 for the Nepal Army Welfare Fund in 2020. Nepal can be an ideal country to host more research on building energy conversion, efficiency and finding new applications of electricity. This has also led to the establishment of big centers. The data center by Switch in Reno, Nevada of 7 million square feet is larger than the US Pentagon, that occupies 6.3 million square feet.[32]

With submarine cables connecting continents to ward off any geo-political challenges, the world is now more digitally integrated than ever. In Nepal, the state utility and private operators currently run small-scale data centres that require exponential scaling. As Bikash Pandey writes for the *Nepali Times*, 'High-tech firms are power hungry, and the climate crisis is driving them to seek renewable sources of energy. Nepal's surplus electricity generation capacity coincides with this surge in global demand to power generative AI data centres.'

According to a *Bloomberg* report from June 2024, 'The data centres globally have the capacity to consume a combined 508 terawatt hours of electricity per year if they were to run constantly. That's greater than the total annual electricity production for Italy or Australia.'[33]

I have proposed the idea of Cyber Gurkhas to several investors exploring opportunities in data centres. Nepal has built a global reputation for security services over the past two centuries—whether through service in the British Army, the Singapore Police Force, or as an elite guard for the Sultan of Brunei. The term 'Gorkha' or 'Gurkha' has become synonymous with the highest standards of security. This legacy can now be leveraged to provide cyber-security through establishment and management of data centres in climatically favourable regions of Nepal.

These data centres, which are substantial energy consumers, can be powered by Nepal's growing hydropower capacity, while physical and cyber-security are managed by Nepali personnel. In the Vision 2030 prepared for the Nepal Army Welfare Fund, we at beed management proposed training retired army personnel to transition into cyber-security roles, thereby supplementing critical technical staff. Nepal is uniquely positioned to leverage its brand credibility to become a competitive player in the global cyber-security solution business as well. This can be done by using electricity to power data centers and meet the increasing global demand for data centers.

While boosting domestic demand and consumption alongside exports is essential for creating markets for hydropower projects, two additional dimensions merit attention. First is the opportunity to tap into green finance capital, which aligns with the clean energy profile of hydropower. Second is the need to approach future developments from a risk management perspective—specifically, mitigating the increasing risks associated with climate change.

Leveraging Green Finance Capital

When the first two commercially financed hydroelectric power projects in Nepal achieved financial closure in 1996, their combined project cost was US$300 million. At that time,

Nepal's GDP stood at US$6 billion, meaning the project cost accounted for 5 per cent of GDP. If we extrapolate this ratio to 2024, with a GDP of US$44 billion, Nepal should ideally be undertaking hydropower projects worth US$2 billion annually.

Financing such large-scale hydropower projects needs to be undertaken on a larger scale that would attract international institutional investors. The enthusiastic domestic market has responded to the public share issue (initial public offering—IPO) of hydropower companies, there would be no dearth of raising capital from Nepalis in Nepal—both within the country and in the diaspora—to meet a portion of funding requirements. Additionally, the global green finance market is expanding rapidly, and Nepal must capitalize on this. The Global Green Finance Market Size was valued at US$4.18 trillion in 2023 and the market size is growing at a CAGR of 21.25 per cent from 2023 to 2033 according to a research report published by Spherical Insights & Consulting.[34] It is estimated that the worldwide green finance market size is expected to reach US$28.71 trillion by 2033.[35]

A study on green finance—conducted in part by beed management—estimated a financing opportunity of US$46 billion in Nepal between 2018 and 2030.[36]

With an increasing number of actors—including government, quasi-government entities, multilaterals, and private institutions—entering the green finance space, Nepal is well-positioned to establish itself as a regional green finance capital not only to finance its own projects but build the capabilities of different parts of management to ensure that it becomes the hub for sustainable finance. Nepal should strive to become a hub for green financing, akin to Singapore's emergence as Asia's financial centre when money markets expanded. Becoming a one-stop shop for sustainable finance would require expertise not just in finance and project management, but also in climate impact assessment, environmental and social governance, insurance and risk mitigation. Combined with Nepal's growing leadership in global climate change discourse—as discussed in Chapter 5—this strategic positioning would significantly elevate Nepal's role in the international financial ecosystem.

When it comes to financing, debt is the easier component to raise. Bonds can be issued provided they are credible and carry high credit ratings. There are enough long-term funds globally that will be willing to buy them as long as it has the right ratings. The question, therefore, is how Nepal will position these instruments, offer legal assurances against policy reversals, and advance the necessary reforms to attract green investment at scale.

In October 2024, the Nepal Rastra Bank issued the Nepal Green Finance Taxonomy to 'encourage the flow of domestic green finance to facilitate green bonds, climate risk reporting and capital needs for the financial sectors.'[37] The institutional framework is now in place.

There are many Nepalis today in the world who have managed large assets and are looking at jumping into new innovative, impact-driven investment opportunities in their home country—something that was not feasible even two decades ago. Nepal must cultivate a cadre of credible champions with a strong track record to lead such initiatives where financial institutions and people will be willing to participate along with having people with the right experience and credibility to run the show. It is a matter of thinking ambitiously and executing purposefully.

Taking Climate Change and Its Impact Seriously

One of the biggest challenges in the development of hydropower projects in Nepal since 2010 has been the private sector's tendency to compromise on environmental, social and governance (ESG) standards in order to minimize project costs. Most of these projects have been financed by domestic financial institutions that also did not insist on following internationally accepted guidelines. Like Nepali vehicles just need Euro 3 air pollution compliance compared to Europe getting ready for Euro 7, Nepali projects have been able to get away with not following international regulations.

This has led to many projects getting impacted whenever there are floods or landslides. Comparisons are frequently made with India, where similarly lax regulations have resulted in major damages to infrastructure in the Indian Himalayas. Developers across the region argue that full compliance adds 15–20 per cent to project costs, thereby affecting returns.

Global multilateral agencies can support making existing projects compliant and also provide grant support to projects to achieve global ESG standard compliance. In a conversation as part of the implementation of the GRID framework, Nepal Economic Forum proposed a mechanism to ensure that the development partners would provide assistance to meet the financing gaps for ESG compliance. International Finance Corporation (IFC) is implementing the Nepal Environmental and Social (E&S) Hydropower Program. This initiative supports Nepal's government, private sector, financial institutions and other stakeholders in creating a sustainability framework and building a local talent pool capable of implementing international best practices.[38]

There is no cutting corners when it comes to environmental impact, but the mindset has to change from just being compliant and ticking the boxes to really looking at taking leadership in this matter for other countries to emulate. There needs to be innovation in financing or leadership in managing environmental impact. There is not much difference in learning and execution across developed and developing countries.

Therefore, Nepal needs to aspire to take the leadership in the hydropower sector.

Dreams of Becoming a Hydro Leader

Nepal must now set a clear goal of becoming a global leader in providing a range of solutions related to hydropower development. In the early days, it was professionals from Montana and Wyoming in the United States who travelled the world discussing hydro projects. Later, Norwegians took the lead, developing projects not only within Norway but across the globe.

In Nepal, the Norwegian contribution began in 1968 with the establishment of the Butwal Training Institute, set up to support the 1 MW Tinau project nearby. In 1978, Himal Hydro was founded, followed by the Nepal Hydro and Electric Company. After the creation of the Nepal Electricity Authority (NEA), Norwegian engagement continued—particularly in capacity building, with the establishment of Hydro Lab Pvt Ltd and through scholarships enabling Nepali professionals to study in Norway.

Suman Basnet, an alumnus of this programme who spent many years in Norway, shared his reflections during a conversation with me: 'With about 3,000 megawatts of hydropower plants in operation in Nepal, and about three times that capacity under construction, we can confidently assert that Nepal has a growing pool of indigenous expertise in the technical, financial, managerial, environmental and social aspects of hydropower development and operation.'

Today, more and more Nepalis are working in hydropower projects globally—from managing projects in Laos, to designing dams in Ethiopia, to offering strategic input in Ghana. Nepalis are increasingly recognised as the next generation of hydropower experts.

This trend has been thoughtfully documented by Professor Mark Liechty in his book *What Went Right: Sustainability versus Dependence in Nepal's Hydropower Development*.[39] The central character of the book is Norwegian engineer Odd Hoftun, who spent over three decades shaping Nepal's hydropower sector. The book outlines the growth of indigenous capacity in Nepal's hydropower. It deals with the range of issues from capital financing to tender bid process to Environmental Impact Assessment (EIA) to the gamut of engineering consulting, construction. It also talks about how the generation, maintenance, transmission and distribution. It highlights the transformation that has taken place, underpinned by Nepalis gaining hands-on experience in delivering complex hydropower projects.

During my visit to Rasuwagadhi Hydropower Limited in April 2025, I witnessed what Liechty described. There is now widespread use of sophisticated, high-precision machining. There has been great experience accumulated over years of tunnelling expertise in the challenging Himalayan geology and climate.'[40] I personally feel that Huftun has built a great foundation, be it Butwal Power Company and multiple training centres. It is now up to us to take it to the next level. In doing so, I look at three critical areas:

First, with multiple projects underway within Nepal, there is a unique opportunity to develop manufacturing or assembly hubs for equipment, along with regular maintenance services. Just as Boeing and Airbus have established global service hubs for aircraft engines, Nepal can position itself to become the place and offer opportunities for companies to be established under a joint venture companies that will not only be able to provide a quick turnaround solutions to project developers while simultaneously training Nepali technicians and creating world-class job opportunities. With a large base of in-country equipment to service and an emerging pool of highly skilled human resources, Nepal can take the lead in this domain. The template of Boeing starting a new hub in Bengaluru[41] in January 2024 can be used as a model to develop these centres.

Second, with more projects coming around the world and renewables becoming the new mantra, Nepal can be the technical education and training hub where young people can not only get certification but also get jobs and then take up international positions like the US and Norwegian professionals did. The global demand for skilled professionals in the renewable sector would increase, and equipped with knowledge and practical experience, Nepalis could develop a global reputation like they have done as Gurkhas in the security personnel industry.

Third, getting hydropower projects insured has remained a challenge since natural calamities in the Himalayas of different magnitudes keep repeating. While managing captive insurance is not possible for individual projects that cannot sustain captive insurance schemes, Nepal could develop a collective captive insurance scheme for hydropower projects that can emerge where risk is shared through premiums and whenever there is a claim, there are funds available. International governments and multilateral organisations keen to support the global energy transition can back the establishment of such insurance facilities. If Nepal aims to become a financial hub for green investment, it is only logical that this complementary risk management mechanism that is critical to making financial feasibility possible would also be based in Nepal.

Nepal's aspiration to transform into a high-income economy by 2043 must be driven by a fundamental transformation of the hydropower sector. To achieve this, there must be a serious recalibration of our scale of ambition. What we need is a vision in which Nepal becomes a global leader in this sector.

Chapter 7

Agricultural Revolution

In a village just outside Tulsipur Sub-Metropolitan City, Dang in western Nepal, I visited a mushroom farming project as part of a field trip for an agriculture market linkages initiative that beed management was working on. This project aimed to explore the gaps between farmers and the market. We were introduced to a woman in her late forties who enthusiastically showed us her newly acquired scooter, which she used to transport mushrooms—neatly packed in plastic trays—to the market. Previously, she had planted only corn and vegetables, carrying them on her back in a basket to sell. But mushroom farming has changed her life as she could afford to buy a scooter because of it.

When I asked how she learnt about mushroom farming, she spoke of a training she had received on managing climate control systems for mushroom cultivation rooms. In this type of farming, controlling the climate inside the room is essential. Traditional methods rely heavily on human judgement, but technology-enabled systems make monitoring and production more efficient. These systems are designed to automatically adjust temperature, humidity and other environmental conditions based on the growth stages of the mushrooms.

She proudly told us that her son, who now works in Japan, had inspired her to take up mushroom farming by sending her videos of advanced climate-controlled rooms used there. Since electricity supply became uninterrupted in 2018, she had started building climate-controlled rooms herself. As a result, both the quality and quantity of her production have improved. She now aspires to acquire the advanced systems her son has been showing her.

In many ways, a different kind of agricultural revolution is taking place here—one driven by technological intervention to enhance both quality and productivity.

Most writings on the Nepali economy begin by introducing Nepal as a predominantly agricultural country. Almost immediately, one reads that this has contributed to poverty. While the share of agriculture in GDP has declined from over 57 per cent in 1981 to 21 per cent in 2023,[1] the proportion of people engaged in agriculture has only fallen from 90 per cent in 1981[2] to 57.31 per cent in 2021.[3] This means that although the share of people employed in agriculture has dropped by one-third, the sector's GDP contribution has declined by two-thirds. This clearly signals reduced productivity and a decline in per capita income for those working in agriculture.

There are many reasons for this state of the agriculture sector, which I have discussed in my previous books. Issues such as managing landholding size, access to efficient irrigation facilities, storage infrastructure, availability of fertilisers and other inputs, training and technical knowledge have been extensively covered in reports by Nepal's development partners.

In this chapter, we will look ahead to a more futuristic scenario. There is a rising demand for agricultural products in both domestic and international markets, and climate-controlled transport solutions are making it more affordable to move these products. There is an evolving demand from the customer for organic products that will put sustainability at the centre of the discourse. Farming is evolving from labour-intensive methods to processes controlled by humans but executed by machines, robots and other tools. Digitalisation is transforming agriculture, particularly through precision farming. Nepal must plan accordingly.

With sufficient energy resources and increasingly accessible technological solutions, there is now a real opportunity to boost agricultural productivity. The next step is to advance climate-smart agriculture to help both mitigate and adapt to the effects of climate change. This chapter concludes by exploring how Nepal can leverage the Himalayas for landscape branding and integrate indigenous knowledge systems. Ultimately, the focus must be on equipping more people to actively participate in this agricultural transformation.

Let us begin with a slightly futuristic perspective on agriculture, focusing on specific trends that are set to transform the sector entirely. The Food and Agriculture Organization (FAO), in its projection towards 2050, states: 'Agriculture in the 21st century faces multiple challenges: it has to produce more food and fibre to feed a growing population with a smaller rural labour force, more feedstocks for a potentially huge bioenergy market, contribute to the overall development in the many agriculture-dependent developing countries, adopt more efficient and sustainable production methods and adapt to climate change.'[4] I agree with this assessment, and it could well serve as a blueprint for Nepal's agriculture sector in 2043.

The biggest challenge for Nepal will be to produce a greater variety of high-quality agricultural products in a sustainable manner, even as the number of people working in the sector continues to decline. For example, while the extensive use of harmful pesticides may temporarily increase productivity and allow a single individual or family can produce a lot, but the consumer is getting educated and demanding better products that use fewer chemicals and those that are grown in a sustainable manner. Consumers now want to know how the food they eat is grown.

Governments, in response, are ramping up their monitoring capacity to ensure that seeds, cultivation processes and final products reaching the market meet strict standards. Therefore, producing more quality produce with less people engaging in agriculture can happen only with the adoption of technology—technology that not only boosts efficiency but also helps adapt to changing climatic conditions.

Machines, Robots and More

When I visited the tea gardens of Ilam, I kept wondering how many labourers would be available in the next decade or two to pluck tea. Tea plucking is a highly specialised task that, until recently, could only be performed by humans. However, countries like Japan have successfully deployed tea-harvesting machines and are now experimenting with developing robots to do the job.[5] In Nepal, given our challenging terrain, we may need to transition from humans picking tea to well-trained robots that would be able to do the same job. This would ensure that productivity increases and plucking can also take place for longer hours without factoring the breaks humans need. This also frees up existing workers for roles that require greater value addition, leading to better pay. They could move into jobs demanding higher skills—such as supervising packaging machines, maintaining and managing robots, or engaging in specialised trades like tea tasting and global tea trading.

Globally, the use of robots is gaining traction in the harvesting of fruits and vegetables. These robots rely on sensors and cameras to detect when the crops are ready to be picked. They then use robotic arms to carefully harvest the crops without damaging the produce. Elsewhere, the use of robots to pluck grapes has been able to help the wine industry evolve. The use of robots has been able to help in the return to organic farming. For instance, one of the major challenges in farming is the weeds that grow. Farmers use strong chemicals for weeding. AI-enabled robots can distinguish between beneficial and harmful weeds, removing only the latter. These robots are relatively inexpensive, and the overall cost of robot production has declined substantially.

Students at the Institute of Engineering in Kathmandu have already begun developing Nepal-centric innovations that are Nepal-centric and would make the cost of production low. These robots can then be developed for multiple agricultural harvests and activities.

Robotics is not the only technology that agriculture has embraced globally. In general, the mechanization of agriculture is taking place at a rapid pace around the world. Put simply, machines powered by electricity are replacing tasks traditionally dependent on human or animal labour. For instance, tractors now plough fields instead of using animals and humans. We can already see this in Nepal. In the Terai, there has been significant adoption of mechanized harvesting. From fewer than ten thousand tractors in 1990, the number had risen to more than 1,50,000 by 2023.[6]

Nepal has also benefitted from access to relatively low-cost technology from China and India—such as power tillers, rice transplanters, combine harvesters and power mills used to process agricultural produce. In 2023, during a field visit to Surkhet—the capital of Karnali Province, located 550 kilometres west of Kathmandu—a farmer showed us videos of various agricultural machines and explained that a local trader in Surkhet imports this equipment from India and China. 'You just need to tell him what you want,' he said. In Rwanda, when we were working on agro-tourism projects and visited farms, we were often told how difficult it was to import agricultural machinery from China and India. Nepal, however, enjoys the strategic advantage of sharing borders with two agricultural powerhouses. Innovations from China and India reach Nepal faster than they do many other developing countries.

What is now needed is the accelerated adoption of mechanization across the agricultural value chain. Local governments can facilitate this process by offering subsidies and financing schemes, along with awareness campaigns and training it would accelerate the process. There are already programmes like the Prime Minister's Agriculture Modernization Project that has the financial and human resources. Local governments can collaborate with such national initiatives to achieve the shared objective of advancing agricultural mechanization.

Agriculture Meets the Digital World

The digitalization of Nepal's agriculture sector has witnessed remarkable progress, with cutting-edge technologies driving transformative change. Innovations such as parametric insurance, AI-driven irrigation, fertiliser and pesticide management, and blockchain systems for warehouse receipts and product tracking are revolutionizing traditional farming practices. In an article for the *Himalayan Times* in December 2024, Nepal Economic Forum Advisory Board Member Mahendra K. Shrestha and Deepali Khanna, Vice President of the Rockefeller Foundation, discussed how parametric insurance can help Nepal build climate resilience: 'Parametric insurance provides a payout when a specific event takes place, such as a cyclone or earthquake, regardless of the extent of the damage. Parametric insurance can also be specifically tailored to the needs of low-income and vulnerable populations, improving accessibility and providing a vital safety net against climate-induced financial shocks.'[7]

In September 2024, the Embassy of Switzerland in Nepal invited proposals from firms working on digital technology in agriculture. We participated in this initiative—the Agri Digitech Challenge—through beed management and received seventy-eight outstanding proposals, from which we shortlisted eight for financial support. This project incentivises the development and adoption of digital solutions through grant funding and technical assistance, facilitating access to Swiss and international expertise.[8] This was an interesting journey for us to learn about different companies that are working on integrating digital transformation and agriculture. For instance, a start-up is Gham Power, which operates the *Super Krishak* app. The app delivers digital agri-advisory services through an AI-powered feature called 'Krishi Doctor'. Farmers can get the disease on the crops diagnosed, get location specific information about soil conditions and nutrient requirements, receive water management advice based on satellite imagery, and access ongoing training. The app also includes a chatbot integrated with Facebook Messenger, making it easier and more accessible for farmers to share their queries and get answers. People can get advice from a team of experienced agri-experts, digital tools and a community of fellow farmers to improve their farming practices which will in turn help upscale their production. They are also using gaming to help the farmers learn. Farmers get coins and badges by completing quizzes and games, making learning both engaging and effective.

Suman Shakya, CEO of Tangent Waves, has been the collaborator with Beed in operating the Agri Digi Tech Challenge. He says: 'The participating companies of the Agri DigiTech Challenge acceleration program showcase the zeal and the ability of companies in Nepal to work on digital technology innovations that are world class. The key tasks will be to TikTok-ify the solutions to create consistent engagement with the end users (farmers) and generate a sustainable business model.' The reach of the TikTok social media platform has been revolutionary in Nepal, at its peak consuming 30 per cent of the country's internet bandwidth. It is to be able to take the different digital technology innovations that are taking place in Nepal to the farmers around Nepal for free over this platform.

As Beed is seen as a company working on agri-digitech solutions, we frequently have companies approach us for advisory services. In one instance, during a presentation by Japanese companies to beed management, they demonstrated 'monorail' solutions that would help people easily transport citrus fruits. These solutions are very easy to build too. It just requires simple rails to be built in the hilly terrain and there are carts for a plucker to sit in and carts for the fruits to be transported in. So, one person can pick fruits instead of many people navigating the hilly terrains and carrying the fruits to traverse steep landscapes and carry produce on their backs.

We identified the potential for such systems in districts like Manang, where apple farming has significant prospects but the population is sparse—fewer than 6000 people, many of whom live outside the district. Whether it be tea, coffee, apple or orange plantations, owners continually emphasise the need for more farm labour or machines to do the work done by humans. The transportation of produce in difficult hilly terrains is always a challenge as it requires human intervention. This is further exacerbated by the migration of labour from these regions. Tech interventions can substitute repetitive, low-value work humans do.

Shift to Precision Agriculture

The global discourse on precision agriculture—a data-driven approach to farming—is gaining traction as a means to improve food production, reduce environmental impact and enhance profitability. Precision agriculture is a farming method that uses technology such as the Global Positioning System (GPS), sensors and data analytics to optimize crop production. It involves monitoring and managing variables using data collected on soil conditions, weather and crop health. These can be assessed at granular levels, mapping specific areas within a given field or farm. The focus is on increasing quantity without compromising quality, and on reducing waste through the optimal use of water and agricultural inputs like fertilizers and pesticides.

For instance, a farmer may use satellite imagery to be able to track areas where there is poor soil moisture and thereby focus on improving the soil condition of the particular patch rather than wasting resources in trying to irrigate the whole plot.

During one of my visits to Ilam in eastern Nepal, 700 kilometres from the capital, I was chatting with local farmers who were eating at the same roadside stop as we were. I began talking to them about how things had been going, and I recall one of them saying: 'Earlier, we needed ploughs and strong hands in agriculture. Now, you need a computer and strong fingers. My neighbour's son brought a drone the other day and showed us how their crops were doing in the hills—forty-five minutes away on foot.' He added, 'I'm happy that I can ask the computer questions in Nepali, and it answers promptly,' referring to Google's Nepali language and voice typing interface.

Digitalisation in agriculture through the broad adoption of digital technologies and data analytics to improve all aspects of farming has begun in Nepal. The next step is to graduate to precision agriculture—a specific application of digitalisation that focuses on using data and technology to optimise agricultural practices at a highly localised and site-specific level. Mobile phone-based farming advisory services (also called 'digital extension') are the most common precision agriculture solutions that are currently helping millions of farmers worldwide, and can be implemented in Nepal very easily. In Rwanda, the government launched the Rwanda Soil Information System (RwaSIS) in November 2024, allowing farmers to get soil information of their plot by logging in the Unique Parcel Identifier of the land. The farmer can get to know the soil composition, erosion risk and fertilizer requirements. The data can then help to provide precision agriculture solutions on what is the best set of crops that the farmer can plant there and how it can be taken care of using the data.

Data can also be used for efficient monitoring of crops and tackling issues such as pests and diseases. As mentioned earlier in this chapter, one of the biggest challenges, such as weeding, can also be resolved through the use of automated weeding machines. These machines will be able to increase the area of operation and, at the same time, reach zones that cannot be accessed by humans. Sensors have an important role to play, from monitoring humidity and temperature to supporting climate-smart decisions. Land can be levelled using laser-guided precision levellers, and both seeding and irrigation can be mechanised and monitored through data.

There is, therefore, an immense opportunity for Nepal to transition into precision agriculture.

Energy to Boost Agriculture

Energy is critical to driving the agricultural revolution. It is required for irrigation—to pump and drain water, the most essential input in farming. Energy is also necessary to operate various farm equipment and then to process agricultural produce. Energy is also required to power devices that are used be it the computers that are storing data or the drones that are flying to collect data. Globally, a common measure of energy usage in agriculture is the *average energy input per agricultural worker*, expressed in kilograms of oil equivalent (kgoe) or, to put it simply, how much energy is contained in one kilogram of oil. The average energy input per agricultural worker refers to the amount of energy, be it fuel or electricity, that is used in agricultural activities, divided by the number of workers involved. Nepal's agriculture sector used only 22 kgs of oil equivalent per agricultural worker in 2021.[9] Energy expert Bishal Thapa, in his column 'Power to the Farmer' in the *Kathmandu Post*, compares this figure with those of other regions: 'The average energy input per agricultural worker in developing countries was 99 kgs. The world average was 394, and for Africa, it was 26. Nepal's energy input in agriculture is at least two to three times lower than what it should be.'[10]

Energy can also help overcome the biggest challenge in Nepali agriculture—irrigation. With the availability of hydro-powered electricity, irrigation can be managed more easily in areas with grid access. In areas where there is no grid access, solar-powered pumps have worked well. Driving through newly built village roads, what continues to catch my eye are the solar panels. These panels generate electricity to operate water pumps, which draw river water into the fields. When I asked the locals about this, they told me they are able to pump around 100 kilolitres of water up a 100-metre hill nearly every day of the year.

Thanks to abundant sunlight, reduced photovoltaic costs, and the ease of installation and deployment, the use of solar panels to power pumps is rapidly proliferating. That's not all—through various programmes, the government of Nepal has subsidized the use of these pumps. There are companies in Nepal that are providing this solution to farmers without the farmers having to buy the pumps themselves. Farmers can either rent the pumps or pay usage-based energy charges. Gham Power, the company I referred to earlier, provides solar-powered irrigation systems financed by local microfinance institutions. These systems are integrated with their device, the 'Gham Power Krishi Meter', which records real-time farm data, helping farmers optimize their operations and enhance productivity.

Energy is also essential for adding value to agricultural produce. For instance, transforming tea leaves plucked by a labourer into consumable tea requires considerable energy. The leaves have to go through the withering trough where big fans take the moisture out, the big machines, powered by electricity, process the leaves and the driers, powered by energy, then produce the final product that can be consumed. Then the packaging machines require energy. This is true for many other agricultural products. Electricity becomes even more critical as greater technology is used, be it robotics, farm equipment or running data centres on farms. Nepal's world of electricity only changed in 2018 because until then, people did not think of a situation where there would be surplus electricity. We get many enquiries from people who want to start cold store chains to store agricultural products and mitigate the price fluctuations due to seasonality. Just as the electric vehicle movement has surged thanks to electricity availability, we must consider how electricity can contribute to accelerating transformation in agriculture.

Climate Smart Agriculture

The World Bank defines climate-smart agriculture (CSA) as 'an integrated approach to managing landscapes—cropland, livestock, forests and fisheries--that address the interlinked challenges of food security and climate change'. It is important to take an integrated approach to agriculture, whether managing soil conservation techniques, crop intensification methods or improved planting and crop management. This extends to livestock as well—some projects are already piloting initiatives that help farming families transition from traditional livestock production methods to more efficient and resilient systems. These aim to improve production, animal health and economic returns while reducing environmental impact.

Funding these transitions is not a major issue, as new international climate funds, such as the Green Climate Fund (GCF), offer opportunities to leverage resources and scale up CSA efforts across the country.

Binija Nepal leads the Green Resilient Agricultural Productive Ecosystems (GRAPE) programme for the key German development agency GIZ (Deutsche Gesellschaft für Internationale Zusammenarbeit). She has worked on climate-smart agriculture for many years. I have moderated sessions for her programmes and always enjoy our conversations. When I asked her about the future of CSA in Nepal, she said: 'In Nepal, the future of climate-smart agriculture will revolve around a comprehensive strategy tackling the intertwined issues of climate change, food security, and sustainable development. Central to this vision will be collaboration among stakeholders, fostering research and innovation, and promoting adaptation measures.'

When we speak to people on the ground who are working on the transition from traditional to climate-smart agriculture, two major issues consistently emerge. First, farmers and those working with farming communities must understand that climate change is real and will impact the future. Therefore, adaptation is not a choice—it is a necessity.

Farmers near Pokhara told us about seed bank projects that have helped conserve indigenous seeds, which are more resilient than the imported hybrid varieties. These native seeds are better able to withstand shifts in climatic conditions. Pests once limited to the lowlands of Nepal are now found in high altitude. Therefore, they believe that a collective sharing of knowledge is important to address these rapid changes.

Second, it is all about economics. If people find better prices and guaranteed markets for their products, they are quicker to adapt to change. We have seen farmers transition to organic tea in Ilam. In Patan, a mile away from my home, Farm Shop, a store dedicated to organic Nepali produce is a great place that my wife and I love to visit. On Saturdays, they also organize a farmers' market that has become popular. From dairy to cheese to different varieties of tea, coffee, spices, legumes, grains, vegetables—the range increases each week. With home delivery services, I have been able to get some of my favourites like Mustang apples right at my doorstep. Yes, there is premium pricing, but it is worth the money you spend.

Leveraging Indigenous Knowledge

The Himalayas are home to indigenous knowledge that explains the myriad ways in which we can both benefit from and coexist with nature. Be it basic food and nutrition or medicinal value, there is much that still remains to be learnt. There are also indigenous practices to manage extreme weather, and knowledge on how to handle fermentation, storage and packaging of products. This knowledge helps locals adapt to the impacts of climate change. Prativa Pandey started cosmetic brand Herveda Botanicals after studying medicinal and aromatic plants of Nepal. A scientist and entrepreneur she told me she is 'dedicating the next ten years to study the medicinal plants and to bring the products and stories to the market.' She says she sees a lot of global potential in leveraging our indigenous knowledge and contributing to the world. She has been able to bring this indigenous knowledge to create and sell luxury products in the beauty industry.

Globally, landscape branding is a popular method to derive premium value. Champagne is a classic example—grapes from a specific region command a higher price when turned into sparkling wine. A similar possibility exists in Nepal. Benjamin Zimmerman, a researcher for *Nepali Times*, says that 'Landscape Branding, whereby agro products are marketed for being endemic to a certain region demanding high market value, has become an incentive for farmers to return to local indigenous crops.' His research in Pokhara highlighted two examples: '*Pokhareli Jethobudho*, a rice native to Pokhara and admired for its aroma, and *Setho Kaguno*, the foxtail millet native to the fields near Begnas and Rupa Lakes. Both products are branded and marketed by the social enterprise Annapaat, guaranteeing farmers a set minimum rate.'[11]

Nepal can learn from neighbouring Bhutan, where they have successfully leveraged knowledge of indigenous products and processes to produce world-class premium goods. Tshering Tenzin, CEO of Menjong Sorig Pharmaceuticals and a speaker at the Himalayan Future Forum in February 2024 on Indigenous Knowledge, gifted me a box of products from their company. It comprised traditional medicines and medicinal soaps. I was impressed by the packaging as well as the global markets these products are reaching. The key ingredients and processes are uniquely Bhutanese. This is precisely what Nepal can aspire to achieve.

Leveraging the Himalayan Brand—High Value, Low Volume and Value Addition

Given Nepal's location next to India and the porous borders, there is no competitive advantage in high-volume items. Nepal needs to find a niche. If it is rice, then Nepal will have a comparative advantage only in certain varieties. The same applies to legumes and other cash crops. Nepal's high mountain terrain can be developed to produce high-value, low-volume products.

For instance, Nepal's cheese production industries have matured, and many of them now produce high-quality cheese, albeit in low volumes. I buy my cheese from François Driard, a French national who started Himalayan French Cheese in 2017. In 2019, the Yak Blue cheese he produces won the Super Gold Medal at the fourth *Mondial du Fromage et des Produits Laitiers* in France's Loire Valley.[12] These cheeses have a growing market in India and beyond. At a supermarket in Delhi, I saw Nepali Yak Cheese sold at INR 4500 (US$50) per kilogram—five times the retail price in Nepal.

The focus, therefore, has to be on building the right backwards integration with dairy farmers, managing the supply chain and transportation, ensuring testing at border labs, and connecting with the right buyers in India. Similarly, with tea, there are Nepali companies that are trying to conquer the world. A *New York Times* column in 2019 ran a story with the headline 'Don't Call it Darjeeling, it is Nepal tea'.[13] Nepal Tea Collective, a US/Nepal-based operation, has been trying to build this high-value, low-volume market since 2016. Amigo Khadka, one of the co-founders, told the *Kathmandu Post*: 'Our loose-leaf teas and organic blends have won 12 international awards, a testament to their premium quality. Having been featured in *New York Times* and *Forbes*, we have been able to build a Nepali tea identity and trusting relationships with international buyers.'[14] Among health-conscious consumers, there is a search for organic products and products that are associated with good health and wellness. The wellness industry is expected to cross the US$10 trillion mark in 2032.[15] The Himalayas can become a great brand in this space, building on the unique blend of natural beauty, traditional healing practices, and spiritual environment along with the number of practitioners and teachers available.

In the streets of Thamel, one can see numerous stores selling Himalaya brand cosmetic products. These are made in India, and Chinese tourists are their biggest buyers. I called the country manager of the Himalaya company to ask whether the products being sold were original or spurious. He assured me that all the products were coming from factories in India. Why not a Nepali product leveraging the Himalaya brand for Chinese markets?

As discussed in the context of landscape branding, it will be important to develop a certification system—like that for champagne—where an authorised body certifies that the product originates from a specific region and that the correct process has been followed. Similarly, there must be a globally acceptable certification system that confirms the material source or value addition is from the Himalayas. Whenever I travel to India, I feel a tinge of envy when I see the brand 'Himalayan Water', marketed by Tata Consumer Products, in hotels and restaurants. Much like the French brand Evian, sourced from a single source in the French Alps, the Tatas have been able to attract premium pricing just by using the connection with the Himalayas.

Whether it's beans, dried mushrooms, rice, herbs or spices, smart branding can help build global recognition. There are already firms that are working in small ways in creating a niche in the product segment they are in. Makkusé, a luxury dessert brand, produces traditional Nepali sweets with world-class packaging and has successfully positioned itself as a premium product. Founder Anushka Shrestha spoke to me about her company's potential and said that scaling up production while maintaining consistency is key, along with tapping into themes like nostalgia and pride in Nepali products—all presented with packaging made from locally produced materials.

There has been a mushrooming of many Nepali firms using local raw materials to produce high-quality products—be it chocolates, ice creams, packaged food or pickles. The key will be to scale them further and ensure they can compete in the global market.

The story of Nepali pickles is remarkable in this respect. Nepali pickles made from specific ingredients like *gundruk* (dried vegetables), *timmur* (Himalayan Szechuan pepper), *dalle* (a variety of chilli) and *lapsi* (Himalayan hog plum) are being produced for diaspora markets. My sister, who lives in Toronto, no longer needs to bring pickle stock from Nepal, as it is readily available in local stores. Interestingly, the bottle of lapsi pickle she bought had been imported by a firm in the UK and then exported to Canada. It carried UK certification so that the product could be exported to Canada. Exports of pickle have been estimated at US$1.1 million in 2023–24.[16] However, these figures may be much higher, as much of the trade is informal—carried in small quantities by people travelling out of Nepal. In India, it is very heartening to see companies like Mother's Recipe, Haldiram that were also traded informally now formally distributed by firms in the UK, US, Europe and other countries. It is only a matter of time like in India, that Nepali companies will move to the next level through proper branding, following international guidelines.

When beed was conducting a study on medicinal plants and their markets, we were surprised to learn that many of these plants were being harvested without documentation and smuggled across the border into India. The story of *Yarsagumba*, a fungus finding its way to Taiwan and China, is very well known. The product is used as an aphrodisiac. The common story one hears is that the product became famous after nine women athletes in China admitted to using this as an energy booster in the 1993 National Games.[17] The final products are sold at prices many times higher than what is paid to Nepali farmers or local traders. Chyangwa Tamang, ward chair of Mugum Karmarong Rural Municipality-2, told the *Kathmandu Post* that 'local traders procure the fungus from villagers for Rs 1.8 million (approx. US$13,000) per kg and sell it to Chinese buyers in Kathmandu for Rs 2.8 million (approx. US$22,000) per kg'.[18] The rural municipality charges a royalty of NPR 30,000 (US$220) per kilogram.[19] In Beijing, they fetch US$110,000 per kilogram.[20]

Taste of Bhutan, a company in Bhutan, has successfully used *Yarsagumba* as an ingredient in tea, honey and capsules. When used this way, the product commands a much higher value than raw cordyceps sold from Nepal. It all comes down to quality, value addition and packaging. The shift now must be towards value addition. This means that for products to achieve international-level grading, we must ensure that all global standards are met and that packaging aligns with the requirements of the destination markets. One recurring story is the significant potential of Nepali tea in China. However, it must comply with Chinese certification norms, be labelled in Mandarin and packaged according to local preferences.

Aneka Rebecca Rajbhandari, co-founder of the Arniko Project—a project that documents Nepal–China relations past and present—is a fluent Mandarin speaker and scholar who keeps reminding us that if you need to conquer the Chinese market, we must package, label and ship products according to the preferences of Chinese consumers. She says, 'It is important to follow all the rules that the Chinese products follow.'

In agriculture, exporting raw materials adds little value. However, value-added processing brings in significantly more revenue and profit. For example, while one can export ginger or cardamom as-is, converting them into powdered form and packaging them properly fetches a much higher price. In a study that beed management was involved in for a client, we were amused to learn that ginger in dried powder form fetches ten times the price of raw ginger. However, this requires facilities for drying, grinding, cleaning and storage. Similarly, instead of exporting raw tomatoes, sun-dried tomatoes or tomato-based products yield higher prices and profit margins.

In 2024, beed management, along with PwC, worked on the Sector Investment Diagnostic and Financing Framework

(SDFF) for the World Bank Nepal. The study concluded with recommendations to focus on and expand the cultivation area for spice crops, vegetables, fruits, cash crops and industrial crops where higher value addition is possible. The study identified twenty-five products across seven target agribusiness segments for deepening the value chain through catalysing interventions from private sector investment and public sector support. These recommendations now need to be implemented.

Towards Agro-Tourism

In Rwanda, during the pandemic years, one of the most interesting projects I was involved in was leading the Beed Team to develop an agro-tourism strategy for the Government of Rwanda. The aim was to explore locations across the country producing diverse agricultural products and assess their potential for experiential tourism—both in high-volume, low-value and high-value, low-volume segments. We took inspiration from the success story of the One&Only Nyungwe House at the Gisakura Tea Estate, Rwanda. Situated on the edge of a tea garden, this lodge has won many global awards and commands a nightly rate of US$3,500 and above. The property has transformed the local economy and livelihoods. Agro-tourism does not need to be limited to small, farmer-run homestays—it can also include large-scale luxury ventures.

Yuvaraj Gurung is the founder of Agro Manang, a company engaged in apple farming. They have been a client of beed management and operate a farm in Manang District, 270 kilometres west of Kathmandu, where motorable roads were only built as recently as 2005. The apple farm also includes a winery and a resort. Their resort—Bhratang Farmhouse—is located in the scenic Bhratang village of Manang district. In his article for the NEF publication *Nefport*, Gurung shared his journey: 'Our focus is in generating revenue from the resort, and to be able to create a small wine-tasting room in the coming year. We believe that schools can organise their excursions around this area as well as treat it as a recreational place for breaks from their long treks in the mountains.'[21]

I have been travelling across Nepal to explore sites that could be developed into agro-tourism hubs. There are small, family-run properties like the Barpeepal Homestay in Ilam in Eastern Nepal, operated by Kedar Sharma and his wife Kiran. Their focus is on culinary delights made using produce from their own farm. Then there are larger operations, such as Srijana Farms in Palpa, which draws visitors from the city of Butwal, just an hour-and-a-half drive away. The Indian city of Gorakhpur in Uttar Pradesh is only four hours away. When I visited in March 2025, a group of Indian tourists were there to watch the World Cup Cricket Final match. They said they were regular visitors to the farm. They enjoy being surrounded by nature and pleasant weather, eating meals prepared with organic produce grown on-site.

Globally, agro-tourism is gaining popularity as farms look to diversify their sources of income. It is important to remember that large tracts of land offer natural beauty, far from the hustle and bustle of cities, where people can spend time in nature and young ones can learn about the origin of the food they see on their plates.

In the Darjeeling district of India, former tea gardens are transitioning to agro-tourism to generate much-needed revenues. In Nepal, based on some of the feasibility studies we have worked on, agro-tourism products could be developed in banana plantations, alongside rice or millet fields, or in hilly regions where tea is grown.

Agro-tourism also creates much-needed jobs, as those working on farms can take on additional roles in the evenings—

working in kitchens, serving food or showcasing local culture to guests. If curated well, these sites can offer exceptional farm-to-table dining experiences. With the rise of experiential tourism, there is increasing demand from travellers to sample local cuisine made from native ingredients, herbs and spices. Combined with Nepali hospitality, this sector holds great promise for the future.

Building World-Class Learning and Training Centres

Nepal has significant biodiversity and wildlife assets managed within twenty protected areas, including twelve national parks that cover about 20 per cent of the country's land area. It is a biodiversity hotspot, ranking forty-ninth in the world. Half the tourists who come to Nepal want to engage with its rich biodiversity.

Since agriculture has often been associated with poverty, it is not taken seriously from the perspective of knowledge building and producing trained personnel. However, some of Nepal's agricultural institutes have produced world-class graduates who are now working in leading institutions around the world. Agriculture and Forest University (AFU), popularly known as the Rampur Campus, located 200 kilometres west of Kathmandu, is a notable example. Research and learning must be made a priority, and more students should be encouraged to enrol in such universities.

Nepal also needs to collaborate with global universities and research institutions to build world-class research facilities to study the diverse biodiversity of the Himalayas and support the ecosystem. There is a need for innovation. Though we have discussed the technological transformations likely to occur, we must consider how Nepal can lead these changes. Why shouldn't some of the future innovations emerge from

Nepal? Global companies and institutions are searching for the next breakthrough—why can't this happen in a research centre in Nepal?

Nepalis have excelled in learning to operate heavy equipment, work on scaffolding and secure high-paying jobs with construction companies in the Middle East. They have also performed well as car mechanics, using laptops to diagnose problems in vehicles and fix them. Now, it is worth considering the growing need for skilled individuals to manage robots and machine learning devices in agriculture, along with their repair and maintenance. This is a promising area for future exploration.

It is also important to be able to have good training in data, information and analysis. Decades ago, everyone grew strawberries when the import prices were high and then due to oversupply, prices crashed. The same is happening with dragon fruit. Herd mentality pushes people to opt for the same set of crops without understanding that when everyone grows the same fruit, the market prices will plunge. We need to know and understand the data related to the production and consumption of different crops. We need data on market demand, supply and pricing. We need to know what is being consumed and where. Companies that would like to scale up will be more than happy to pay for such data, as their survival depends on understanding the markets.

Domestic Consumption Will Continue to Rise

Finally, we should not overlook the potential of a country of 30 million. The average food bill of a Nepali has been rising, and from once being content with a meagre daal bhat (rice and lentils), with vegetables and the occasional addition of meat, the average Nepali palatte has evolved. There is now a demand for food from around the world. Food service delivery has further driven this demand. In addition, e-tailers have made it possible to get a product from one part of Nepal to another. Sitting in Kathmandu, I can now have beans and red rice from Jumla in the west, cheese from Ilam in the east and apples from Mustang delivered to my doorstep. Before e-commerce and online platforms, these products could only be acquired by visiting those regions or finding a store in Kathmandu that stocked them.

The pandemic pushed these companies to innovate, and logistics firms handling deliveries have also grown in number. The pandemic has also made people more health-conscious. As a result, there is now greater focus on consuming more organic food that travels shorter distances and is not preserved. As discussed in earlier sections, it will be important to understand domestic demand and production in a holistic manner.

Looking at the Long-Term Big Picture

Nepal in 1995 adopted a twenty-year Agriculture Perspective Plan (1995 to 2015) to boost agricultural productivity and its contribution to GDP. The Agriculture Development Strategy 2015 to 2035, prepared by the Ministry of Agriculture, focuses on areas typically supported by development partners: 'dimensions of increased food and nutrition security, poverty reduction, competitiveness, higher and more equitable income of rural households, and strengthened farmers' rights.'[22] However, there has been no significant research on transformational agriculture. As we look towards 2043, many of the issues that will need to be addressed will only yield results over the long term.

We also need to take a long-term view of food security, particularly in the context of potential geopolitical challenges with India. Nepal is heavily reliant on India for many agricultural products, largely because Indian goods, produced with government subsidies, are more competitive. However, we have seen that during times of domestic shortage, the Indian government understandably imposes export restrictions to prioritise its own markets. As a result, the Nepali market is significantly affected—both in terms of supply and price—by developments in India.

Finally, we must evaluate which products offer Nepal a comparative and competitive advantage, and which do not. It is essential to understand consumer behaviour. Why do large quantities of Nepali rice go into producing homemade alcohol, while we prefer to consume imported rice from India? Just as we import garlic and onions from China during major shortages, what other food items could we source from China at competitive prices?

In Nepal, many international organizations have conducted studies related to agricultural value addition. These efforts have involved various subsidies and support from development partner programmes. Over the years, I have been involved in many such initiatives and studies. However, development funding is beginning to decline, with USAID closing, development partners rethinking strategy and Nepal graduating to a middle-income country. The transformation now required is for private sector firms to take the lead in the discourse, identifying needs and gaps, and calling on development partners to support those specific areas—rather than the traditional top-down approach. The shift from subsistence agriculture to commercial agriculture must be grounded in extensive research, thorough analysis and a long-term strategic plan.

Chapter 8

Towards Sustainable Tourism

'What a day!' my friend, who had just returned from a whirlwind journey, sighed as he sipped a drink at a jungle lodge in Chitwan National Park. This was Asia's largest national park, located 200 kilometres west of Kathmandu. He had begun his day with an early morning, hour-long helicopter ride from Kathmandu to Lukla, the entry point to Mount Everest. He was mesmerized by the sight of the Lukla airport, regarded as one of the most challenging airports in the world. He then flew another twenty minutes to have breakfast at the scenic Syangboche, situated at 3,780 meters. By midday, he was back in Kathmandu to enjoy a sumptuous local meal before taking a twenty-minute flight to Bharatpur in Chitwan, where he arrived amidst lush jungles.

He told me he travels a lot, but there are not many places in the world where, within a single day, you can experience so much. This one trip alone had offered breathtaking views of the mountains, mid-hills and plains. You can watch the sun rise in the hills and then see it set over the plains. There is diverse flora and fauna, along with rich cultural heritage and traditions to absorb—all in one place.

Land-linked to China and India, with two billion people within three hours' flying distance from Kathmandu, the potential of Nepali tourism is immense. My interest in tourism began when I started my career in Nepal's first five-star hotel—Soaltee—in 1989. The hotel went through many transitions, from being managed initially by the Oberoi Group of India to later being rebranded as Crowne Plaza under the InterContinental Hotel Group (IHG). My office was located within the hotel complex, which gave me the opportunity to observe various facets of its operations. In the early 1990s, there were only a few luxury hotels, all concentrated in Kathmandu. My experience began with doing internal audits of the hotel, airline General Sales Agency (GSA) operations and travel company within the group. I later got involved in finances and project management. I leveraged my learning of strategy building and acquisitions for the largest travel company in Nepal. These have provided me with some much-needed insights into the tourism industry.

As I continued to travel across the world and, especially through my work as a tourism consultant to the Government of Rwanda, I have had the opportunity to reflect on Nepal's tourism from different perspectives. Since 2012, beed management has been engaged in product development for the Rwanda Development Board (RDB), the government agency responsible for tourism. We developed multiple offerings, including cultural tourism products, water tourism products and eco-tourism products, and identified the markets where these could be promoted. Our experience in Rwanda later led to a project in Saudi Arabia, where we were asked to assess tourism products just as the government was about to embark on an ambitious tourism development plan.

Drawing from these experiences, I share a few thoughts in this chapter on how Nepal's tourism has evolved over the years and how its potential can be further developed. I also touch on a few areas where discourse has been limited: the rise of domestic tourism, future trends that will affect Nepal and the leadership opportunities for Nepal within the broader tourism ecosystem.

What Makes Nepal a Tourist Destination for Foreigners?

Nepal gained global attention when it opened up to the outside world in 1950. Maurice Herzog and Louis Lachenal of France climbed Annapurna I on 3 June 1950. Then, on 29 May 1953, Tenzing Norgay Sherpa of Nepal and Sir Edmund Hillary of New Zealand reached the summit of Mount Everest, the world's highest peak at 8,848 meters.

In 1962, Nepal started keeping a record of people visiting the country and in that year alone, 6179 tourists visited the country. The number crossed the half-million mark in 2007 and reached one million in 2019.

In 2024, Nepal received 1.15 million international visitors arriving by air. In addition, over a million people entered Nepal by land from India, along with a smaller number from China—particularly from the Tibet Autonomous Region.

The international tourists visiting Nepal can be grouped into five major categories. The first are those who come to enjoy the natural beauty of the majestic mountains, the diverse topography of the country and the wilderness of the jungle. Then there are those who come mainly for the culture—to visit UNESCO heritage sites, experience festivals and immerse themselves in cultural celebrations. The next category comprises tourists seeking religious and spiritual experiences—with visits to Lumbini, the birthplace of the Buddha, and other significant Buddhist sites, as well as places of worship revered by Hindus. The fourth category includes those drawn by adventure sports—from bungee jumping to mountain climbing, rafting, trekking, cycling and more. Finally, there is MICE tourism: people travelling for meetings, incentives, conferences and exhibitions. There has been growth across all five segments over the past decades, and the future of each appears promising, especially when viewed in light of global trends.

Domestic Tourism and Changing Trends

I began writing about the potential of domestic tourism in 2006, when the Nepal Tourism Board recognized the need to boost this segment.[1] There were a number of factors that contributed to this shift: the end of the Maoist insurgency in 2006, improved road and air connectivity, the proliferation of social media, changes in social structure and behaviour, the development of new tourism products and the rise in the number of people from the diaspora returning to Nepal.

For ten years during the insurgency (1996–2006), followed by political transitions until 2010, Nepalis did not feel safe travelling within their own country. There were army checkpoints with long queues, and in some areas, insurgents extorted or abducted people. This is no longer the case today.

In addition, road connectivity has significantly improved. In 2024, the Department of Roads reported a total of 65,000 kilometres of roads, most of which were built and maintained by local municipalities. With 26 per cent of households owning two-wheelers or four-wheelers,[2] travel decisions have become more spontaneous. Various forms of transport—jeeps, microbuses and traditional buses—have improved connectivity between towns, making travel easier for smaller groups. Rideshare and social media platforms have also made it easier to book transport. A Russian ride-sharing app, InDrive, specialises in helping users find available seats on vehicles travelling between cities. When I needed to visit Dharan in eastern Nepal for a family emergency, I simply found a car for hire on Facebook—and a comfortable vehicle with a friendly driver awaited me at Biratnagar airport. Finding a car with working air-conditioning in the hot and humid plains of Nepal used to be a challenge. We had to call friends and request their vehicles!

Air connectivity has also improved dramatically. In 2024, it was not surprising to hear that at peak, there were forty-nine flights a day between Pokhara and Kathmandu. Again in 2024, 4.47 million Nepalis travelled by air within their own country, many of them as tourists. The proliferation of social media has become the most effective promotion for tourism. From bikers recording videos on their GoPros to people sharing pictures and clips across different platforms have enticed more people to travel. It also created a sense of peer pressure and during the pandemic, when it was expensive and difficult to travel outside Nepal, your own country threw in many surprises.

There have also been many behavioural and societal transformations contributing to the rise in domestic tourism. Families have become more nuclear and dispersed across the country, which meant that during the annual festival of Dashain, around October or for weddings or periods of grief, there would be travel. The taboo on women travelling alone has practically vanished. Thirty years ago, you could not spot women on two-wheelers undertaking long journeys along highways. Today, Nepal is considered one of the safest places in South Asia for women to travel. Solo female travellers now vlog about their journeys, breaking traditional boundaries.[3] The taboo around where and from whom one can eat are also fading. People are no longer concerned about the caste of the cook or whether a menstruating woman prepared the food. The availability of reasonably good food along highways, in towns and cities has encouraged greater mobility. During my travels, I am always surprised to find charming coffee shops and tidy eateries serving local dishes. A domestic chain like The Burger House or Crunchy Fried Chicken, according to its owner Basanta Lama, has 151 branches across the country.[4] Again, social media platforms have played a crucial role by offering ratings for eateries and lodging. The transformation has been mind-boggling.

In March 2025, when I was driving through Jajarkot and Rukum districts in the Karnali province, I was stunned by all that had changed since the peak of the insurgency in 2004. The governance ecosystem has improved with Nepalis not having to pay tolls, taxes and other levies to travel within their own country. I booked a hotel in Rukumkot on a global platform like booking.com. The proliferation of digital platforms enabling bookings and payments and references from social media platforms and sites has made travel easier for domestic tourists. Property owners have better control of the operations with digital payment platforms. WhatsApp, Viber and other free messaging platforms have made it easier to contact hotels, travel companies and service providers. While international tourist arrivals have seen steady growth, domestic tourism has practically exploded.

New Products and Diaspora Tourists

New tourism products have entered the market, and activities once considered the domain of international tourists are now sought after by domestic tourists as well. Ten years ago, there was only one cable car in the country, which transported devotees to a temple in Kurintar, a hundred kilometres west of Kathmandu. Today, cable cars have become immensely popular nationwide, connecting both famous and lesser-known temples and destinations. During the pandemic, Kushma, located 60 kilometres west of Pokhara, emerged as a hub for bungee jumping and other adventure activities. More than fifty lodges have now opened in the town to accommodate the rising number of tourists visiting Kushma.

An article in the *Nepali Times* stated: 'After it took TikTok by storm last year as a selfie spot, The Cliff in Kushma has become a go-to destination for adventure sports. People from the far corners of Nepal as well as overseas come to this bridge over the Kali Gandaki gorge to bungee or swing jump. The pedestrian suspension bridge has a span of 520 meters and hangs 228 meters above the river, connecting Kushma of Parbat to Balewa of Baglung. This is supposedly the second-highest bungee jump in the world, after Macau Tower in China.'[5]

Similarly, trekking routes such as Mardi Himal, Annapurna Base Camp and Langtang now see more Nepali than foreign trekkers. The number of Nepalis visiting popular destinations like Chitwan and Pokhara from across the country has also grown significantly. Through beed, when we work on hotel projects, owners tell us about the new design changes they are adopting, keeping in mind the requirement of Nepali travellers: Barbeque pits, a compatible food menu and willingness to provide late service.

Famous Farm, a boutique nature resort in Nuwakot, was once intended primarily for foreign tourists and rarely saw domestic visitors. However, when we visited in December 2023, it was full of Nepalis. The staff explained how they now need to stock more firewood because, unlike foreign tourists who retire early, Nepalis prefer to stay up late. In another lodge we visited, the hotel provided the first round of firewood for free, but guests had to pay extra to keep the fire going. The service staff told us that international tourists tend to return to their rooms after dinner, whereas Nepalis often stay up late into the night. Consequently, different pricing mechanisms have emerged to cater to this new clientele.

Lastly, it is the diaspora that is travelling across Nepal when they return—this is what is pushing domestic tourism. They are not only travelling themselves but also encouraging their relatives, friends and family to travel. Hotels like Chandragiri Hills Resort in Kathmandu or Rupakot Resort near Pokhara have become must-visit destinations for members of the diaspora. In these resorts, Nepalis now outnumber international tourists. In *Nefview*, Narayan Baral, who has recently returned to Nepal and taken a road trip, writes: 'Regardless of where I went for the trip, ranging from Pokhara to The Pink City or Waling, Syangja, the smooth road trip from Butwal to Bhairahawa, I was constantly surprised with the resemblance to my road trips in the US—striking me with the range of progress Nepal has gone through in the last 23 years.'[6]

Visiting Nepalis are delighted when they are served a Nepali breakfast like *aloo dum* and *sel roti* with gourmet plating, or when they receive personalised service that they could never afford while travelling in Australia, North America or Europe. Second-generation Nepalis, especially those from the US, are rediscovering their fascination with Nepal. They compare the cost of holidays in Nepal with their average spend in the US or Europe and recognize the tremendous value for money. When I met my friend's children who live in Boston and who now make Nepal their biannual holiday destination, they told me that you can enjoy some of the best heritage and nature experiences for a hundred dollars, while similar experiences in Europe might cost five hundred. Then there are the helicopter rides—for a few hundred dollars, one can enjoy breakfast in the mountains with stunning views or go on a pilgrimage to Pathivara in eastern Nepal.

Global Trends That Will Impact Nepali Tourism

I've identified seven trends that are transforming global tourism, and some of these will deeply impact the future of Nepali tourism.

Bleisure travel: The pandemic legitimized remote working and the ability to combine work and leisure. This is popularly known as *bleisure* (blending business and leisure) travel. One can now be on a work trip, take a break, return to work and then head home—without raising eyebrows. A friend in Dubai, who works as an expatriate and moves frequently between countries, told me that his wife recently took up a remote job. This allows her to keep her job even if their location changes.

The pandemic also saw the rise of digital nomads[7]—people, especially—young people who choose to work from locations they would otherwise visit for a holiday. Countries like Estonia, Croatia and Dubai introduced liberal work permit rules, enabling people to work remotely from these destinations. If Nepal reorients its work permit and visa systems to allow individuals to live and work in the country, a new segment of tourism could emerge. For instance, there are people interested in biodiversity, art, music, culture, Himalayan anthropology and more who might wish to make Nepal their second home. Countries like Thailand, Malaysia and Indonesia are already offering long-term visas. Nepal needs to follow that route.

Buying tourism products and services in a jiffy: While tourism products and services have become easier to purchase through mobile applications and other technology-backed enablers, augmented and virtual reality is entirely changing the game. Soon, one will be able to book a hotel or choose a destination by viewing it through wearables. It is quite different to see a picture or video of a trekking route on your phone compared to experiencing it through high-quality wearable devices. In Dubai, the Jumeirah Group offers AR-powered virtual tours on its website, allowing guests to explore luxurious properties virtually before making a reservation. This immersive experience has been shown to increase booking conversions by offering a realistic preview of what guests can expect.

Films and vloggers push tourism: The documentary *14 Peaks* on Netflix recently inspired many people to visit Nepal for climbing. Similarly, the Bollywood film *Uunchai*, which follows a group of friends heading to Everest base camp, has worked wonders for Nepal's tourism. Today, videos, reels, series and movies from different countries, delivered to your drawing room via streaming platforms, help showcase tourism products and destinations. In the past, travel writers or publications like *Lonely Planet* decided where you went, where you stayed, what you ate and what you did. Now, there is an abundance of co-created content to guide those same choices. One vlogger or influencer can transform a country's tourism prospects. A video on Nepal's 'mad honey' has garnered over 12 million views on YouTube. *Republica* reported: 'Travel vlogs like "Ghumante" with 271,000 subscribers, "Nepal" with 175,000 subscribers, "Srijana Siju" with 119,000 subscribers, and other popular vlogs such as *Yatri*, *Parikrama* and *Muna Chiya* have truly attracted people from around the world to explore new and diverse places in Nepal. These vlogs provide detailed and unique videos about hundreds of tourist destinations across Nepal's eastern, western, northern and southern regions, sharing them globally online.'[8]

Tourism Is Moving from Product to Experience

It is not about the temple or the palace, but about understanding the history, culture and living heritage that surround them. With the Internet, travellers are more informed than ever. As a result, they seek experiences beyond what they have read or heard from others. In the heritage walks I conduct as a hobby to raise funds for my ancestral temple—Hiranyavarna Mahavira, popularly known as the Golden Temple in Patan—I emphasize on the rituals that take place there and contextualise the temple's thousand-year history by linking what is written with what is actually happening in that moment. Travel is no longer just about visiting a centuries-old temple, but about witnessing what takes place inside it.

Luxury Tourism Will Be the Key

In Jomsom, I recently visited the Shinta Mani Resort, a luxury resort that is part of the Bill Bensley collection and is making waves. In January 2024, *Condé Nast Traveler*, the iconic travel magazine, featured the resort on its cover, drawing global attention to this high-end tourist destination.[9] It was then that I began to think that perhaps Nepal can do more in luxury tourism.

From tea houses to tented camps, Nepal's tourism offerings now include a wide range of products at different price points. This segment is growing and one that Nepal needs to keep an eye on. The global consulting firm McKinsey projects the luxury tourism industry to cross US$2.2 trillion by 2030[10] and, assuming it quadruples every decade, it could exceed US$5 to US$7 trillion by 2043. This represents a significant opportunity, especially as most luxury travellers will be from China and India.

Bhutan has been a trailblazer in the region in promoting luxury tourism, with a particular emphasis on high-value, low-volume sustainable travel. Countries can learn from Bhutan on how to manage luxury tourism—from ensuring impeccable services at the airport for private jets to delivering exceptional hotel experiences, transportation and appropriate responses to medical or other emergencies.

Since 2022, I have been conducting high-end 'Unleashing the Vajra Journeys' in Bhutan, which are based on three principles: exploration, immersion and reflection. I hope to bring these journeys to Nepal as well in the future.

Weekend getaways and staycations: My friends from India who come to Nepal on work trips generally like to time their visits so they can spend the weekend here. They often tell me how well value for money works for them. They say it is worth even the flight ticket, as the experience and service in Nepal are much better than in India and come at a fraction of the cost. My friends' children who visit from India say one thing in unison: in India, if you want to eat international food and drink good wine or high-end beverages at a restaurant, it is beyond the reach of the middle class, but in Nepal, it is affordable and accessible. Even in highway shacks, one can find good wine and single malt whisky to go with Korean or Western food.

Lord of Drinks, or LOD, a club in Thamel, Kathmandu, features among the top fifty clubs in the world. Barc, a speakeasy bar, has been ranked 39th among the fifty best bars in Asia.[11] Earlier, Indians came to Nepal for temple visits, shopping or to go to the casino. The younger generation now seeks world-class fun that is safe and affordable. There are half a billion young people next door in India. Nepal needs to think carefully about what it can offer them.

Wellness tourism: This is the next big segment that will take off, growing well beyond the pilgrimage and religious tourism markets. Different studies project the volume of wellness tourism to cross the two trillion-dollar mark by 2030.

A prime example is the Buddhist monasteries mushrooming across Nepal that sell well under the 'Tibetan Buddhism' brand. These are centres where one can stay for extended periods to engage in wellness and spiritual experiences. Kerala in India and Thailand in Southeast Asia are excellent examples of how tourism can centre around wellness and spirituality. That said, it is not as though tourists who visit these places do not go to bars or indulge in other kinds of activities. The definitions keep evolving as countries explore different ways to create a differentiated product. Nepal has the added advantage of combining its natural beauty as a USP with these products and experiences.

At the Shinta Mani resort, I was introduced to an eleventh-generation traditional healer known as an *Amchi*. I was told that guests return for repeated consultations with him as his treatment has been very fruitful for many.

Similarly, a friend in Bangladesh, Shazia Omar, runs Dhaka Flow, a wellness platform that regularly hosts wellness retreats in Nepal. Bangladesh, with its 170 million population, is separated by just 14 kilometres, and flights take only an hour.

Opportunities for the Private Sector

Historically, Nepal's tourism and hospitality sector has taken off without much support from the government. It has largely been led by the private sector. Nepal's flag carrier, for instance, has limited international reach, and this vacuum has been filled by international airlines. The domestic aviation sector too is dominated by private players. When people ask me what Nepal's national carrier is, I respond with 'Qatar Airways' as this airline flies more Nepalis than the national flag carrier or any other airline.

But jokes apart, Nepal's tourism and hospitality industries have produced hundreds of thousands of trained professionals who are working in Nepal and across the world today. Be it on the east coast of the US, in the UK, Scandinavian countries or Australia, Nepalis are widely employed in the hospitality sector. It is heartening to meet so many of my former colleagues from the Soaltee Hotel when I visit restaurants and hotels around the world.

While the private sector will continue to innovate, this sector can take off in a big way if the government pays some attention to it and helps facilitate the transition and transformation of the industry in the long term. Specifically, here are six issues to consider in this respect:

Pushing value over volume: Promoting sustainable tourism and ensuring the carrying capacity is not compromised is important. For instance, the permit for a Mount Everest expedition needs to be raised to half a million dollars. The government also needs to ensure that waste management and the environmental impact left by climbers are adequately addressed. With drones now being used to remove waste and transport materials, we can push the boundaries of sustainability. The current fee for the permit of US$11,000, which was increased to US$15,000[12] in 2024—is too little to climb the tallest mountain in the world.

In Rwanda, the cost of permits to observe gorillas in their natural habitat for an hour was increased from US$500 to US$750 in 2012, and then to US$1500 in 2017.[13] Only eighty permits are on offer in a day. While cheaper pricing is available in neighbouring countries, people come to Rwanda as this money has been invested in the conservation of the gorilla population, which has grown over time. Interestingly, luxury hotels have opened in the area, as tourists willing to pay US$1500 for a permit are also willing to pay premium rates for accommodation.

Similarly, Bhutan charges what is known as the 'Sustainable Development Fee (SDF)' for tourists, and this model has been effective. Even Indian tourists, who otherwise do not require a visa, must pay an entry fee to visit Bhutan. In Mustang, Nepal, foreigners visiting the northern part of the district—Upper Mustang—must pay US$500 for a ten-day trekking permit and US$50 for each additional day. I have met foreign tourists on motorbikes in that region who told me the fee was well worth it for the opportunity to witness the stunning landscape and heritage sites.

I continue to advocate that sustainability is not only about staying in low-end homestays or pasting slogans about eco-tourism. It is about shaping the product towards sustainability across the entire value chain. The balance between income generation, conservation of nature and culture, consumption and the future must all be considered. Lisa Choegyal, a sustainable tourism specialist who has worked in Nepal for the past fifty years, told me in a conversation: 'Despite the preaching of academia and idealists, the first rule of sustainable tourism is to be financially viable and to make money. Otherwise, you will not be in a position to help anyone – neither the locals nor climate change, heritage, nature or wildlife.'

World-class airports: Airports must become world-class through increased investment and improved management. Additionally, the management of the national carrier must be handed over to one of the world's top airlines. This requires government intervention. Once again, the example of Rwanda becomes relevant, where 49 per cent of their national carrier has been sold to Qatar Airways and 60 per cent of the airport to Hamad International Airport, Doha. Nepal Airlines holds slots at many international airports that need to be activated, and we require a larger fleet flying from different Nepali airports to different airports outside Nepal. Nepal now has three international airports. However, rather than building more airports, we need to manage the current ones well.

In January 2025, in Zurich, I was in suggesting the management of the Zurich Airport to make plans to take over Nepal airports and make it world class through an efficient management system. Zurich Airport, for example, is set to operate the second airport of New Delhi in India. For the future of tourism, there is no alternative but to open up Nepal's airlines and airports to global players. I had once reviewed a proposal submitted to the government by a private airline from East Asia seeking to take Bhairawa Airport on a long-term lease and operate low-cost short-haul routes. The proposal was ultimately buried due to political wrangling. Yet options like these are crucial to accelerating growth and ensuring better management.

Leveraging China and India outbound: Nepal has been fortunate in that tourists continue to throng to the country despite its limited promotional activities compared to other destinations. Nepal's biggest advantage is its location between China and India—the two largest outbound tourist markets in the world. If current trends continue, India's outbound market is projected to reach 150 million and China's 400 million by 2043. Both markets are price sensitive and have distinct needs, behaving very differently from other international tourists. Nepal must therefore develop more customized experiences for each of these markets and promote them effectively. For India, overland tourism is likely to be a major attraction, as the Indian Himalayan region becomes saturated. Nepal offers a more diverse range of food, accommodation and entertainment options. A November 2023 report by the leading global consulting firm McKinsey outlines key areas of transformation in the Indian outbound market that countries should look at.[14]

Indians have constituted a major share of tourists to Nepal even before Western markets opened up, but Chinese tourists only began arriving in large numbers from the early 2000s. Most are first-time visitors. A 2018 McKinsey report seeks to bust the myth surrounding Chinese tourists, who are often viewed in a stereotypical manner—as travellers interested only in shopping, eating their own cuisine and frequenting Chinese-run establishments.[15]

Chinese tourists also have a unique segment within themselves. One such group that I encountered in Bangkok during the Chinese New Year holidays comprised single women seeking luxury, global cuisine and immersive cultural experiences. Interestingly, women outnumber men in outbound travel, and safety is a critical factor for them when choosing travel.[16]

Leveraging Lumbini, religion and spirituality: One of the biggest changes the Nepali tourism market noticed since 2010 was the arrival of Chinese tourists interested in visiting Lumbini, the birthplace of Buddha, and other places of Buddhist importance. It is estimated that there are more than 300 million Buddhists in China who are asserting their belief. Therefore, China has been interested in Buddhism in Nepal.[17] This has been the case since the time Nepali artist Araniko built the first Buddhist temples in Beijing. Thousands of Chinese men and women visit the Miaoying Temple, also known as the White Stupa in Beijing, built by Nepali craftsman Araniko and his team in the thirteenth century.[18]

The World Bank commissioned a study that resulted in a report on the formulation of the Buddhist Circuit Strategy for South Asia. The strategy has been iterative, adapting to evolving contexts and based on demonstrations and lessons learned. It began with field visits to some of the main places associated with Buddha's earthly journey. This process of retracing Buddha's footsteps was informed by scholarly research on Buddha's teachings (Sutras, Tripitakas and Vinayas) delivered in these places. Resulting maps and a conceptual framework were presented to Elders and Monastics in Southeast Asia and worldwide for review and validation of their accuracy and authenticity.[19]

Similarly, the Government of India has embarked on extending the Ramayana Circuit to Nepal, touching upon Janakpur, the city in the southern plains, the birthplace of Sita, Ram's wife and a central character in the Ramayana mythology.[20] Similarly, after the visit of Indian Prime Minister Narendra

Modi to Muktinath in Mustang District, a holy temple revered by Buddhists, Jains and Hindus alike, there have been large inflows of pilgrims to this area. Earlier, Pashupatinath Temple in Kathmandu was the only holy place Indian pilgrims used to visit. Now, newer religious tourism destinations are emerging across the country. If many of them are connected by cable cars now or in the future, they will become more accessible. In 2022, more than 20 per cent of the people visiting the Manakamana Temple on cable cars were from India. Pathibhara in eastern Nepal, 43 kilometres from the Indian border, is very popular too. People who cannot walk take the chopper. In 2024, a charter for five persons cost US$3000.

There is Maula Kali in Gaidakot too, which is connected by a cable car and is less than 100 kilometres from the Indian border. This is apart from Kalinchowk in the mid-hills, which offers great views and is 200 kilometres by road from the Indian border.

Towards experiential hubs: Nepal needs to emerge as a pioneer in a new kind of tourist offering called experiential hubs. These would attract a mix of people from different parts of the country and abroad. Visitors could come for short- or long-term stays. Typically, these hubs would be integrated with the local community, whether in terms of design and hard infrastructure or soft skills. This could be Nepal's gift to the world.

These hubs could offer people the experience of being in nature and engaging in activities of their choice. From adventure and sports to culture, wellness and spirituality, these hubs can be built and managed with sustainability at the core of their existence. They could also serve as a way to create more jobs for locals and offer opportunities for both small- and large-scale businesses to integrate with them.

There are many people who want to retire and spend their final years in Nepal. Countries like the Bahamas have managed to attract investment and high-net-worth retirees to the Caribbean by partnering with global firms that specialize in investment migration programmes. Perhaps Nepal can learn from that too.

Destination for events: Nepal is already a popular destination for conferences, weddings and social functions, but this segment has the potential to grow significantly. With bleisure (blending business and leisure) travel emerging as the future, Nepal offers the ideal platform to mix business with pleasure. Air connectivity and service infrastructure are key for the MICE segment, as demonstrated by the popularity of destinations like Singapore, Bangkok, Cape Town, Nairobi and Dubai.

Today, birthday parties, baby showers and wedding anniversaries are becoming grander than ever, turning celebrations into lucrative opportunities for destinations. Every festival or social occasion is increasingly becoming a money-spinner. Nepal has a very attractive visa regime, and whenever a South Asian event needs a neutral venue, Nepal often becomes the preferred location. A Pakistani who cannot travel to India, or an Indian unable to get a visa to Bangladesh, can obtain a free visa to Nepal. The world needs to know how easy it is to enter Nepal.

Creative city: In October 2023, Kathmandu was listed as a 'film city' under the UNESCO Creative City Network (UCCN). This recognition of Kathmandu's diverse art and culture can be leveraged to position the city as a hub for filmmaking. This would further involve establishing training institutions, producing films and managing the backend activities involved in film production.

If Nepal could earn the confidence of Hollywood, there would be no need to spend US$20 million to recreate a Nepali village in Australia for the shooting of a film.[21] Small efforts in this direction are already underway. Incessant Rain, a company founded by US-based Nepalis Kiran and Deepa Joshi, provides backend animation and visual effects for Hollywood blockbusters. They have now launched Rain Academy, which trains Nepalis to access world-class employment through the company. They also advise Women in Animation (WIA) Nepal, an initiative that equips women with the skills needed to work as animators.[22]

In May 2025, the biopic of Tenzing Norgay, one of the first to summit Mount Everest, was being shot in Nepal, starring popular Hollywood actor Tom Hiddleston.[23] More than 300 foreign cast members were in Nepal, and the city was abuzz with the number of hotel rooms the production company had booked across multiple properties.

Developing global service training centers: The hubs discussed earlier would require impeccable service—and who better to deliver it than a Nepali with an inherent smile.

Already, there are hospitality institutions in Nepal that have gone global. These institutions should be incentivised to expand and enhance their reach. At the same time, global companies must be encouraged to support training for Nepalis in airports, hospitality establishments, transport services and other allied sectors. If one of the world's busiest airports—Hamad International Airport in Doha—can operate with the help of a significant Nepali workforce, or if Qatar Airways employs a large number of Nepalis, then perhaps it is time for these companies to establish global training centres in Nepal to provide better on-the-job training.

Large hotel chains and networks that promote eco-tourism and sustainable tourism can also train Nepalis and bring others to be trained here. Nepal can, therefore, be the home for training centers for guides to go on mountain and trekking guides—much like how Botswana, South Africa and Kenya have become hubs for training naturalists and safari guides.

The future of tourism is not going to be about products only, but experiences. Hence, large-scale investment in building 'soft' infrastructure must be prioritized.

Chapter 9

Digital Transformation

In August 2024, I was invited by friends Prasanna Dhungel and Deepti Bhattarai to visit the Nepal office of GrowByData, a technology company working in the field of market intelligence. They gather marketing intelligence that helps global brands gain competitive insights. Founder Prasanna is proud to share that they work with some of the world's leading companies, including Amazon. From starting in a room with five people in Boston in 2014, by 2024, they had grown to employ 100 people across their Boston and Kathmandu offices. He says he collaborates with over 100 brands through half a dozen agencies. When the *Kathmandu Post* interviewed him, he was asked why he established a company in Nepal. He cited three key advantages: 'Firstly, Nepal offers access to top talent in software and data analytics. Secondly, the significant time difference allows for 24-hour operations, providing productivity gains. Thirdly, US businesses can benefit from cost advantages in Nepal.'[1]

Nepal's digital transformation has progressed quietly, often overlooked amid the country's political headlines. In 2020, beed management launched the Nepal Private Sector Assessment Report, conducted for the United States Agency for International Development (USAID). Many who read the report were surprised to learn that 37 per cent of Nepal's exports came from the Information, Communication and Technology (ICT) sector.[2] The report was also one of the first major research projects that looked at exports of services. In 2024, my estimates of Nepal's total exports in this sector were closing in on US$900 million, though the report by the Institute for Integrated Development Studies (IIDS) had the official figure of export of US$515 million in 2022.[3] The study also stated that 'over 106 IT service export companies and 14,728 IT freelancers in software development and technology and 51,781 ITeS freelancers engaged in exporting IT services through various digital platforms.'[4] In July 2024, the government has set a target of NPR 3 trillion (US$2.4 billion) of ICT exports in ten years.[5]

The growth in this sector has been exponential. Total formal IT service exports reached US$515 million in 2022, representing a growth of 64.2 per cent since 2021.[6] An Investment Board document from 2017 proudly stated that in 2013, the export revenue from ITES and BPO was approximately US$3,572,905.[7] So, the jump has been over 1000 times in a decade!

Initially, most export-oriented businesses were US-based, but Australia is catching up. Australia has a population of 1,79,050 people of Nepali origin.[8] Alaya, formerly called Home Loan Experts Nepal (HLE), is the offshore arm of a mid-sized mortgage firm based in Sydney. It began with five employees in 2017 and employed more than 400 people by 2024. The key reason for this expansion has been the ability to find skilled resources at nearly half the cost. For instance, while an Australian support team member costs AUD 74,800 per year, a Nepali worker costs only AUD 34,800.[9]

It is not just about firms in the ICT space. Many Nepalis now hold key positions in global technology companies. In July 2023, at our annual NEFMeet event organized by Nepal

Economic Forum, we had Amit Shrestha, Chief Financial Officer (CFO) of Microsoft Mexico, as the keynote speaker. It is always a matter of honour to host Nepali professionals who have taken up significant roles in global organizations.

My interest in the technology sector began during my earlier job with the Soaltee Group, when we started Surya Infotech in 2002 and began exploring different investments in technology companies. Meeting many people in the technology space helped me understand how technology was progressing and impacting human lives. While we worked with different technology companies from Nepal and abroad, it was in 2020, through Nepal Economic Forum, that we started the Centre for Digital Transformation. This gave us more exposure to the policy space, which continues to evolve rapidly.

In this chapter, we will discuss the future of digital transformation in Nepal by examining the drivers of this transformation. What are the observable trends? Where is it headed? And how can Nepal learn from and leverage the opportunity between India and China? We will conclude by discussing the need for skilling, understanding the Fourth Industrial Revolution, and recognising the need for a mindset shift.

Key Drivers for Digital Transformation

Amit Shrestha, CFO of Microsoft Mexico, explains digital transformation as 'the incorporation of digital technology into various aspects of business, essentially changing how it operates and delivers value. It is the move from physical to digital, disrupting existing business models and creating new ones. Simply put, this is about looking at all the processes and seeing how we can do things better, efficiently and effectively. The journey is about taking data and turning it into action while adding value to the business in the fastest and most relevant way. This is also seen as the "Fourth Industrial Revolution" that will transform many facets of our lives, including how we work and socialise with one another.'[10]

Digital transformation has largely been possible due to five key drivers. First, we leapfrogged directly to smartphones without having to go through the landline and dumb-phone era. Audio and video have become the primary means of communication, making it unnecessary for people to understand language technicalities or possess typing skills. Second, the proliferation of internet connections through affordable services available across the country. Keshav Nepal, CEO of WorldLink, Nepal's largest internet service provider, shared in a conversation that internet penetration grew from 2.5 per cent in 2010 to 45 per cent in 2024, with broadband household subscribers increasing from 1,37,000 to 3.15 million.

Third, the language interface has changed to Nepali. Apart from a few portals in English, 2340 online news portals registered with the Press Council[11] are in Nepali and other regional languages of Nepal. Nepali typing and translation facilities have eased the use of devices. One can now read international content in any language, translated into Nepali.

Fourth, the availability of electricity to charge and operate devices, along with supporting infrastructure, has enabled the proliferation of the Internet. Finally, free platforms are now widely accessible. For instance, TikTok and Instagram have become e-commerce platforms where users do not have to make any payments for the basic versions. TikTok, released in 2016, accounts for up to 40 per cent of Nepal's internet bandwidth.[12] The controversy surrounding this app, owned by a Chinese company, led to its ban in November 2023—three years after India banned it—though the ban was lifted in September 2024.

If we could place ourselves inside a time machine and go back to 2014, many of the services available now had not even emerged at that time. E-commerce platform Daraz entered Nepal in 2016. Aanchal Kunwar, the CEO of Daraz, revealed at an event hosted by the Nepal Economic Forum that 40 per cent of their sales and 35 per cent of their vendors were located outside the Kathmandu Valley.[13] This shows that e-commerce platforms are connecting customers and vendors even beyond the capital.

Foodmandu, the pioneer in food delivery apps, secured its first major investor in 2016, paving the way for many others to follow. The ride-hailing app Tootle began in 2017, and Pathao, a Bangladeshi company, entered the Nepal market in 2018 and is currently the market leader in this segment. In July 2023, when the payments app Khalti managed the digital payment system for a concert by Indian singer Arijit Singh in Kathmandu, they told me that they sold US$1.1 million worth of tickets for a single show. This was unprecedented in Nepal.

One of the major digital transformations that has taken place in Nepal is in the area of digital payments. I remember when the company F1 Soft, a firm providing digital solutions, was entering the digital payments market with its digital wallet e-Sewa. They wanted to revolutionize the way payments are made in Nepal. They were seeking to strengthen their operations to build the foundations for growth. With the success of e-Sewa, they launched the payment platform Fonepay in 2019.[14] Now, Fonepay has become synonymous with paying via QR codes. Between mid-July 2021 and mid-August 2021, the NRB recorded approximately 1.3 million QR-based payments, totalling NPR 5.1 billion (US$35 million). Fast forward to 2024, and this figure has surged to 160.93 million transactions, amounting to approximately NPR 500 billion (US$3 billion), marking multifold increases.[15]

Online banking has taken off in a big way in Nepal, with 8 million people using mobile banking and 16 million using internet banking. The Nepali stock markets dematerialized

(DEMAT) their securities in 2021. This means people no longer need paper share certificates, as their shares are stored in digital accounts. The percentage of the population holding demat accounts in Nepal was 12.62 per cent, while the same figure for India was 5.32 per cent in 2021. Interestingly, there are more women engaged in online stock trading—there are 1.6 million active accounts belonging to women and 2.1 million to men, nearly four women for every five male investors![16] In India, based on data provided by equity research firm Trendlyne, among the country's top ten investors, only one is a woman.[17]

The government has also pushed its own online platforms, such as the Nagarik (Citizen) App—a mobile application launched by the Government of Nepal to provide government-related services through a single online platform. These services include access to the national ID, driving licence, passport, citizenship, voter ID and other documents, all within a single app. So, there is no need to carry physical documents. When traffic police fine you, they simply scan your licence, and a message is sent to your phone. You then pay using digital wallets or online.

In office in April 2025, the team was scrambling to put together a bid in response to a call for proposals for a consulting assignment with an international firm based in Nepal. One of the requirements was the submission of a Police Clearance Report. My memories of obtaining this report involved running around to different offices and police stations. I started to get worried. My colleague said we could just apply through the Nagarik App—and we all did. The process was easy, and the report arrived the next day. The app has shifted many government services online.

Niraj Bhusal, who works with the Government of Nepal and is involved in improving the Nagarik App, counts it among his key interests and responsibilities. I have enjoyed interacting with him and learning about the challenges the app is facing and the direction in which the government is moving towards faceless bureaucracy and e-governance. He wrote, 'The Government of Nepal plans to develop and expand the Nagarik app as the primary digital tool to make public services accessible, enabling as many services as possible to be delivered online, transforming traditional service delivery into faceless bureaucracy and e-governance, reducing the need for service recipients to visit government offices, and enhancing public service delivery.'[18]

Tax filing is now completely online, as are other services such as applying for passports and documents like labour permits. The government has also tried to incentivize online transactions by offering a 10 per cent VAT refund on digital payments. Amit Agrawal, the CEO of the payment platform Khalti, shared with me that they were able to receive about Rs 4 million in VAT refunds by paying their internet service provider vendor online.

The government is becoming increasingly ambitious. Dipesh Bista, the CEO of the National E-Governance Commission—a high-level government body formed and chaired by the prime minister—shared his vision of completing the next census in 2031 within a week. He even claimed it would be possible to count the cows on a farmer's land in real time using satellite imagery and embedded devices. The focus has also been on making the National ID the basis for delivering digital services to citizens, similar to the Aadhaar card in India. He envisions government services being delivered to people's doorsteps, just as goods or food are delivered by online platforms. Like those platforms that charge for delivery, he argues that the government should also charge a fee for delivering services directly to citizens. He cited the example of the visa service company VFS, which offers premium services that include helping people write visa applications at home, collecting passports and delivering them back. He believes the government can adopt a similar approach.

Social and cultural practices have also kept pace with digital transformation. Invitations to events are now delivered online, and various online platforms have been created to host social and cultural events. When a social function is organized, invitations are sent via WhatsApp groups, a Facebook page is created or a dedicated website is developed.

Religion too has gone digital. Today, one need not be physically present to perform or participate in religious rituals—they can be conducted online. When my friend married her partner, the family priest logged in virtually from within the same city and ensured all the wedding rituals were properly observed. This trend began during the lockdown, when online offerings and rituals gained acceptance. The digitization of indigenous knowledge has also made it possible for people to access rituals, chants and processes that were previously at risk of being lost. With more cultural and religious events being streamed on social media, people can now attend functions both online and in person simultaneously.

My cousin and her friends have come together to create an online platform over Zoom to listen to Buddhist teachers, discuss dhamma and conduct group meditation. They now meet offline as well and call themselves the 'zoom-dhamma friends' group.

Technology Megatrends

In their 2024 report titled *McKinsey Technology Trends Outlook*, McKinsey and Company list fifteen trends to watch that will shape the future. These include the rapid development of artificial intelligence through machine learning. The report highlights the pace of progress in Large Language Models (LLMs). It uses an analogy: prompting a model used to be like adding a research paper, but now it's like adding twenty novels. Among the fifteen trends are Generative AI, Applied AI, Next Generation Software Development, immersive reality and more.

Nepal has already made early progress in a few of these areas. Sameer Maskey, an American Nepali entrepreneur, founded Fusemachines, a company that develops AI-driven solutions. The company, listed on NASDAQ, employs over 300 people in Nepal. Maskey believes he is on a mission to #DemocratizeAI, as his company claims, aiming to bridge the gap between AI advancement and global impact. In pursuit of this goal, it seeks to bring the most advanced technology solutions to the world.[19]

Elsewhere, Bal K. Joshi founded Xuno, a fintech platform that promotes 'borderless transactions pioneered in landlocked Nepal'. In a conversation with him and his COO, Rupesh Krisha Shrestha, they explained how users can initially remit money from the US—and later from across the world—at a fraction of the cost charged by traditional financial services. Joshi aspires to build Nepal's first unicorn.

Nepal is also rapidly becoming a hub for outsourced software development. Pramod Poudel leads Soft-Ed, a company working in higher education and education technology through various educational programmes. Since 2018, it has been at the forefront of ICT education and edtech. He says, 'Given the increasing importance of digital literacy and high demand for professionals in computing, cybersecurity, data science and artificial intelligence, we predict a continued rise in enrolments at SoftEd group of associated institutions. Our higher education wing should at least triple student numbers to about 5000 in the next decade. As Information and Communication Technologies continue to permeate every aspect of our lives, our education technology wings should be able to widen their client base to 1000 schools, with a minimum of 3,00,000 school students directly using our products and services. This forecasting is all in confidence that the SoftEd group is well positioned to equip the next generation of students with the skills and knowledge they need to succeed in the digital era.'

One of the key areas of focus will be building trust around data and digital-enabled products and services. Digital transformation also brings challenges, including cybercrimes, data misuse and growing security risks. It is therefore essential to build trust while bridging the digital divide and promoting digital transformation. Nepalis have already embraced digital payments significantly—they trust that adequate measures are being taken to mitigate the risks.

Another key area is innovation in connectivity. The adoption of 5G would mean download speeds of 10 to 20 gigabits per second—one hundred times faster than 4G. A movie that takes fifty minutes to download on a 4G platform would take less than a minute to download.[20] This would immensely benefit telemedicine and virtual teaching platforms, for instance. A country like Estonia has already taken the lead in this—they have enabled free Wi-Fi with good speed in cities and towns. Nepal can leverage its position of being land-linked to China and India to achieve similar progress.

As a friend from Traveloka, a leading global technology company in Indonesia, said to me at a conference, 'You are lucky. Unlike us, there is no need for submarine cable connections. You can connect with the latest technology being developed in China and India, perhaps a connection with physical wires in quick time.' I will discuss other ways in which we can leverage our links with India and China later in the chapter as well but before that, a quick mention of a few other factors that will be key in Nepal:

Cloud computing has seen a phenomenal surge over the years, and the establishment of data centres has increased internet speed and reduced latency. This has also made virtual work more efficient. If we look at the top five largest data centres in the world, each consumes more than 100 MW of power.[21] Therefore, there is a significant opportunity to capitalise on Nepal's clean hydroelectric power to operate data centres. (I've discussed this in an earlier chapter on hydropower as well.)

Nepal can also contribute to the development of quantum technology, which will be critical in addressing climate impact, telemedicine and quantum communication. We can partner with both Indian and Chinese firms that are competing in this space.

Leveraging Links with India and China

Nepal is situated between two nations that are leaders in digital transformation. However, divergent technologies are emerging from both countries, and Nepal needs to strike a delicate balance to gain maximum leverage.

China's digital economy reached US$7 trillion in 2023 with 1.08 billion internet users. The country has also embarked on creating a Digital Silk Road, connecting its neighbours by making payment platforms acceptable in other countries and encouraging the proliferation of social media platforms like TikTok. China has seen major integration of retail sales, service delivery and digital urbanisation, with more than half of the world's smart cities.[22] President Xi Jinping laid down the vision of 'Digital China' in 2012. His vision aims to create a nation of smart, internet-connected cities, where data is treated alongside labour and capital as a key factor driving the economy and help China compete more effectively globally.[23] Deep Seek, an AI company, took the world by storm in February 2025.

As reported in *Rest of World*, 'Since DeepSeek's launch, a swathe of Chinese companies—from automakers to appliance firms—have joined the frenzy to incorporate the homegrown artificial intelligence model into their products and services.' The report further quoted the company: 'DeepSeek's reasoning model, R1, and large language model, V3, have achieved performance levels comparable to those of leading Western competitors but at a much lower cost.'

China is embarking on a Digital Silk Road (DSR), building a digital ecosystem with China at the centre. This includes payment systems, e-commerce platforms, digitalisation, digital public infrastructure and financing the ecosystem. For Nepal, the key is to learn from and build upon the innovation happening in China. Nepal also has the advantage of accessing cost-effective hardware and technology solutions from China. For instance, I often notice the thousands of distribution or junction boxes used by various Internet Service Providers (ISPs) in Nepal. This hardware is custom-made in China specifically for the Nepali market.

Similarly, India too has had ambitious plans for digitalization. Digital India, a vision of Prime Minister Narendra Modi launched in 2015, aims to transform India into a digitally empowered society. The digital economy, estimated at US$200 billion in 2022, is expected to increase fivefold to US$1 trillion by 2030.[24] With 850 million internet users, India's digital transformation is expected to be built around fintech, start-ups and the digital delivery of services.

In digital payments, India has surpassed China. However, in terms of the size of the digital economy, China remains far ahead, owing to the sheer scale of its economy. India has evolved into the world's back office, but its presence in software and hardware products remains relatively limited. China, on the other hand, is a global leader in both hardware and software.[25]

Nepali companies have gained access to a variety of events and knowledge platforms proliferating in India, with the Government of India supporting such initiatives to help Nepali firms participate in major Indian events. In April 2025, twenty Nepali start-ups were supported by the Embassy of India to take part in the second edition of the three-day Startup Mahakumbh.[26] This is a large startup event that happens each year in India that brings different startup companies together. Likewise, Nepali companies and professionals are taking part in fintech festivals and other industry gatherings across India. Access to learning and networking at these events presents a significant opportunity for Nepali entrepreneurs.

One of the biggest lessons Nepal can draw from India is the success of the trilateral linkage between Jan Dhan bank accounts, the Aadhaar (National Identity) card and mobile phones—popularly known as the JAM Trinity. This system has enabled the delivery of public services in real time and promoted financial inclusion. Rather than people having to visit government offices, banks or other institutions, services have now moved to their phones. Nepal has also rolled out a National Identity Number and is working to link it with mobile phones and bank accounts. There is much to learn from India—both in terms of what has worked and what has not.

Nepal, therefore, has a unique opportunity to leverage its geographical position—being land-linked to two of the world's leading technology powerhouses, which are producing products and services at competitive costs. Within a few months of their launch, electric vehicles produced in China reach Nepal. My friends in Africa are always jealous of this, as it takes months for people there to even hear about new models, let alone have them arrive.

The founders of an instant noodle manufacturing company in Nepal shared how easy it is to access high-quality machines with sensors and electronic components from both India and China. You can mix and match equipment in ways that would be difficult to imagine in many other countries. This is the advantage Nepal needs to build on.

The next series of innovation—whether in robotics, VR, AR or AI—is likely to emerge from China or India and Nepal will benefit from the rapid pace of developments in the neighborhood.

Digital Nepal Framework

Emulating China and India, Nepal launched the Digital Nepal Framework (DNF) in 2019. It has been seen as an ambitious government initiative aimed at raising digital literacy and supporting the advancement of ICT in Nepal. I personally believe that for digital transformation to succeed, agility and innovation are critical, given the ever-evolving nature of the field. While frameworks provide a necessary technical roadmap, it is equally important to learn from relevant case studies—for instance, what other small countries have managed to accomplish. For me, Estonia, a country in Eastern Europe with 1.37 million people, and Rwanda, a nation of 14 million in Africa, continue to be inspiring examples.

Learning from Estonia: Estonia is considered to be one of the world's first movers in digital transformation, particularly in the delivery of government services. They have even digitized voting, with more than half the population casting their votes electronically. Their cities and towns are equipped with free Wi-Fi. They have implemented X-Road, a communication protocol that enables the secure and automatic cross-use of data between information systems. Citizen trust in digital platforms and e-governance is rooted in their global standing—they rank third in the world in cybersecurity.[27]

Perhaps, the key lessons to learn from Estonia are that you make the key lessons Nepal can learn from Estonia are: move data, not people; use technology to deliver services to citizens rather than create bureaucratic obstacles; focus on people, not just sophisticated technology, as it is the people who will drive digital progress; and finally, do not be afraid of taking bold steps. Like Estonia, which has developed IT solutions, it now exports to the EU and other countries, Nepal too can develop and export digital solutions to countries of similar size and population across the world.

Lessons from Rwanda

Rwanda is regarded as a country making pathbreaking strides in digital transformation in Africa. It has a Digital Transformation Directorate General under the Ministry of ICT, responsible for developing policies and addressing skills gaps that emerge as digital transformation proliferates. *Irembo*, the e-government platform launched in 2015, provides access to government services through a user-friendly portal. From obtaining passports to driver's licences, visas or any other service involving a government department, everything can be accessed through this platform, with payments made digitally. There is no human interface anymore. The government has also licensed and trained Irembo agents who support people who do not have smartphones or need help to fill the paperwork. In every nook and corner of the country, one can see these agents that are providing services to people, making them not make that long trip to the nearest town or city saving time and money. Generally, there is no additional cost for the person seeking the service as the agents get paid commissions based on the number of transactions they complete. This is a great digital platform that Nepal can learn from.

Mindset Change

Digital transformation is the only way forward, as we are literally living in two worlds today. In one world, we use the most advanced social media platforms, consume content online, use email and other software like any other global citizen. We chat on platforms that are constantly updated and improved in real time. We are proficient at playing online games or participating in wagers. This same level of digital efficiency must be replicated in other areas of our daily lives.

Eliminating paper and manual processes remains a major challenge. For example, banks still ask for copies of citizenship documents, passports and other government-issued identification each time a customer interacts with them. Emails are printed and attached to memos that are handwritten and require multiple physical signatures. Simply implementing and accepting digital signatures could drastically reduce the use of paper and cut down on redundant administrative work. Going online should not mean that one must always remain 'on-line'. With falling hardware and software costs and an increasing number of open-source applications, what is truly required is the right *mindware*. The key lies in eliminating physical paperwork and human intervention wherever possible.

The widespread adoption of digital payments and access to finance can also be extended to other domains. If people can trust digital platforms for financial transactions, that same trust can be cultivated for other purposes as well. Invoices and payment records can remain entirely online without the need for printing. Similarly, land documents can go online, where people can just have a digital record of the land or apartment they own. The International Civil Aviation Organization (ICAO) has announced a sweeping overhaul of global air travel procedures through the introduction of a Digital Travel Credential (DTC) system. This significant transformation in aviation over fifty years aims to replace traditional boarding passes and check-in protocols with biometric and digital identity technology to create a seamless, paperless travel experience. Nepal has to adapt to the changes quickly. People should be able to trust electronic delivery receipts for goods like they trust the electronic payment system. It is about thinking at every step whether one can digitize the process or not.

Way Ahead—Skilling, Industrial Revolution 4.0 and Human Interface

Looking ahead, for digital transformation to take place, I see three key drivers. First, integrating technology education as a basic skill and expanding digital literacy. Second, catching up with the world through Industrial Revolution 4.0. And third, effectively managing the human side of technology.[28]

MySecondTeacher is an academic platform developed in Nepal and used by students, teachers and institutions globally. It employs around five hundred people engaged in curriculum design and teaching methodology using technology. Nepali companies have already demonstrated global capabilities in managing education curriculum, now is the time to see how they can move towards developing an ecosystem that will ensure technology becomes a basic skill that students need to get used to.

In many countries like Singapore, coding and computational thinking are already integrated into the education system for primary and secondary students. In Rwanda, the government has established the Rwanda Coding Academy, a hybrid model offering both traditional education and vocational training that enables students to adopt coding as a practical skill. India has embarked on the National Digital Literacy Mission. In 2024, China announced a coordinated national plan to boost digital literacy by 2025 through coordinated efforts of different government agencies.[29]

Nepal must reframe its education system along similar lines. Sumana Shrestha, who entered politics after a career in technology consulting, holds a degree from MIT and has worked at the Boston Consulting Group. She was appointed as education minister in March 2024. On her website Sumana, she writes: 'Investment in education should focus on skills and employability of students post-graduation. Generating human resources deft at technological skills through informal education and trainings by organising bootcamps will be prioritised. Graduates of such bootcamps will be guided through hiring processes across various tech jobs.'[30]

Industrial Revolution 4.0

Moving on, the technological revolution of the past four decades has been unprecedented. We have witnessed remarkable innovations being swiftly replaced by even better ones, rendering some earlier breakthroughs almost forgotten. Initially, there were widespread fears that technology would make humans redundant. In reality, it has created more jobs than were generated during earlier phases of the Industrial Revolution.

Banks, which were once limited to taking your money, giving you some interest, lending you money and taking some interest, started to do things that bankers in the 1970s could never have imagined—such as dealing in investment products, including hedging and complex financial instruments. Today, for nearly every financial service taking place anywhere in the world—whether transferring money, issuing credit cards or selling insurance—there is a bank involved and profiting.

The smartphone revolution has fuelled the rise of social media, which in turn has further propelled the smartphone industry. The world may have shrunk in terms of connectivity, but it is bursting at the seams with choices. More people are required to make apps function, recognize faces in apps, and do all the menial work to ensure technology works. For instance, in order to make augmented and virtual reality work well, you need millions of people behind the scenes. Countless human hours go into ensuring that you receive an instant response to a translation command. It is a fascinating, intricate world that has been built.

In earlier industrial revolutions, Nepal failed to play a significant role. But in this revolution—what I refer to as Industrial Revolution 4.0—Nepal has the opportunity to play a transformative role by unlocking the potential of its human capital. The World Economic Forum defines the Fourth Industrial Revolution as a fundamental shift in how we live, work and relate to one another. It states: 'The Fourth Industrial Revolution is about more than just technology-driven change; it is an opportunity to help everyone, including leaders, policy-makers and people from all income groups and nations, to harness converging technologies in order to create an inclusive, human-centred future. The real opportunity is to look beyond technology, and find ways to give the greatest number of people the ability to positively impact their families, organisations and communities.'

Nepalis can lead these human-centric transformations, and the country has a genuine opportunity to build global leaders.

Finally, in the coming decades, the focus will be on humans building platforms to compete with other humans—whether through AI, blockchain technology or the metaverse. This will require billions of hours of human effort to improve these technologies. The world is increasingly driven by competition—between firms within countries and across borders.

Nepal, with over half its population under twenty-five years old, is home to a large pool of talented young people who could write code, create new platforms and potentially build future unicorns. The playing field has been levelled, allowing people from all walks of life—regardless of income, caste, creed, sex, religion or other divides—to access free tools such as Gmail and Zoom. This means that someone in Nepal now has the same opportunity as anyone else in the world to use the virtual space to innovate, create and sustain. This is the future.

Dima Syrotkin, CEO of Panda Training, argues in his latest blog on Medium that the next trillion-dollar start-up will be an education company.[31] In Nepal, we have seen many people reskill themselves and explore a sea of training and knowledge platforms. CloudFactory, an AI data platform company founded by Mark Sears in Nepal in 2010, brought about a quiet revolution by engaging thousands of Nepalis in microtasks that helped train machines to learn—such as recognising faces. It was inspiring to witness so many young Nepalis engaging with different platforms to share knowledge on a wide range of topics.

There has also been a marked rise in the number of people pursuing education in this field. Kathmandu University in 2023 added the Bachelors of Technology in AI. There are nineteen government colleges and twenty-five private ones that are engaged in IT education.[32] Perhaps, with tremendous information technology. With growing technological capabilities and a solid track record in exporting ICT services, Nepalis now have a genuine opportunity to dive into this domain.

Who knows—the next unicorn could very well be developed in Nepal!

Human Centric Approach

In November 2019, I had the honour of being on a panel with French Buddhist monk Matthieu Ricard on the topic 'The Future of Compassion in the Context of Artificial Intelligence and Technology'. We discussed how the key driver of technology is the human behind it; technology itself is neither right nor wrong—it is the intent and action of its creator or user that determine its outcome. We need to recognise where the online ends and the offline begins.

Take food delivery, for instance—yet another area where technology has brought major improvements. The number of restaurants to choose from and the amount of food options available over the Internet are massive, which has expanded the horizon of consuming food beyond what could have been imagined before. But it is important to remember that no matter how 'online' food delivery systems are, the delivery is still offline and done by humans who are, by nature, fallible. The same is true of ride-sharing apps. Ultimately, no matter how efficient the online interface is, service delivery is only as good as the human component behind it. We must realize that the human dimension remains critical.

Nepal has both the quantity and quality of human capital. An Asian Development Bank (ADB) study on Bangladesh revealed that with every 1 percentage point increase in internet users, the gross domestic product (GDP) could increase by 0.11 per cent.[33] There is a strong correlation between demographic dividends, digital innovation and economic growth. Two-thirds of Nepal's population falls within the productive age group of fifteen to sixty-four, with another 28 per cent below fifteen years of age. We have until 2050 to capitalize on this demographic dividend.

Digital innovation in Nepal has accelerated at an unprecedented pace, with Nepalis increasingly leveraging global platforms to create solutions for domestic and international markets. The economic growth witnessed over the past decade has been largely driven by digitisation and the rise of ICT companies that sell their products in Nepal and beyond. In the journey to 2043, this growth needs to be further fuelled and the steps that the country takes now will be crucial.

Chapter 10

Reaping the Demographic Dividend

In the 1990s, there was a sudden surge in employment within the financial services sector when private banks began their operations. Until then, apart from government jobs and occasional roles in a few international agencies, there were limited job opportunities in Kathmandu. For those outside the capital, prospects were even bleaker—you had to move to the city to find any meaningful work. These banks created jobs that offered good pay, perks, privileges and prestige. Banking soon became the first-choice career for those who studied business or commerce. Until then, any profession outside medicine, engineering or the government was often looked down upon. All of this changed with the expansion of private banks—and it was all driven by people in their thirties and early forties.

Perhaps I remember those times so vividly because I had just started my career in 1989. Nepal's banking sector was transformed. There was innovation in terms of providing different new products for the customers be it savings or credit. New product development initiatives emerged with customized products for customers like anywhere else in the world. From having to use influence to get access to banks to take out your own money, banks had started coming to one's doorstep. This is what demographic dividends can achieve—young people leading others in their generation, driving economic and national transformation.

Before the 1990s, finding a job was extremely difficult if you did not belong to a privileged caste or ethnic group. Connections with influential individuals in the palace or government were often essential. When I applied for a trainee position at the Soaltee Hotel, the two individuals who vouched for me had held senior positions in government. I was fortunate—they happened to be the fathers of two Nepali friends I had studied with in Kolkata. I did not know anyone apart from my family members and acquaintances in Patan, who worked mostly in the handicrafts industry. It was impossible to get anywhere without a reference.

For the youth today, however, the story is quite different. One can participate in a reality show and make it big. Or one can upload a video of one's song on social media and watch it go viral. Access has been democratised. People can apply for global education and jobs from their rooms, and even secure financial aid to study, work or travel abroad. Falling prices of equipment, innovation, electricity and internet services have transformed not only the kind of work people do but also how they do it. Information is readily available online, and translation software has made it accessible across languages. multiple courses one can do online to advance one's skills. Online platforms have made it easier for people to connect with other people and build a learning circle or leverage connections for jobs. In more ways than one, these are the pillars on which demographic dividends will be reaped and Nepal is in a particularly privileged position when it comes to this.

In April 2023, in an interview with *The Kathmandu Post*, Professor Yogendra Gurung, head of the Central Department of Population Studies at Tribhuvan University, said: 'A country's ability to achieve economic development through the mobilization of the working age population is called its demographic dividend. The government's policy now should be to take advantage of this window of opportunity [in Nepal].'[1] Let me explain the 'window of opportunity' Gurung is referring to.

Nepal is currently benefitting from a demographic dividend—specifically a 'population dividend' or 'youth bulge'—in which young people constitute the largest segment of the population. In other words, Nepal is experiencing a demographic window of opportunity where the proportion of the working-age population exceeds the number of dependents.

The question is what can be done with this window of opportunity before it closes. Before offering my recommendations, let me briefly explain the concept of demographic dividends and how they work.

Understanding Demographic dividends

I've been interested in demographic dividends since the early '90s when global discussions on the ageing population in Japan began. In 2024, through the Nepal Economic Forum, we started partnering with the United Nations Population Fund (UNFPA) to understand the opportunities and the timeline for reaping demographic dividends. *Nefport*'s October 2024 issue specially focused on this topic. UNFPA defines demographic dividend as 'the accelerated development that can arise when a population has a relatively large proportion of working-age people coupled with effective human capital investment.'[2] There is a particular section in the UNFPA Arab States report that I find especially relevant here: 'To realize a demographic dividend, a country must undergo a demographic transition – a shift from high fertility and mortality to low fertility and mortality. Mortality generally falls as child survival rates improve, mainly because of improved health and sanitation standards. Decline in fertility often follows, and as families have fewer children, household resources are freed up to make investments in their long-term well-being.'[3] The key issue to understand is that the relative speed of fertility and mortality transitions contributes to how long this window of opportunity lasts. Research shows that while in developed countries the transitions occurred over a relatively long period—over 100 years—the demographic transitions in the contemporary developing world are considerably shorter. These shifts are especially evident in Southeast Asia. Research has shown that the demographic dividend is not simply a matter of increased labour participation rates. It also involves life-cycle savings, a deepening of investment, foreign capital flows, consumption, healthcare and schooling etc.[4]

Countries in East Asia have become global examples of how nations can push economic growth through demographic dividends. Strong family planning measures reduced fertility rates. Population growth slowed and resulted in accelerated economic development. In a meeting with me, Ambassador Chan Heng Chee, the Ambassador-at-Large, Government of Singapore and Global Co-Chair of Asia Society, shared that the transformation of Singapore was a consequence of leveraging their demographic dividend, with education being the vital tool. Singapore's educated and disciplined youth helped the country become a global financial centre. Education and citizen welfare drove economic transformation alongside savings.

Now, Singapore is working on converting demographic dividends into longevity dividends.[5] The anticipated longevity dividend for individuals includes an expanded period of life with good health and well-being, allowing them to be productive members of society in both paid and unpaid roles.

In Africa, Botswana and Tunisia are two countries that have made strong progress in lowering population growth and increasing income because of sound economic policies, good governance and social priorities such as investments in education and health. Comparing 2010 to 1980, families in both countries have fewer children but much greater purchasing power.[6]

In April 2024, at the launch of the South Asia Development Update of the World Bank, Pakistani economist Durr-e-Nayab echoed what Singapore and the African countries believe about demographic dividends: that demographic dividends occur when demography meets economy. Nayab talked about how, when her team analysed the meteoric rise of the South Korean economy, they realized that it was the investment South Korea had made in human capital that led the transformation of the country. Without investing in human capital, whether in health, skills or education, demographic dividends cannot be reaped.

Nepal's Window of Opportunity

Nepal has undergone major demographic changes in the past three decades—transforming from a high fertility–high mortality society to a low fertility–low mortality society within a comparatively short time. This conversion is a tremendously affirmative result of the state's development.[7]

In the thirty years between 1991 and 2021, Nepal's population grew from 18.491 million to 29.164 million—a jump of 50 per cent. In 2021, there were more people who belonged to the 'earning' category than those considered dependent. This has changed the economic growth trajectory of Nepal and marks the beginning of the reaping of demographic dividends.

In February 2025, Ameet Dhakal, editor of *Setopati*, wrote a much-read piece on this transformation of the Nepali population in the economy with the catchy title: 'Nepal's Income Increased Threefold; Worries Doubled'. Originally written in Nepali, I decided to translate the piece and make it available for a larger audience.[8] In the piece, he says: 'In 2023, the population reached 29.7 million. Of this, the working-age population (15–59 years) is 18.4 million. Nepal has never had such a large working-age population in its history. Moreover, since 2021, our 'dependency ratio' has been the lowest in history. That is, now, 100 Nepalis have to work and support 62 dependents. Whereas in 1990, 100 Nepalis had to work and support 90 dependents.'[9]

Prof. Samir KC, a research scholar at the International Institute for Applied Systems Analysis (IIASA), Austria has been working on population projections. Ameet Dhakal quotes his work and says that in the next ten years, by 2035, the working-age population of Nepalis will reach 21.12 million. 'This number will reach 22.7 million in the next twenty years— i.e., by 2045. This means that an additional 4 million Nepalis will enter the labour market in the next twenty years.'[10]

It is important to understand the phenomenal growth in population, especially when people discuss migration. Many do not understand the context of this large increase in population that has led to a rise in migration. More people are entering the job market due to the young population. Since there are not enough jobs in Nepal, they migrate.

Further, until 1990, the contribution of women in the formal economic sector was limited. However, by the 2021 census, many women were employed in entrepreneurship or had migrated outside Nepal to work. For instance, in the financial industry, including banking and insurance, until 1990, the number of women in the industry could be counted on one's fingers. By 2024, Nepal, at 45 per cent, had the highest participation of women in South Asia.[11] Therefore, to understand Nepal's potential in the lead-up to 2043, it is important to consider both the increase in the overall working-age population and the growing contribution of women to the workforce.

Then there are other factors. Overall, population growth has slowed. The shift to urban centres has increased the cost of living and thereby reduced family sizes. Additionally, with more women entering the workforce, they are having fewer children. As in Southeast Asia, the push towards education helps control population growth. Nepal's fertility rate has declined from a high of 2.62 per cent as per the 1981 census to 1.35 per cent in 2011 and 0.92 per cent in 2021.[12] The 2021 census data shows that the active population aged fifteen to sixty is 62 per cent and population above sixty is 10 per cent, and the rest 28 per cent are below fourteen.[13]

Interestingly, with life expectancy increasing, the traditional retirement age of fifty or sixty is no longer valid. People remain economically active well into their seventies and eighties, which means fewer years of dependency on savings.

According to calculations by the Population Council, the demographic window of opportunity for Nepal will last for a total of fifty-five years. It began around 1992—twenty-five years before 2017—and will begin to close around 2047—thirty years from 2017.[14]

The 2021 census also reveals that 61.96 per cent of Nepal's total population falls within the age range of fifteen to fifty-nine years. This is an increase from 56.96 per cent in 2011. It means that 65.5 per cent of Nepal's total population is economically active. This active population will drive the transformation to 2043.

When it comes to defining what it means to be 'economically active', the census, when collecting data, considered persons aged ten years or above as economically active. This presents a unique opportunity for Nepal to utilize the population bonus for economic growth and prosperity. Like I've said before, it is important to recognize that effective investment in human capital is necessary to fully capitalize on the benefits of having a young population.

There is also consensus among economists and demographers that a larger working-age population can boost productivity and lead to economic growth, as more individuals can participate in the labour force. Additionally, as more people work and earn, there will be an increase in consumer demand for goods and services, which can further stimulate economic growth.

Recommendations to Leverage Demographic Dividends

Demographic dividends can be reaped in five different ways. First, the labour supply increases in both quantity and quality. There are more people engaged in economic activities and, with education, skills and global opportunities, their per capita income is increasing. Nepal is expected to have one of the highest rates of labour force growth in Asia and the Pacific region. The engagement of labour in productive jobs pushes economic growth and development. Engagement in sustenance agriculture generates low incomes but as this shifts to commercial agriculture, the value increases substantially. The increase in labour productivity in agriculture frees up people who can then move into entrepreneurship or work for larger organisations, thereby increasing income and savings. It is, however, the acceleration of investment that will lead to the building of larger enterprises that will create higher-value jobs. About 6,00,000 young people enter the job market each year, and the objective will have to be to create meaningful jobs for these young people that bring the best out of productivity and value.

Second, these people who are earning more will also be spending more. An increase in consumption drives the economy. Smaller family sizes and nuclear working families boost sales in restaurants, hospitality and travel. They will also be investing in housing and other capital assets. Studies have also shown that a younger population spends more on digital services, as this segment of the population has grown up using mobile phones and had ready access to internet connections. They become early adopters of innovation and technology, thereby pushing spending.

Technological innovations are also driven by the demand for easier access to goods and services. For instance, just the need to buy a music concert ticket online prompts the development of multiple businesses that can provide this service.

Third, a reduction in household size means there will be less expenditure, which in turn increases disposable income. Parents can invest more in quality education and healthcare for their children when family size reduces. The mushrooming of private schools across the country—which are expensive given income levels in Nepal—shows that there are people willing to pay to secure their children's future. Similarly, there is not only spending on basic healthcare, but also on cosmetic surgeries, especially cosmetic dental treatments. In 1990, when there were just forty dentists in the whole country, dentistry was all about the basic treatment. By 2024, it is very hard to find a young child from a middle class family who has not engaged in cosmetic dentistry treatment. This increased opportunity has pushed the number of dentists to more than 5000 in 2023.

Fourth, with improved quality of work and greater flexibility through remote working, more mothers are participating in economic activities. Economic growth in East Asia has been fuelled by the increased participation of women in the economy. Empowering adolescent girls and young women is essential to accelerate the demographic transition.

As I've discussed earlier in the chapter, Nepal has seen a huge transformation in women's participation in the workforce. From 1980 to 2021, the literacy rate among women aged fifteen to twenty-four rose from less than 15 per cent to over 90 per cent.[15] One-third of those employed in government jobs are women. However, they are yet to achieve proportional representation in senior management and board positions in private companies. This means there is still room for women to move up the ladder and continue the trend of transformation that has taken place over the past three decades.

Fifth, the increase in income and reduction in expenses result in savings that are then invested across various sectors. The insurance industry typically experiences major growth once per capita income levels cross US$2500. The life insurance industry has already surpassed the billion-dollar premium mark. Housing booms occur as people seek to buy second homes or properties as investments. In Nepal, with more than 81 per cent of people living in their own houses, this trend is steep. This pushes property prices and results in increased returns, which then get reinvested. The savings also get channelled into the stock market and with participation becoming easy through online trading and dematerialization of security, there are more people investing and reaping benefits from activities of companies. This in turn builds the equity market and investments that are necessary to spur economic growth through investments.

Act before the window closes

While Nepal's demographic dividend offers an opportunity for economic growth, it is not infinite. This window will inevitably close as the current working-age population transitions into an ageing, aged, and eventually super-aged population. This shift will make sustainable social and economic protection even more important.[16]

It will be important to spread this message widely across Nepal. International visitors are often surprised when they learn about Nepal's demographics. Companies and institutions recognise the potential only after they see the numbers. Since public discourse is generally dominated by older men who have passed their prime, the mention of youth often unsettles them. This needs to change.

At the Himalayan Future Forum we hosted in February 2024, we included a youth fellowship programme where twenty-five young people were selected to attend the event. During the feedback session, they remarked that a few speakers didn't even realize that there were young people in the room, and that they too needed to be addressed and engaged in the conversation.

Empowering the youth is really about handing over the reins of politics, bureaucracy, business and institutions to younger people, while guiding them. I always tell the story of my late mentor, Prabhakar Rana. When he decided to step down at age sixty-five and hand over the reins of the business to his son, he truly let go. He did not intervene. He would provide guidance when asked, but otherwise left it to the next generation to take things forward.

In our work on restructuring family businesses, we still see considerable reluctance from older family members to pass the baton to younger members—especially women. In politics, we are seeing more young people emerge, and those who are first-time politicians tend to work hard. However, second- and third-generation young politicians from dynastic families often struggle to step out of the shadow of their grandfathers, fathers, uncles and elder brothers.

Skilling human capital

The next stage in reaping the demographic dividend will be to ensure that more meaningful jobs are created in Nepal. For this to happen, not only must there be financial investment, regulatory reforms and a shift in attitude from both government and private sector, but also investment in human capital.

This should be approached through an opportunity lens. Skilling centres that help people find better jobs or become better entrepreneurs need to mushroom. To make this a reality, Nepal must open up to the best international firms willing to establish themselves here. If Nepal is to become the best training ground for naturalists working in jungles or trekking guides taking you through amazing journeys, we then need to aim to build the best institutions in the world and churn out world class professionals of international calibre. The same logic applies to hospitality, healthcare, education and other fields.

Quantity should not be our concern; the focus must be on quality. Smaller countries like Switzerland and Singapore have succeeded by investing in the quality of human capital. In Nepal, like other South Asian countries, the focus has been on producing more doctors. However, for every doctor you have, you need double the number of nurses, four times the number of health assistants and eight times the number of support staff.

The apprenticeship programme in Switzerland and the respect for the work one does have been fundamental in transforming the country over the past century. My globe-trotting professor-friend from Switzerland called excitedly to tell me she is getting married to a construction worker who speaks little English, and that she is settling down in a mountain home with the three dogs he owns. She told me her travels would now have to end, as his job does not allow him much leave. I keep wondering how we would have reacted to this news if it had been someone from our own family. Dignity of labour is something we must instil in today's youth.

In a world rapidly transforming through innovations in communication and technology, skilling to match these changes has become crucial. Whether young people want to work for others, be self-employed or pursue entrepreneurial ventures, there are certain non-negotiable skills. In a country where society does not ostracize corrupt people or the respect for the rule of law is poor, it is important to build a culture of values, transparency and integrity. Young people who avoid shortcuts to success, people who invest their time and resources to acquire these skills and create a peer learning group of sharing and growing have delivered better than those who don't.

The quantum leap Nepal can make on the path to 2043 will depend largely on how well it can reap its demographic dividend. The key question is: how can Nepal ensure that the value addition of its youth increases through enhanced productivity and opportunity? The socio-economic transformations will rest on how much Nepal can stretch itself in terms of realizing the necessity of contribution of the youth.

Chapter 11

The Global Nepali

In 1977, the then Indian Prime Minister Morarji Desai refused to include Nepali as an official language in the Indian constitution, considering it a foreign language.[1] This triggered the Nepali *Bhasa Manyata Andolan* (recognition of the Nepali language in the Indian constitution). Back then, I was in school in Kalimpong, West Bengal. We participated in processions, and this topic was hotly discussed at family gatherings. It was in 1992 that the Nepali language was finally declared an official language in India.

In 2023, I happened to be back in Kalimpong during the Nepali New Year.[2] I saw people clad in traditional Nepali costumes carrying out a celebratory parade. It took me back to my school days, over forty years ago, and brought back memories of the pride we felt in the Nepali language that had driven us to take part in the demonstrations. It got me thinking again about who a Nepali is. Is the identity restricted to those who hold the citizenship of the country? I know of a Bhutanese national who lived as a refugee in Nepal and later moved to the US and Australia, but still identifies with Nepali music, songs and cuisine. Can he be called a Global Nepali, for instance? A person's identity is more closely linked to the language and culture they identify with than to the citizenship they hold.

Today, out of the 100 most spoken languages worldwide, Nepali stands at the fifty-seventh position with almost 15.8 million native speakers.[3] The language, culture, food, music and art emerging from this community comprise the collective identity of the Global Nepali. And it is this Global Nepali that is the focus of this chapter.

In the next few pages, we will discuss what drives the movement of Nepalis, the role of connectivity and technology, and finally, the world of the Nepali diaspora and what the future looks like.

Nepal's History with Migration

Nepalis have historically had ties with different parts of the current nation-states of China and India. The first batch of migrants to leave the Kathmandu Valley was perhaps those who accompanied Princess Bhrikuti to Tibet in the seventh century.[4] Thereafter, in the twelfth century, the Nepali craftsman Arniko started the culture of migrating for work when he travelled to then Tibet and China to build monasteries and cities. With Tibetan Buddhism flourishing, artisans from Nepal found work constructing monasteries and furthering their craft in the Himalayan kingdoms.

In 1846, there was a large exodus of people after the Rana rule was established. This was in part due to the hardships people faced under the regime as well as to take advantage of growth in the larger Himalayan region. It began with the establishment of tea plantations in Assam and Darjeeling in British India, which was a labour-intensive business.[5] People then moved further to Malaysia and Burma, which were then part of the British Empire. The only connectivity back then was through overland travel—so parts of eastern British India and Tibet, then an independent nation, became destinations for people to work and settle.

In the first part of the twentieth century, the two World Wars created a large market for mercenaries. Nepalis fought as mercenaries in the British Army, sending remittances that formed the bulk of Nepal's economic receipts and served as a source of funds for consumption. This peaked during the Second World War. Thereafter, Gorkha soldiers became part of the defence forces of many countries, including the British Army, Indian Army, Singapore Police and the Sultanate of Brunei. Until 1970, the remittances from these soldiers were the largest receipts in Nepal's economy.[6]

In fact, before the Second World War, global travel was largely unrestricted. If a Nepali stepped outside the borders of the Kathmandu Valley, the world opened up for him (the male pronoun is apt here, given how this generally applied only to Nepali men). Stepping into British territory prior to 1947 meant one could seamlessly travel from present-day Afghanistan to Malaysia. They could settle down, own property and live a better life elsewhere than under the Rana regime in Nepal. Nepalis could even own property in Tibet until 1959, and it was only when one had to cross from Tibet into China that paperwork became necessary. Nepalis had the great privilege of being plugged into the biggest economic power of the time, the British Empire, and much of the wealth of many Nepali families comes from money earned in Burma (present-day Myanmar), India and Tibet.

The Shift Today

While earlier migration waves were largely necessity-driven, the new generation of migrants in the twenty-first century is making a conscious choice to move to high-income countries such as Australia, Canada, Japan and Europe for professional growth and long-term stability.

A key example of this shift is the increasing number of Nepali students and skilled professionals migrating abroad. Australia, for instance, has seen a significant rise in Nepali student enrolments, with many pursuing degrees in nursing, IT and business—fields that offer strong prospects for permanent residency and high earnings. Similarly, Canada's Express Entry system has attracted a growing number of Nepali professionals, particularly in healthcare and finance, where skilled workers can secure well-paying jobs and benefit from social security systems. Another example is the surge in Nepali nurses migrating to the United Kingdom under its Skilled Worker visa programme, reflecting the demand for professionals in essential sectors.

This shift is also evident in the changing profile of migrants. Unlike in the past, when migration was predominantly undertaken by individuals from low-income backgrounds seeking survival wages abroad, today's migrants often come from middle- and upper-middle-class families with greater access to education and resources. The transformation in migration patterns highlights how Nepal's migration landscape is evolving beyond economic necessity. It is no longer just about escaping poverty; rather, it has become a strategic decision aimed at securing a better future, accessing world-class education and achieving social mobility in a competitive global environment.

Passports and Visas

It was only in 1994, after the promulgation of the Nepal Immigration Rules, that passports could be easily acquired within a week across district headquarters all over Nepal. This meant that every Nepali had the opportunity to travel, get an education degree or work outside the country. The process, despite the chaos, meant people could get a passport even within a day. In fact, the government converted the printing and selling of passports into a lucrative business. In April 2023, in Lisbon, Portugal, the Government of Nepal held a month-long 'passport camp' to renew passports for Nepalis living in Portugal and, in a few weeks, made a revenue of NPR 52.2 million (US$4,50,000).[7] A sixty-six-page passport costs NPR 20,000 (US$150) in 2024, making it one of the most expensive passports in South Asia.[8] However, Nepalis do not mind paying this for a one-day service. Till April 2025, 4.4 million e-passports have been issued.[9]

When I first made my trip to the US in 1997, I remember being told that the US embassy received fewer than ten applications a day from Nepal. In the past twenty-five years, the US consular office in Nepal has become one of the busiest in the world, processing hundreds of applications a day. US embassy officials have shared with me how surprised they are when they realize the number of visa applications they receive from Nepal alone. This is true of other embassies too—they are surprised at the traffic in their Nepal office.

With many of the documents required to travel—like labour permits, no-objection certificates for education-related travel and other materials—going online, and better and cheaper air connectivity across the region, this trend will only surge. When I had to travel to the US in the late nineties, I went through Bangkok, then Narita in Japan, to Chicago in the US before reaching my destination. Now I can choose multiple options through Doha, Istanbul, Dubai and airports in India each day for a one-hop flight to any city in the US or Europe.

The Significance of Diaspora

As of 2023, as per the *World Development Report* published by the World Bank, about 184 million people—2.3 per cent of the world's population—live outside their country of nationality,[10] making the modern-day diaspora a significant part of the global population. In 2023, remittance flows to low- and middle-income countries (LMICs) are estimated to have reached US$669 billion. Major reasons are resilient labour markets in advanced economies and the Gulf Cooperation Council (GCC) countries continuing to support migrants and helping them send money home.[11]

The United States continued to be the largest source of remittances for Nepal. The top five remittance recipient countries in 2023 are India (US$125 billion), Mexico (US$67 billion), China (US$50 billion), the Philippines (US$40 billion) and Egypt (US$24 billion).[12] Within South Asia, remittances grew from US$75 billion in 2009 to US$189 billion in 2023. Remittance by the Nepali diaspora has crossed the US$10 billion mark in 2023, representing about 24 per cent of Nepal's Gross Domestic Product (GDP). A Nepal Economic Forum (NEF) study indicated that informal remittances are equal to formal remittances, which means that in 2023, total remittances—both formal and informal—exceeded US$20 billion. Even if we assume a 25 per cent remittance-to-GDP ratio, the projections for 2030 are around US$25 billion, and for 2043, US$100 billion![13]

Up until the 1990s, the diaspora was never seen as an important contributor to a country's economic growth. Several global events led to a shift in this thinking: The liberalization of economies in the 1990s opened up global travel; the opening of Chinese, Indian and East Asian economies; the boom in Gulf economies created further demand and trade. The former Soviet republics started to transition from a command economy under the USSR to market economies, and Africa, as a continent with potential, started to be discussed. The WTO and other trade agreements brought Central and South America closer to the world. A demand for travel to business and tourism destinations across the world also started to open up. Embassies began to mushroom along with bilateral and multilateral agency offices, which in turn created new career opportunities.

The technology revolution accelerated the entire shift. The diaspora, therefore, started becoming an important source of contacts, investment and soft power.

Take the case of India. India's global image catapulted when people of Indian origin began to secure coveted positions in global corporations and institutions. Politicians like Indian Prime Minister Narendra Modi gained more appreciation at home every time he hosted major events with the diaspora community outside India.

In Nepal too, for Nepali politicians, diaspora organisations that pledged their allegiance to them became important sources of funding and votes back home. The Mayor of Kathmandu, for instance, has immense support among diaspora Nepalis, and so does the Rastriya Swatantra Party (RSP). Both have successfully managed to leverage the power of the diaspora.

When governments realized the significance of the diaspora, they instituted a series of new measures catering to it. In India, the Person of Indian Origin (PIO) scheme has ensured that the diaspora can play a role in the country's growth and development. The government has also made it easier for the diaspora to return.

In Nepal, the diaspora as an identity began to be discussed in the early 2000s; Nepalis abroad started being referred to as Non-Resident Nepalis (NRNs), on the lines of Non-Resident Indians (NRIs). In 2023, finally, through a Supreme Court ruling, NRNs received many privileges apart from political rights. My friends in New York were elated when they realized that even the children of their US-born son would be able to own property in Nepal and engage in social and cultural groups.

Things have also changed in how governments respond to crises faced by the diaspora. When the war in Gaza began in October 2023, Nepal's foreign minister travelled to bring back fellow Nepalis from Israel. There was also public pressure for government action when Nepalis who had gone illegally to fight for the Russian army were killed.

International organizations have also started recognizing the role of the diaspora. The World Bank for instance, is making efforts to understand the role of the diaspora and how to leverage it for a country's growth and development. In fact, the World Bank *Annual Report 2023* focused on Migrants, Refugees and Society. At the launch of this report in Nepal, the Country Director Faris Hadad-Zervos rightly said: 'It's not whether migration is good or bad, but rather how we can better manage migration so that it serves as a force for development and prosperity for all countries.'[14]

Scaling New Heights

While their home countries are realising their worth, the global Nepali is also scaling new heights in their adopted countries. Be it personal successes—an e-commerce company, Daraz, hired Aanchal Kunwar, a Nepali in the US, as its CEO to manage the business in Nepal—or acting as cultural ambassadors for Nepal by spreading the country's rich culture, literature and art, the diaspora transforms and transfers Nepal's social values, ideas and culture to other parts of the world.

Of course, none of this is without challenges: those who are approaching or have reached retirement are trying to figure out how to lead the rest of their lives—whether to be in Nepal or in the US. The choice is between building a couple of houses in Nepal that one can visit regularly, or shuttling between the two countries at regular intervals while setting up a platform in Nepal that will provide both professional and personal engagement. Social media networks are promoting interest among second-generation Nepalis to explore Nepal through stories centred on trekking, cultural escapades and the diverse cuisine. Young American Nepalis are travelling with friends and discovering Nepal as they would other countries, while steering clear of the usual itinerary of relatives, predictable food and guffaws around politics.

When I asked Preeti Adhikary, the founder of The Great Nepali Diaspora, about her passion for the work she does, she offered an interesting perspective: 'I started The Great Nepali Diaspora (TGND) in August 2022 because our diaspora is so fragmented in terms of location, industry and ethnicity. We have strong social ties but not professional ones. By connecting the global professional talent with roots in Nepal, I wanted to nudge Nepalis across diverse industries to network and spark opportunities for collaboration and camaraderie. Elements like visibility, transparency and accountability will enable us to uplift our community and Nepal. My long-term vision for TGND is to be connected to every Nepali's life cycle, whether at home or abroad. I see seamless transitions and a connected migration story instead of buzzwords like brain gain and/or drain.'

The Future Potential of the Global Nepali

The question, however, is where do we go from here?

A study by the NEF has estimated that the total number of Nepalis settled in Australia, Canada, the UK and the USA will cross one million by 2030.[15] In Japan, Nepalis represent the largest South Asian population, nearing 2,00,000 in 2024.[16] With Japan's ageing population and its special bond with

Nepal, more Nepalis will be working there. Schools in Japan operated by Nepalis now also allow students to sit for Nepal's school examinations.[17]

Nepal is one of the sixteen countries on the E9 visa, and in March 2024, South Korea announced that it would be opening up more areas of work for E9 visa holders.

To say that the workforce in Nepal is preparing for this would be an understatement: Nepalis continue to queue to sit for language proficiency tests, with thousands taking tests in languages that bear no resemblance to any of the 123 spoken in Nepal. In 2019, a record 92,000 Nepalis took the test. China is expected to be the next major destination, particularly in the elderly care and service industries. It is only a matter of time before that market expands further.

The Gulf Cooperation Council countries remain a major draw, with economic activity in the region showing no signs of slowing down. In Europe, Nepalis are already moving in droves to destinations like Romania and Poland. In April 2025, a *Nepali Times* report stated: 'According to Gabinete de Estratégia e Estudos (GEE) in Lisbon, the number of Nepalis in Portugal had crossed 21,000 even by 2022, and it is expected to be much higher now. This year, Nepal established a resident embassy in Lisbon.'[18]

Nepalis also travel abroad to study, and this trend is not likely to decline in the coming decades, as long as universities and educational institutions continue to rely on income from foreign students. Nepal remains among the top fifteen countries sending students to the US and has one of the highest per capita student migration rates relative to its population. In 2024, after China and India, Nepalis were the third-largest group admitted to Australian universities, with 65,815 students.

The biggest transformation will come when more women begin to travel for education and employment abroad. Currently, they are estimated to make up close to 10 per cent of the migrant workforce, but the numbers are growing. Women who wish to be financially independent and steer their lives on their own terms are increasingly seeking global opportunities.

Chapter 12

Towards Transformation

I have been dubbed by many as Nepal's CEO—Chief Eternal Optimist—and people continue to ask me how I can remain so optimistic about Nepal's future. My answer is simple: over my thirty-five-year career, I've witnessed the remarkable ways in which this country has transformed itself and the immense potential it still holds to grow and reshape its destiny. It has also shaped who I am today. Therefore, I can only remain positive about its future.

However, while I am an optimist, my optimism is rooted in reality. In this final chapter, I present a list of non-negotiables that I believe will be key to our progress towards 2043.

Political Transformation

The first set of non-negotiables involves a firm belief in democratic values and freedom of speech. Democracy is, in fact, associated with higher economic growth. In a study published in January 2019 in the *Journal of Political Economy*, Daron Acemoglu, an MIT economist, along with co-authors Suresh Naidu, Pascual Restrepo and James A. Robinson, examined 184 countries between 1960 and 2010. During this period, there were 122 instances of democratization and seventy-one cases where countries shifted from democracy to a non-democratic form of government.[1] The study found that democracy significantly enhances development. Countries transitioning to democratic rule experienced a 20 per cent increase in GDP over a twenty-five-year period compared to what they would have achieved under authoritarian regimes.

South Korea, for instance, underwent dramatic change after 1987. The shift to democracy following three decades of repressive authoritarian rule confirmed the modernization thesis that economic development ultimately leads to democracy.[2] This also holds true for Nepal. From 1960 to 1990, during authoritarian rule, GDP rose only modestly from US$600 million to US$3.6 billion in thirty years. In contrast, between 1990 and 2006, it increased from US$3.6 billion to US$10 billion. After the end of the Shah rule in 2006, Nepal's GDP rose from US$10 billion to US$44 billion by 2024.[3]

In 1950, most land and assets were owned by the Shah and Rana rulers. The 1960 land reform institutionalised private ownership, albeit with land ceilings, but the reforms of the 1990s enabled private sector growth and development. I continue to argue that Nepal, like many other countries, has demonstrated that democracy does indeed deliver better economic outcomes.

In March 2023, the US Deputy Secretary of Commerce, Don Graves, speaking at the Center for Strategic and International Studies (CSIS), stated that 'democracy creates conditions for private sector growth, and a flourishing private sector in turn ensures that democracy delivers'.[4] With rapid advances in technology and innovation, the fear of opaque regimes is growing, as authoritarian regimes do not have to face the public in elections, parliament or public spaces, so can get away with anything. This will further push democratic values and accountability. However, there is always the fear of a rise of authoritarianism that will challenge the fundamentals of democratic values and inclusive economic growth. In March

2025, demonstrations took place in Nepal advocating a return to authoritarianism under a monarchical system, rejecting democratic values. I maintain, however, that these are sporadic reactions rooted in frustration.

As Nepal looks towards 2043, democracy and an open, pluralistic society must prevail. While events in 2024 may lead people to think that this space is shrinking, Nepal has the opportunity to continue to work on tolerance, diversity and freedom of engagement. To complement this, a strong judiciary is important to keep the legislature and executive in check. In 2023, when a series of scams surfaced, these cases were brought before the courts, resulting in prison sentences for many prominent political leaders and bureaucrats. This sends a strong message to investors and the global community—that wrongdoers will be punished and corruption will not be tolerated.

Ensuring Freedom of Speech

One of the hallmarks of Nepal's transition to democracy has been the protection of freedom of speech and the freedom to convene. Siddharth Varadarajan, founding editor of *The Wire*, was the keynote speaker at the Himal Media Mela in 2023. He stated, 'In Nepal, media freedom is seen as something sacrosanct. It is powerful that Nepal is a meeting place for Southasia when other countries are happy to close their borders to ideas'[5] While many political leaders in Nepal have attempted to gag the media, introduce restrictive regulations or curtail public assembly, they have consistently failed and have ultimately been forced to back down. In March 2023, the home minister from the Rastriya Swatantra Party, part of the ruling coalition, announced a series of regulations enabling media surveillance. They had to be withdrawn in forty-eight hours.[6] Leaders with popular support cannot dent this. People in the government try to provide advertisements to media outlets to ensure that they are spared from the critical eye of the media, but they hardly succeed. Further, with a very fluid political scenario with ever-changing governments, such moves can only be for the short term. Democratic practices have allowed independent media to survive and also for social media platforms to proliferate.

When the elections for 2022 were being held, the folks at the global technology company Meta, taking care of Facebook, were surprised that there were no viral videos promoting violence or hate speech, unlike in many other countries. Nepal appears to exhibit a form of unwritten self-regulation. In October 2022, through the NEF, I participated in training programmes with Meta for members of the Election Commission and the communication teams of political parties. The fact that they took self-regulation, self-censorship and managing community management practices left a strong impression on Meta's team.

Post-1990, Nepal's openness has made it the most preferred destination in South Asia for hosting regional events, especially those involving delegations from countries hostile to each other. For instance, it is difficult for an Indian citizen to obtain a visa to Pakistan and vice versa, and the same applies to travel between India and Bangladesh. This is particularly true for activists, journalists or individuals in the arts. Nepal, however, welcomes everyone with open arms. While we have unrestricted movement with India, visitors from SAARC countries receive a free thirty-day visa. Barring nationals from twelve countries, every citizen of the world can obtain a visa on arrival. Nepal has never demanded reciprocation. Bhutanese citizens, for example, can visit Nepal under this free visa policy, whereas Nepalis must pay the Tourism Development Fee, equal to that charged to third-country nationals, to enter Bhutan.

In the coming years, as regional meets rise and the focus shifts to the growth in South Asia and the need to connect better with China and Southeast Asia, Nepal's openness can become its biggest selling proposition, not only earning revenues through hosting events, but to be able to become a convening centre.

Economic Transformation

In the anthology *State of Nepal*[7] I wrote a chapter titled 'Squandering a Promising Economy'. It told the story of Nepal's economic growth in the early 1990s, when the country undertook a wave of reforms and subsequently rolled them back. I had then proposed that Nepal should pursue the path of a capitalist welfare state, a state that believes in private enterprise while ensuring the welfare of its citizens. The government in such a system has two key roles: first, to create an enabling environment for private enterprise to flourish; second, to ensure equitable delivery of welfare to all citizens.[8]

I continue to advocate this model as essential for Nepal's prosperity by 2043 and consider it the second non-negotiable.

Nepali capitalism, in my view, should rest on the following principles: First, the right to privately own property. There can be ceilings on land ownership, but these should not deter large-scale projects. People should be free to own private property, but inheritance beyond a regularly reviewed threshold should be taxed. While taxing inheritance[9] is not a popular idea, I continue to advocate it, as it discourages rent-seeking behaviour, especially in the context of rapidly escalating real estate prices.

Second, it will be important for businesses to be able to start and exit easily. When I speak with private equity investors, their main concern is the difficulty of exiting from investments.

Third, it is important that there is fair competition and no collusion with either people or firms consuming or supplying goods and services. In Nepal, aside from the business of selling momo (dumplings),[10] there are cartels—both formal and informal—that exist in nearly every sector, as highlighted by research conducted by the NEF on cartels.[11] Collusions can defeat the very principle of a free market.

Fourth, mobility of people, goods and services—both within Nepal and across borders—must be seamless, provided legal and regulatory norms are fulfilled. If a business requires international capital or resources, accessing them should be easy to obtain that. Similarly, if Nepalis have the opportunity to move goods and services outside Nepal or work outside, there should be easy clear-cut procedures to follow. It should also be able to set up companies outside Nepal without undue restrictions. I was part of a task force in 2004 that sought to amend legislation prohibiting Nepalis from investing outside Nepal. After twenty years in the May 2025 Budget Speech, some provisions for investing outside Nepal has been provided,[12] but we need to go the full hog.

Finally, perhaps the most important area of intervention would be education, where the concept of private wealth and capital should be explained well so that the future generation grows up with the right concepts.

Shunning Crony Capitalism

For capitalism to work, it will also be important to ensure that the image of the private sector is transformed. The private sector should be seen as comprising law-abiding corporate citizens who reject protectionism, respect the rule of law, improve internal governance and transparency, and earn the trust of their stakeholders. In an increasingly globalised world, it must also be understood that the sooner one is able to compete internationally, the faster one can grow.

Countries of different economic systems have suffered from different forms of crony capitalism. Nepal is not an exception. Earlier, royal family-based patronage systems and later, post multi-party democracy, protection by political leaders have made crony capitalism explode. Crony capitalism can be dealt with through two pronged efforts. First, to minimize the role of the government, especially in-person involvement. Digital procurements have gone a long way in eliminating interactions with individuals. Second, ensure more stringent global practices are followed. It is not that crony capitalism instances do not exist in the most regulated economies, but the instances are rare and more importantly, discovery of a malpractice leads to consequences.

Welfare State

There are different definitions of what comprises a welfare state. However, for me, a welfare state is one that takes care of its citizens, especially those who cannot afford to take care of themselves. Classically, a welfare state is defined as one committed to providing basic economic security for its citizens by protecting them from market risks associated with old age, unemployment, accidents and sickness. It ensures contributions through taxation and to national security systems, which are then used to provide economic and social security. Nepal has the highest tax per GDP ratio in Southasia which means there is enough means. The Social Security Fund that came into operations in 2011 has till March 2024 collected NPR 52.63 billion (US$400 million)[13] and been making disbursements to members of the fund. Similarly, the Nepal Army Welfare Fund has around US$600 million[14] and Police Welfare Funds around

US$40 million.[15] Financial resources are not a constraint, therefore, but ensuring that welfare schemes reach the real beneficiaries is the key challenge.

Towards Inclusion

Economist Branko Milanović warns that while global inequality between countries is decreasing, inequality within countries is increasing. Wealth creation and welfare schemes must remain equitable. In India, in 2023, 1 per cent of the population held 40 per cent of national wealth and accounted for 22 per cent of national income.[16]

Perhaps one can learn from the Nordic model when it comes to inclusion. The Nordic countries demonstrate that major egalitarian reforms and substantial welfare states are possible within prosperous capitalist countries that are highly engaged in global markets. They also show that humane and equal outcomes are achievable within capitalism.

The Green Resilient Inclusive Development Action Plan, launched jointly by the Government of Nepal and development partners in 2021, states: 'Rising inequality and exclusion impede development. Recovery efforts should therefore leave no one behind, reduce disparities in opportunities and outcomes, and help excluded groups realize a fair share of benefits.'[17]

The World Trade Organization (WTO), in its 2023 report, emphasized the need for re-globalization to be more inclusive than previous versions of globalization. 'The idea of re-globalization is to re-invest in the multilateral trading system to make globalization not only more sustainable and more resilient, as discussed elsewhere in this report, but also more inclusive at all levels: in terms of people, business and economies.'[18]

Nepal's economic journey to 2043, therefore, must ride on two key pillars: promoting a capitalist state and ensuring far-reaching welfare programmes that ensure 'no one is left behind'. Pushing private sector growth and development will be key, along with ensuring that businesses play by global rules, open up to the world, renounce current protectionist behaviour and stop leaning on cartels. Nepal must seize the opportunities created by young entrepreneurs and Global Nepalis. It must also leverage its goodwill to attract the global investment community to invest in transformative projects such as large-scale infrastructure, which can create jobs and accelerate economic growth. This, in turn, increases the resources available for welfare activities that are critical to addressing income and opportunity inequalities. The infrastructure for efficient delivery already exists; what is needed now is the will to make it happen.

Social Focus

The final big non-negotiable is societal transformation. Any economic or political transformation is futile if it isn't accompanied by societal transformation. I propose these five key areas of societal transformation that Nepal will need to focus on:

Tackling corruption: If I were asked about a big factor that has kept Nepal from realizing its full potential—my answer would be corruption. Corruption remains rampant, and no single leader has been able to tackle this issue effectively. Corruption occurs in all societies, but the real question is whether society regards corruption as a problem and ostracizes the corrupt. Does it tolerate impunity, or will it demand accountability?

In *Unleashing Nepal*, I have written about the 'two laddoo' syndrome: in a culture where we compete to bribe the gods, we do not find bribing mortals an issue. (Laddoo is a sweet generally offered to the gods, especially the elephant-headed god Ganesha.) Culturally, it is acceptable to be corrupt and embrace bad governance. This needs to change—and it must begin with small actions, like submitting that bill for an extra six plates of chilli chicken when you were drinking beer during an official meeting, or returning to the office on time instead of delaying the trip by a day to claim an extra day's travel allowance. Or, by ensuring transparency when you award a contract to your friend or relative by declaring a conflict of interest. Small steps are the only way to begin.

Building equitable society: Nepal's 240 years of Shah/Rana rule is checkered by inequity. Post-2006, while attempts have been made to address inequality, the transformation has not been equitable. Certain communities have benefitted more than others, and the system favours some and not others. A privilege-hungry, ritual-oriented society does not go far if it is not backed by solid content and knowledge.

There are people who are less privileged due to the geography they live in, the caste they belong to, their sexual orientation, physical disabilities or gender, but it is important they also get the same privileges as the rest. I remind myself and others that if I did not have a last name associated with high caste and an address in a well-known neighbourhood of Patan, would I have had the same opportunities?

We should never forget that an insurgency that emerged to fight inequity took ten of Nepal's key years and more than 13,000 lives. It changed the lives of hundreds of thousands of people as they migrated, left their homes, settled in other countries or changed their perception of life. We cannot let such a violent uprising repeat to fight inequality.

Lesser litigation and more justice: Nepal is increasingly becoming a more litigious society. Every major decision is challenged in a court of law. As of 16 July 2024, the Supreme Court had

28,434 pending cases. Of these, 15,545 are over five years old.[19] Another 1,62,172 cases are pending in different courts of Nepal, per the Supreme Court Report for July 2024. This means there is one case pending for every twenty Nepalis. There are litigations among family members, business partners, inheritors of properties, people booked for offences and many against various decisions made by the government. In 2024, people even went to court over frivolous matters, like questioning the qualifications of the Governor of the Central Bank. Every time the government makes a decision, it is challenged in court. A former secretary of the Government of Nepal, Suryanath Upadhaya, supported by hyper-nationalists, went to court challenging Nepal's decision to export power to India, which was fortunately quashed.[20] Competing firms use courts to delay procurement processes, and hardly any issue goes by without being challenged in court.

Strengthening the judiciary, digitalizing records and tackling corruption will be critical in the future. We must create alternative rapid dispute resolution mechanisms, especially for business-related issues, so that economic projects are not held hostage. Laws need to be less ambiguous, and the chances of human intervention at the behest of interest groups must be eliminated.

Pride of being a Nepali: At events in Nepal, I ask people to reflect on what they say about who they are and the country they come from. The answers I hear are often negative. Nepalis have to learn to provide a positive narrative about themselves and their own country. Yes, negative news sells, and negative reels, posts and tweets get more attention than positive ones, but it is also important to look at what's working and what we can be proud of. And there is a lot to be proud of: the rich history of the nation state and the transformations each of our lives have had, be it in terms of education, healthcare, transportation, communication or work opportunities.

We need to change the narrative when we introduce Nepal and Nepalis, as discussed in Chapter 1. We are not from a small country, but a country with a sizeable population. We are the land-link bridge between the two most populous countries in the world, which will be the top two economies by 2040. We are culturally diverse and blessed by nature's bounty. We are now spread across 180 countries, living better lives than our ancestors and previous generations in different parts of the world. Finally, our biggest brand is what I call the brand 'smile'[21] that can be synonymous with the brand of the proud Nepali.

These cannot be achieved through government-led programmes or top-down interventions; rather, they have to emerge from the bottom up. Social media influencers have a role to play here. When Amrit Gurung, the lead singer of the band Nepathya, sings '*Rato Chandra Surya* (red moon and sun)', the insignia in the Nepali flag, people start to wave flags at concerts, and even those sitting at home, watching on screens, start to get goosebumps. That is what stories, songs and narratives can do!

Imbibing a Learning Culture

Nepalis are adaptive and learn about cultures well when they move outside Nepal, but learning does not happen at the same pace when they stay back in Nepal. The next decades will see technology exploding at a speed we have never seen before. Therefore, being able to position oneself with the right learning mindset is super important.

We also need to learn about basic human values that are so well ingrained in us, be it empathy, compassion or willingness to help. Buddhist monk Matthieu Ricard, who is regarded as the world's happiest man, talks about value-based education. According to this, the potential wisdom and goodness in human beings need to be brought to the surface, polished and taken care of. He stresses that the power of transformation in human beings and their minds should not be underestimated. When we are considerate about one another, we will create a positive economy and bridge the gap of inequality. This ensures that compassion has a bright future, because it is the only future.[22]

Conclusion

From thinking of ourselves as a small country between China and India, or equating ourselves with Bhutan and Sikkim (a country of eight hundred thousand and an Indian state of half a million people), it will be a task for us to change our perspectives and think of ourselves as the centre of Asia. It is not financial power that will make Nepal the centre of Asia, as Dubai or Singapore has managed to do, but the non-financial, soft elements like our culture and Buddhism, or our ability to find new tools and solutions to global issues such as climate change. Or perhaps, it will be a consequence of remaking ourselves as the cosmopolitan centre of the continent, a place that has a mix of rich heritage and contemporary innovations in art, culture and literature. In this transformation, if the governments get proactive, the pace will be accelerated, but we need champions and campaigners outside the government too in order to achieve this dream.

In the seventy-five years since Nepal opened itself up to the world, Nepalis have captured the imagination of people around the world. The natural beauty, mountains and people have drawn more and more visitors to explore Nepal. We have also seen increasing interest in Nepal as an investment destination. Like I keep saying, a country situated between the two fastest growing nations in the world cannot be ignored. It takes a bit of time, a bit of stepping back and re-examining, but there is little one can argue against Nepal having the potential to become the centre of Asia in the future. I hope that after reading this book, there will be more people who begin to believe in this dream along with me.

Acknowledgements

I had spent a week at a tea garden bungalow in Gisovu, Rwanda, to write the concept note of the book. Writers draw concept notes, editors make the book happen. From discussing the concept to drafts to the final book, I owe a lot to Archana Nathan, my editor at Penguin Random House India, for getting this book to this stage. A big thank you, Archana.

The writing of the book began at the beautiful apartment at Kent Vale, National University of Singapore. Thank you to Iqbal Singh Sevea, Hernaikh Singh and the National University of Singapore Institute of South Asian Studies (NUS-ISAS) for hosting me. As a senior fellow, I got access to many resources useful for the book, and it was wonderful to chat with Kishore Mabhubhani and Ambassador Chung Hang Chee to get insights. This helped me to write a book on Nepal that would be useful to many other countries in the world.

My travels allow me to meet people with whom I can have long conversations and get diverse perspectives. In Nepal, I spend considerable time talking to people, who have provided me with new perspectives on the country.

Jack McCarthy has been a sounding board, friend and coach. I owe a lot to him for pushing me to the limits. The classes at Babson College, where I made regular class visits, made me think of how to look at the world in the next twenty years when the students in the classroom would probably be in the peak of their careers.

Acknowledgements

I am grateful to have a team at Nepal Economic Forum (NEF) and beed, and the access to the resources and publication of these two institutions helped me immensely in research and writing. Thank you, Arnico Panday, Elisabeth von Cappellar, Francois Xavier-Leger, Giuseppe Savino, Kenichi Yokoyama, Kul Chandra Gautam, Mahendra Shrestha, Saloni Sethia and Shraddha Gautam from the advisory board of NEF. Thank you to senior fellows and the alumni community. My association with Bower Group Asia (BGA) began in 2014, and conversations with Ernie Bower, team members and clients continuously push me to provide perspective to international clients and audiences.

I miss the late Prabhakar Rana, a visionary thought leader from whom I learnt the art of looking at the future. I also miss late Bibek Debroy, who inspired me to have the discipline in writing. Late Gwen Robinson and Ambica Shrestha, I feel sad you will not see the book take final shape. Conversations with Gurcharan Das, Mahendra P. Lama, Namita Gokhale, Raja Mohan, Shamika Ravi and Shiv Shankar Menon have been super-useful, and their writings continue to inspire me. I am also grateful for the conversations I had with Amrit Gurung, Aneka Rebecca Rajbhandari, Bishnu Rimal, Christopher Giercke, Danielle Meuwly, Felicity Volk, Jean-Hervé Lorenzi, Jorg Frieden, Lisa Choegyal, Luc Lureth, Martin Raiser, Mrigendra Rijal, Pierre Jacquet, Prativa Pandey, Rameshore Khanal, Rob Fenn, Riina-Riikka Heikka, Shankar Sharma, Swarnim Wagle, Tariq Karim, Teresa Daban Sanchez, Veronique Lorenzo and Yuvaraj Khatiwada during the course of writing the book. A big thank you to friends not mentioned above who read the manuscript and provided blurbs—Bruno Macaes, David Gellner, Gita Wirjawan and Helen Clark.

A big thank you to Milee Ashwarya, publisher at Penguin Random House India for her constant guidance. Thank you to Yash Daiv, Alkesh Biswal and others in the PRH family. Thank you to Isha Sharma and Eva Kafle for your support in the research and finalization of the book.

Finally, a big thank you to the two pillars of my life, my wife Alpa and daughter Suyasha, who continue to make compromises to family schedules to accommodate my writing. They are my biggest source of feedback, helping me not only to become a better writer but to improve my life and living. Thank you!

Notes

Introduction

1   The International Monetary Fund's (IMF). *World Economic Outlook* (WEO). October 2024.
2   World Integrated Trade Solution. Nepal Trade Summary 2004. https://wits.worldbank.org/CountryProfile/en/Country/NPL/Year/2004/Summarytext (accessed 26 February 2025).
3   Human Flight. 2023. *Nepali Times*, (10 May), https://nepalitimes.com/editorial/human-flight (accessed 26 February 2025).
4   Nepal's Tax-to-GDP ratio is the highest in South Asia: Are we spending it wisely? 2024. *National Policy Forum*, (14 June), https://nationalpolicyforum.com/posts/nepals-tax-to-gdp-ratio/ (accessed 27 February 2025).
5   Budget 2023: Tax for higher-end cars to rise again; ARF to go up from 220 per cent to 320 per cent. 2023. *Straits Times*, (15 February), https://www.straitstimes.com/singapore/transport/budget-2023-tax-for-higher-end-cars-to-rise-again (accessed 27 February 2025).
    Pushpa Sharma. 2023. Environment Versus Economy: Nepal's Dilemma with Electric Vehicles. ISAS, (8 December), https://www.isas.nus.edu.sg/papers/environment-versus-economy-nepals-dilemma-with-electric-vehicles/ (accessed 27 February 2025).
6   Government of Nepal. 2023. *Nepal Living Standards Survey IV 2022–23*. Department of Statistics. P. 37.

7 World bank Open Data Gross Fixed Capital Formation Nepal, https://data.worldbank.org/indicator/NE.GDI.FTOT.ZS?locations=NP (accessed 15 March 2023).
8 Nepal Rastra Bank. 2023/24. *Current Macroeconomic and Financial Situation of Nepal*.
9 Informal remittances are amounts that are earned by workers that are remitted through informal channels like Hundi or bringing electronics and gold in bulk for the purposes of sale.
10 Sujeev Shakya. 2022. Decoding remittances. *Kathmandu Post*, (21 March), https://kathmandupost.com/columns/2022/03/21/decoding-remittances (accessed 27 February 2025).
11 Chandan Sapkota. (n.d.). Nepal's Top Remittance Source Countries in 2021. Sapkotak Blog. https://sapkotac.blogspot.com/2022/12/nepals-top-remittance-source-countries.html (accessed 27 February 2025).
It is estimated that $1.7 billion was sent from Nepal to India ($1.6 billion, which is close to remittance inflows from India).
12 Rukmini Shrinivasan. 2019. India Was the Top Recipient of Remittances Worldwide in 2018. *Economic Times* (20 July). https://economictimes.indiatimes.com/nri/forex-and-remittance/india-was-the-top-recipient-of-remittances-worldwide-in-2018/articleshow/70310386.cms?from=mdr (accessed 27 February 2025).
13 Ramesh Kumar. 2022. Kathmandu's Unreal Real Estate Prices. Nepali Times (5 February). https://nepalitimes.com/here-now/kathmandu-s-unreal-real-estate-prices (accessed 27 February 2025).
14 Nepal Rastra Bank Prepares Real Estate Index to Measure Price Fluctuations. 2021. *Basobas,* (November 29), https://basobaas.com/blog/nepal-rastra-bank-real-estate-index-measure-price-fluctuations (accessed 27 February 2025).
15 Local measure of land—one ropani is 5476 square feet.
16 Nepal Planning Commission. 2020. 15th Plan, Chapter 2, Long Term Vision 2043, p. 23.

17 The world in 2050. PwC. (2017). https://www.pwc.com/gx/en/research-insights/economy/the-world-in-2050.html (accessed 27 February 2025).

18 ODI Global. (n.d.). Global China 2049 Initiative. https://odi.org/en/about/our-work/global-china-2049-initiative (accessed 27 February 2025).

19 World population projections. (n.d.). Worldometer. https://www.worldometers.info/world-population/world-population-projections / (accessed 27 February 2025).

20 Nepal Planning Commission. 2020. 15th Plan, Chapter 2, Long Term Vision 2043, p. 23.

21 Nilanjan Ghosh et.al. 2023. Leap to the Himalayas: A 10-Point Agenda for a 5x Nepal. Observer Research Foundation (1 October).

22 Anon. 2005. Alchemy Wins Nepal Tourism Board Account Worth $2 Million. Exchange4Media (27 July), https://www.exchange4media.com/advertising-news/alchemy-wins-nepal-tourism-board-account-worth-$-2-million-17196.html (accessed 27 February 2025).

23 Sujeev Shakya. 2016. Nepal economic vision 2030: Leveraging private sector growth and investments. Nepal Economic Forum, (20 July), https://nepaleconomicforum.org/nepal-economic-vision-2030-leveraging-private-sector-growth-and-investments (accessed 27 February 2025).

24 Vision for Singapore (n.d.). Remembering Lee Kuan Yew. https://www.remembering.gov.sg/life-and-contributions/mr-lee-and-singapore/vision-for-singapore (accessed 27 February 2025).

25 Frank Kanyesigye. 2013. Rwanda: The Rising Revenues of Rwanda's Tourism. AllAfrica, (17 February), https://allafrica.com/stories/201302180130.html (accessed 27 February 2025).

26 Ibid., p. 49.

27 UN list of Least developed Countries. (n.d.). *UNCTAD*. https://unctad.org/topic/least-developed-countries/list (accessed 27 February 2025).

28 Countries Approaching Graduation and Already Graduated (n.d.). LDC Portal—International Support Measures for Least Developed Countries. United Nations. https://www.un.org/ldcportal/content/countries-approaching-graduation-and-graduated (accessed 27 February 2025)

Chapter 1

1 National Census Nepal. 2021. The 2021 Nepal Population and Housing Census Support Project.
2 National Statistics Office. 2021. National Population and Housing Census 2021.
3 The Central Bureau of Statistics (CBS) Nepal Labour Force Survey (NLFS), 2017/18.
4 Gender Equality in Nepal, Facts and Figures, Government of Nepal Ministry of Women, Children and Senior Citizens, April 2024.
5 National Census Nepal. 2021. The 2021 Nepal Population and Housing Census Support Project.
6 Future-proofing Nepal's population strategy. 2024. UNFPA (14 July), https://nepal.unfpa.org/en/news/future-proofing-nepals-population-strategy (accessed 27 February 2025).
7 *Embassy of India Kathmandu, Nepal.* (n.d.). https://www.indembkathmandu.gov.in/media-detail/256 (accessed 27 February 2025).
8 Nepalese government approves China rail link. 2024. *International Railway Journal* (15 July), https://www.railjournal.com/infrastructure/nepalese-government-approves-china-rail-link/ (accessed 27 February 2025).
9 Sino-Indian Rivalry in Rail Connectivity in Nepal. Observer Research Foundation. (2024). https://www.orfonline.org/expert-speak/sino-indian-rivalry-in-rail-connectivity-in-nepal (accessed 27 February 2025).

10 Birat Anupam. 2020. The Story of Nepal's 'Zone of Peace' Proposition to the World. *People's Review* (21 September), https://www.peoplesreview.com.np/2020/09/21/the-story-of-nepals-zone-of-peace-proposition-to-the-world (accessed 27 February 2025).

11 Embassy of Nepal. (n.d.). https://nyc.nepalconsulate.gov.np/wp-content/uploads/2019/09/Visa-Application-Form.pdf (accessed 27 February 2025).

12 Section 18(3) of the Constitution of Nepal (2015) explains that the State shall not discriminate against, inter alia, 'sexual minorities'.

13 Bibek Bhandari. 2023. Why Nepal Could Be the Next Big LGBTQ Travel Destination. *CNN* (29 June), https://edition.cnn.com/travel/nepal-lgbt-tourism-intl-hnk-cmd/index.html (accessed 27 February 2025).

14 Nasala Prajapati. 2024. Youth Participation in Preserving the Intangible Cultural Heritage of Kathmandu Valley. Nepal Economic Forum, (May 20), https://nepaleconomicforum.org/youth-participation-in-preserving-the-intangible-cultural-heritage-of-kathmandu-valley (accessed 27 February 2025).

15

16 David N. Geller. 2016. *The Idea of Nepal*. Himal Book (11 December), https://soscbaha.org/wp-content/uploads/2019/11/mcrl2016.pdf, p. 8.

17 Ibid.

18 History of Kirat - Federation of Indigenous Kirat Associations, Central Committee. 2022. Federation of Indigenous Kirat Associations, Central Committee, (9 August), https://kiratfederation.org.np/history-of-kirat/ (accessed 27 February 2025).

19 Laxmi Gautam. 2025. Kirat Community Celebrating New Year (Yale Tangwe) Today. Kantipur, (14 January), https://ekantipur.com/en/pradesh-1/2025/01/14/kirat-community-

celebrating-new-year-yale-tangwe-today-33-42.htm (accessed 27 February 2025).

20. Pradeep Rai. 2021. Yeledong and Maghe Sankrati | Kirat Rai History and Yalambar. Himalayan Indigenous Cultures - History, Tribal, Tradition, Festival Info - Indigenous Cultures of the Himalayas, (20 February), https://himalayancultures.com/articles/yele-dong-and-maghe-sankranti/ (accessed 27 February 2025).

21. Nepal Monarchy: Thakuri Dynasty. (n.d.). http://royalnepal.synthasite.com/the-thakuri-dynasty.php (accessed 27 February 2025).

22. Encyclopaedia Britannica, Malla Era, Encyclopaedia Britannica (n.d.), https://www.britannica.com/event/Malla-era (accessed 27 February 2025).

23. Nepal Constitution 2015, https://ag.gov.np/files/Constitution-of-Nepal_2072_Eng_www.moljpa.gov_.npDate-72_11_16.pdf, p. 6.

24. Yogesh Poudel. 2019. 12 Years After Madhes Movement, Gains Are Yet to Be Institutionalised. Kathmandu Post, (20 January), https://kathmandupost.com/national/2019/01/20/12-years-after-madhes-movement-gains-are-yet-to-be-institutionalised (accessed 27 February 2025).

25. Kunda Dixit. 2015. U.N.'s Mixed Messages on Nepal's Constitution. IPS News, (9 September), https://www.ipsnews.net/2015/09/opinion-u-n-s-mixed-messages-on-nepals-constitution/ (accessed 27 February 2025).

26. Encyclopaedia Britannica. 2025. Treaty of Sagauli. Encyclopaedia Britannica. https://www.britannica.com/event/Treaty-of-Sagauli (accessed 27 February 2025).

27. Government of Nepal. The Act Restricting Investment Abroad (ARIA). 1964.

28. Sujeev Shakya. 2021. Let Nepalis invest abroad. *Kathmandu Post* (8 March). https://kathmandupost.com/columns/2021/03/08/let-nepalis-invest-abroad (accessed 15 March 2025).

29. National Policy Forum. 2025. Nepal's Tax to GDP Ratio. *National Policy Forum.* https://nationalpolicyforum.com/posts/nepals-tax-to-gdp-ratio/ (accessed 27 February 2025).
30. Sandeep Kumar. 2023. Taxman Launches New Fiscal Year with VAT on Air Travel. *Kathmandu Post* (18 July) https://kathmandupost.com/money/2023/07/18/taxman-launches-new-fiscal-year-with-vat-on-air-travel (accessed February 27, 2025).
31. Understanding Nepal's Taxation System. Pioneer Law Associates. (n.d.), https://pioneerlaw.com/resource/understanding-nepals-taxation-system (accessed 27 February 2025).
32. World Bank. 2025. GDP (Current US$)—Nepal. *World Bank.* https://data.worldbank.org/indicator/NY.GDP.MKTP.CD?locations=NP (accessed February 27, 2025).
33. Government of Nepal, National Planning Commission, 15th Year Plan, p. 29.
34. Government of Nepal, Nepal Statistics Office. Nepal Living Standards Survey IV 2022/23, p. 269
35. Ibid.
36. Anon. 2019. With lockdown eased, Nepal Sees a Resurgence of Weddings and Ceremonies Amid Covid-19 Risk. *Nepal Live Today,* (6 July), https://www.nepallivetoday.com/2021/07/06/with-lockdown-eased-nepal-sees-a-resurgence-of-weddings-and-ceremonies-amid-covid-19-risk (accessed 27 February 2025).
37. ETOnline. 2021. How is Nepali consumer different. *Economic Times,* (3 May), https://brandequity.economictimes.indiatimes.com/news/marketing/how-is-nepali-consumer-different/82364021 (accessed 27 February 2025).
38. Nepal's informal economy is 38.6 per cent of GDP. 2024. *Kathmandu Post,* (26 January), https://kathmandupost.com/money/2024/01/26/nepal-s-informal-economy-is-38-6-percent-of-gdp (accessed 27 February 2025).
39. The State of Private Sector: Contributions and Constraints' jointly Published by the Federation of Nepalese Chambers

of Commerce and Industry (FNCCI) and the International Finance Corporation (IFC), a member of the World Bank Group. May 2024.

40 Nepal Rastra Bank. 2007. Annual Bank Supervision Report https://www.nrb.org.np/contents/uploads/2019/12/Annual_Reports-Annual_Bank_Supervision_Report_2006-2007.pdf (accessed 27 February 2025).

41 Nepal Economic Forum. (2024). Nefport 57—Decoding the Creative Industry.

42 *The Economic Journal of Nepal*, Vol. 42, No. 3 & 4, July-December 2019 (Issue No. 152) © Cedecon-TU Contribution of Insurance Business in Nepal Khom Raj Kharel 14.

43 IIDS, Unleashing IT: Advancing Nepal's Digital Economy, July 2023.

44 Private Vs Public Schools. 2014. *Edusanjal*, (5 April). https://edusanjal.com/news/private-vs-public-schools (accessed 27 February 2025).

45 Government of Nepal, Department of Tourism, Tourism Statistics, 1998.

46 Nepal's tourism paid for 1.19 million jobs in 2023. 2024. *The Kathmandu Post*, (10 June), https://kathmandupost.com/money/2024/06/10/nepal-s-tourism-paid-for-1-19-million-jobs-in-2023 (accessed 27 February 2025).

47 Nepal Electricity Authority. (1990). Profile of Progress. https://www.nea.org.np/admin/assets/uploads/supportive_docs/NEA per cent20FY per cent201985-90.pdf (accessed 27 February 2025).

48 Nepal Plans to generate 30,000 MW of Power by 2035. 2023. *Kathmandu Post*, (September 13), https://kathmandupost.com/national/2023/09/13/nepal-plans-to-generate-30-000mw-of-power-by-2035 (accessed 27 February 2025).

49 Why the MCC Compact Courted Controversy in Nepal. 2020. *Kathmandu Post*, (9 January), https://kathmandupost.

com/national/2020/01/09/why-the-mcc-compact-courted-controversy-in-nepal (accessed 27 February 2025).

Chapter 2

1. Baha is a type of courtyard with a monastery and living community.
2. Government of India. Ministry of External Affairs. Treaty of Peace and Friendship Between the Government of India and the Government of Nepal. 31 July 1950.
3. Government of India, Ministry of Commerce and Industry. 'Treaty of Transit between Government of India and Government of Nepal'. 1 June 2023.
4. Embassy of India, Kathmandu, 'Entry of Indian Registered Vehicles in Nepal'.
5. Embassy of India, Kathmandu, 'Public Facilitation – Vehicle Permit'.
6. Government of India, Ministry of Commerce and Industry. Revised Indo Nepal Treaty of Trade. October 2009.
7. Prasai S. World Bank (2021). Business Across Borders: India-Nepal Links Thrive and Grow.
8. Anon. 2022. Experts Doubt Implementation of Latest Trade Deal with China. *Kathamndu Post*, (April 1), https://kathmandupost.com/money/2022/04/01/experts-doubt-implementation-of-latest-trade-deal-with-china (accessed 27 February 2025).
9. Government of Nepal, Department of Customs, Customs Rules 2007, Appendix 5.
10. Ramesh Mishra. 2024. Most of the Foreign Students Who Come to India for Higher Education are Nepalese. *Kantipur*, (31 March), https://ekantipur.com/en/diaspora/2024/03/31/most-of-the-foreigners-who-come-to-india-for-higher-education-are-nepalis-39-52.html (accessed 20 March 2025).
11. World Bank. 2023. World Development Report.

12 Khabarhub. 2022. Chinese Citizens Obtaining Work Permits in Nepal 4.5 Times Higher Than Nepalis Working in China, (20 March), https://english.khabarhub.com/2022/20/242601/ (accessed 20 March 2025).
13 Real GDP Long-Term Forecast. OECD. (n.d.). https://www.oecd.org/en/data/indicators/real-gdp-long-term-forecast.html (accessed 20 March 2025).
14 The World in 2050. The Long View: How Will the Global Economic Order Change by 2050? PricewaterhouseCoopers. (n.d.). https://www.pwc.com/gx/en/research-insights/economy/the-world-in-2050.html (accessed 20 March 2025).
15 United Nations, Department of Economic and Social Affairs, Population Division, World Population Prospects. (n.d.)., https://population.un.org/wpp/ (accessed 27 February 2025).
16 Anon. 2025. USAid Shutdown Isn't Just a Humanitarian Issue—it's a Threat to American Interests. The Conversation, (February 4), https://theconversation.com/usaid-shutdown-isnt-just-a-humanitarian-issue-its-a-threat-to-american-interests-248939 (accessed 20 March 2025).
17 Amin Mohseni-Cheraghlou. 2024. The Bretton Woods Institutions Need Revitalizing. Luckily, they are no strangers to reform. Atlantic Council. https://www.atlanticcouncil.org/blogs/econographics/the-bretton-woods-institutions-need-revitalizing-luckily-they-are-no-strangers-to-reform/ (accessed 20 March 2025).
18 Jim Tankersley, Emma Bubola, Andrew Higgins and Aurelien Breeden. 2025. Trump Is Leading a Global Surge to the Right. *New York Times*, (23 January), https://www.nytimes.com/2025/01/23/world/europe/trump-europe-right-immigration-ukraine.html (accessed 20 March 2025).
19 World Economic Forum. 2024. WTO Director-General at Davos: Globalization and the Future, (28 January 18), https://

www.weforum.org/stories/2024/01/wto-director-general-davos-globalization/ (accessed 27 February 2025).

20. Global South seeks democratic, Diversified Re-Globalisation: S. Jaishankar. 2023. *The Hindu*, (27 August), https://www.thehindu.com/news/national/global-south-seeks-democratic-diversified-re-globalisation-s-jaishankar/article67241015.ece (accessed 27 February 2025).

21. Microsoft Corp (MSFT) stock Price & News—Google Finance. (n.d.). Google Finance. https://g.co/finance/MSFT:NASDAQ (accessed 20 March 2025).

22. International Monetary Fund. (n.d.). United Kingdom: IMF DataMapper Profile. https://www.imf.org/external/datamapper/profile/GBR (accessed 20 March 2025).

23. https://www.imf.org/external/datamapper/profile/GBR

24. Provincial Annual Per capita GDP in NRS. (n.d.). https://data.nsonepal.gov.np/dataset/provincial-national-accounts/resource/ca6c56c4-95af-4993-9c2a-5651cfa8780f (accessed 20 March 2025).

25. Elon Musk. (n.d.). Forbes. https://www.forbes.com/profile/elon-musk/ (accessed 20 March 2025).

26. Elena Moore, Camila Domonoske and Jeongyoon Han. 2024. Trump Taps Musk to Lead a 'Department of Government Efficiency' with Ramaswamy. NPR, (13 November), ps://www.npr.org/2024/11/12/g-s1-33972/trump-elon-musk-vivek-ramaswamy-doge-government-efficiency-deep-state (accessed 20 March 2025).

27. Bruno Venditti. 2025. Visualizing Over $1 Trillion in Wealth at Trump's Inauguration. VisualCapitalist, (January 24), https://www.visualcapitalist.com/visualizing-over-1-trillion-in-wealth-at-trumps-inauguration/ (accessed 20 March 2025).

28. Aimee Picchi. 2024. Elon Musk's Net Worth Tops $400 Billion, A First for Any Person. Here's Where He Gets His Wealth.

CBS News, (December 11), https://www.cbsnews.com/news/elon-musk-net-worth-400-billion-bloomberg (accessed 20 March 2025).

29 RSF. 2023. NDTV Takeover Signals End of Pluralism in India's Leading Media. Reporters Without Border, (2 January), https://rsf.org/en/ndtv-takeover-signals-end-pluralism-india-s-leading-media (accessed 20 March 2025).

30 Global Development Policy Center. 2023. A New State of Lending: Chinese Loans to Africa Boston University, (18 September), https://www.bu.edu/gdp/2023/09/18/a-new-state-of-lending-chinese-loans-to-africa (accessed 20 March 2025).

31 World Bank. 2025. Global Economic Prospects: Low-Income Countries in the Twenty-First Century, (12 March), https://www.worldbank.org/en/news/video/2025/03/12/global-economic-prospects-low-income-countries-in-the-21st-century (accessed 20 March 2025).

32 Mahbubani, K. (2022). The Asian 21st Century. In China and Globalization.

33 Khanna Parag (2019). The *Future Is Asian*. New Delhi: Simon and Schuster.

34 Arendse Huld. 2024. China-ASEAN Trade and Investment Relations. China Briefing, (August 9), https://www.china-briefing.com/news/china-asean-trade-and-investment-relations/ (accessed 20 March 2025).

35 Stephen Foley. 2024. Davos Entourages Will Face 10-Fold Price Increase Next Year. SWI, (13 November), https://www.swissinfo.ch/eng/multinational-companies/davos-entourages-will-face-10-fold-price-increase-next-year/87953242 (accessed 20 March 2025).

36 William Burke-White. 2020. The World Economic Forum Deserves Criticism, But We Need it Now More Than Ever. Brookings, (January 28), https://www.brookings.edu/articles/the-world-economic-forum-deserves-criticism-but-we-need-it-now-more-than-ever (accessed 20 March 2025).

37 CCG holds 9th China and Globalization Forum. (n.d.) Center for China and Globalization. http://en.ccg.org.cn/archives/80328 (accessed 20 March 2025).
38 World Economic Forum. 2024. BRICS Summit: Geopolitics and the Future of the Bloc. (November 20) https://www.weforum.org/stories/2024/11/brics-summit-geopolitics-bloc-international/ (accessed 20 March 2025).
39 Statista. (n.d.). GDP (PPP) Share of World GDP: G7 vs. BRICS. https://www.statista.com/statistics/1412425/gdp-ppp-share-world-gdp-g7-brics/ (accessed 20 March 2025).
40 Jayanty Nada Shofa. 2025. De-Dollarization: Indonesia, India Look Forward to Local Currency Trade. *Jakarta Globe*, (27 January) https://jakartaglobe.id/business/dedollarization-indonesia-india-look-forward-to-local-currency-trade (accessed 20 March 2025).
41 BRICS Pay as a challenge to SWIFT network. (n.d.). *Interpreter*. https://www.lowyinstitute.org/the-interpreter/brics-pay-challenge-swift-network (accessed 20 March 2025).
42 Government of Russia. (n.d.). Official Document from the Kremlin. http://static.kremlin.ru/media/events/files/en/RosOySvLzGaJtmx2wYFv0lN4NSPZploG.pdf (accessed 20 March 2025)
43 Sujeev Shakya. 2023. Building BRICS for the Future. *The Hindu*, (3 October) https://www.thehindu.com/opinion/op-ed/building-brics-for-the-future/article67372620.ece (accessed 20 March 2025).
44 Ghulam Ali. 2024. China and India Rebuild Trust on the Path to Reconciliation. East Asia Forum, (25 December) https://eastasiaforum.org/2024/12/25/china-and-india-rebuild-trust-on-the-path-to-reconciliation/ (accessed 20 March 2025).
45 Commonspace.eu. (n.d.). G20 Summit in Delhi Turns into India's 'Coming of Age' Party as Country Starts the Process of Adopting a Name-Change. ommonspace.eu. https://www.commonspace.eu/news/g20-summit-delhi-turns-indias-

coming-age-party-country-starts-process-adopting-name-change (accessed 20 March 2025).

46 Press Trust of India. 2023. PM Modi Closes 2023 G20 Summit, Pitches for UN Security Council Expansion. NDTV, (11 September), https://www.ndtv.com/india-news/pm-modi-closes-2023-g20-summit-pitches-for-un-security-council-expansion-4378262 (accessed 20 March 2025).

47 US Department of State. (n.d.). *I2U2 Initiative*. https://www.state.gov/i2u2 (accessed 20 March 2025).

48 S. Jaishankar. 2023. S. Jaishankar on India's Growing Global Role. The Economist, (13 November), https://www.economist.com/the-world-ahead/2023/11/13/s-jaishankar-on-indias-growing-global-role (accessed 20 March 2025).

49 India's Non-Alliance Culture Enables It to Balance Relations with Both Russia and US: Jaishankar. *Economic Times*, (n.d), https://economictimes.indiatimes.com/news/india/indias-non-alliance-culture-enables-it-to-balance-relations-with-both-russia-and-us-jaishankar/articleshow/108732641.cms (accessed 20 March 2025).

50 Jagannath Panda. 2023. India in a World of Asymmetrical Multipolarity. Institute for Security and Development Policy, (22 March), https://www.isdp.eu/publication/india-in-a-world-of-asymmetrical-multipolarity (accessed 20 March 2025).

51 Press Information Bureau, Government of India. 2023. Press Release. https://pib.gov.in/PressReleaseIframePage.aspx?PRID=1985077 (accessed 20 March 2025).

52 National Development and Reform Commission of China. 2024. Press Release. https://www.ndrc.gov.cn/xwdt/ztzl/NEW_srxxgcjjpjjsx/yjcg/yw/202401/t20240123_1363634.html (accessed 20 March 2025).

53 Michael Schuman. 2023. Why China Won't Win the Global South. Atlantic Council, (16 October), https://www.atlanticcouncil.org/in-depth-research-reports/report/why-china-wont-win-the-global-south (accessed 20 March 2025).

54 Office of the Leading Group for Promoting the Belt and Road Initiative. (n.d.). *Belt and Road Portal.* https://eng.yidaiyilu.gov.cn (accessed 20 March 2025).
55 https://eng.yidaiyilu.gov.cn/special/xjpyydyl
56 Green Finance & Development Center. (n.d.). Countries of the Belt and Road Initiative (BRI). https://greenfdc.org/countries-of-the-belt-and-road-initiative-bri/ (accessed 20 March 2025).
57 Keith Bradsher. 2025. China's Trade Surplus and Global Economic Shifts. *New York Times*, (12 January), https://www.nytimes.com/2025/01/12/business/china-trade-surplus.html (accessed 20 March 2025).
58 Kjelds Munkholm. 2025. Analysis of China's Trade with ASEAN and Vietnam's Export Dynamics. LinkedIn, (14 November), https://www.linkedin.com/pulse/analysis-chinas-trade-asean-vietnams-export-dynamics-munkholm- per centE5 per centAD per cent9F per centE5 per cent8F per centAF per centE5 per cent92 per cent8C-3eyte/ (accessed 20 March 2025).
59 EU trade relations with China. 2025. Trade and Economic Security, (19 March), https://policy.trade.ec.europa.eu/eu-trade-relationships-country-and-region/countries-and-regions/china_en (accessed 20 March 2025).
60 The People's Republic of China. (n.d.). United States Trade Representative. https://ustr.gov/countries-regions/china-mongolia-taiwan/peoples-republic-china (accessed 20 March 2025).
61 Noriyuki Doi and Saki Akita. 2023. Yuan Exceeds Dollar in China's Bilateral Trade for First Time. Nikkei Asia, (24 July), https://asia.nikkei.com/Business/Markets/Currencies/Yuan-exceeds-dollar-in-China-s-bilateral-trade-for-first-time (accessed 20 March 2025).
62 Shivangi Acharya and Riddhima Talwani. 2023. India Cenbank to Give Banks Guidance to Resolve Rupee Trade Issues. Reuters, (14 July), https://www.reuters.com/world/india/india-cenbank-give-banks-guidance-resolve-rupee-trade-issues-official-2023-07-14/ (accessed 20 March 2025).

63 The Hindu. 2024. India in Trade Deficit with Nine of Top 10 Trading Partners in 2023-24. The *Hindu*, (18 March), https://www.thehindu.com/business/Economy/india-in-trade-deficit-with-nine-of-top-10-trading-partners-in-2023-24/article68217897.ece (accessed 20 March 2025).

64 Brookings Institution. 2024. Is There Going to Be an India-China Deal? (5 February), https://www.brookings.edu/articles/is-there-going-to-be-an-india-china-deal/ (accessed 20 March 2025).

65 New Business Age. (n.d.). https://www.newbusinessage.com/Articles/view/17784 (accessed 20 March 2025).

66 The People's Republic of China. (n.d.). United States Trade Representative. https://ustr.gov/countries-regions/china-mongolia-taiwan/peoples-republic-china (accessed 20 March 2025).

67 Achyut Tiwari. 2022. Giving Yarsagumba a Chance for Regrowth. *Nepali Times*, (19 August), https://nepalitimes.com/here-now/giving-yarsagumba-a-chance-for-regrowth (accessed 20 March 2025).

68 Wang Mingjie. 2024. Chinese Tourists Return to Global Markets. *Chinadaily*, (7 November), https://www.chinadaily.com.cn/a/202411/07/WS672c9e6ca310f1265a1cc1bc.html (accessed 20 March 2025).

69 Trifon Tsvetkov. 2024. 5 Key Facts You Need to Know About the Chinese Tourism Market. Regiondo, (29 February), https://pro.regiondo.com/blog/5-key-facts-you-need-to-know-about-the-chinese-outbound-tourism-market/ (accessed 20 March 2025).

70 The Feed. 2025. This Chinese Company Has Overtaken Tesla as World's Largest Maker of Pure Electric Cars. *Economic Times*, (January 4). https://economictimes.indiatimes.com/news/international/us/this-chinese-company-has-overtaken-tesla-as-worlds-largest-maker-of-pure-electric-cars-heres-how-it-outsmarted-elon-musk/articleshow/116947090.cms?from=mdr[H1] (accessed 20 March 2025).

71. Sebastian Moss. 2025. Nvidia Records Largest Market Cap Loss in US History, as DeepSeek Wipes out $600bn. Data Center Dynamics, (28 January), https://www.datacenterdynamics.com/en/news/nvidia-records-largest-market-cap-loss-in-us-history-as-deepseek-wipes-out-600 bn/(accessed 20 March 2025).
72. WIPO. 2024. WIPO IP Facts and Figures 2024. Page 11. https://www.wipo.int/edocs/pubdocs/en/wipo-pub-943-2024-en-wipo-ip-facts-and-figures-2024.pdf (accessed 20 March 2025).
73. Amy Hawkins. 2023. China Overtakes US in Contributions to Nature and Science journals. *Guardian*, (24 May), https://www.theguardian.com/world/2023/may/24/china-overtakes-us-in-contributions-to-nature-and-science-journals (accessed 20 March 2025).
74. We Were Market Leader in EVs in Nepal, We Would Like to Regain That Spot. 2024. *Kathmandu Post*, (7 August), https://kathmandupost.com/money/2024/08/27/we-were-market-leader-in-evs-in-nepal-we-would-like-to-regain-that-spot (accessed 20 March 2025).
75. Norway: Nearly All New Cars Sold in 2024 Were Fully Electric. 2025. Reuters, (2 January), [https://www.reuters.com/business/autos-transportation/norway-nearly-all-new-cars-sold-2024-were-fully-electric-2025-01-02/](https://www.reuters.com (accessed 20 March 2025).
76. China's Two Mountains Framework: Varied Responses from Southeast Asia. (n.d.). Fulcrum. https://fulcrum.sg/chinas-two-mountains-framework-varied-responses-from-southeast-asia/ (accessed 20 March 2025).
77. Leap to the Himalayas: A 10-point agenda for a 5x Nepal. (n.d.). orfonline.org. https://www.orfonline.org/english/research/leap-to-the-himalayas-a-10-point-agenda-for-a-5x-nepal (accessed 20 March 2025).
78. Nepal and the World. (n.d.). Institute of South Asian Studies, National University of Singapore. https://www.isas.nus.edu.sg/papers/nepal-and-the-world/ (accessed 20 March 2025).

79 Nepal and the World. (n.d.). Institute of South Asian Studies, National University of Singapore. https://www.isas.nus.edu.sg/papers/nepal-and-the-world/ (accessed 20 March 2025).
80 Abebe Bocher. 2023. Rwanda's Success Story Is a Tale of African Solutions. Abren, (20 July), https://abren.org/rwandas-success-story-is-a-tale-of-african-solutions/ (accessed 20 March 2025).
81 Sujeev Shakya. 2025. Revitalizing Switzerland-Nepal connections. Nepal Economic Forum, (21 January), https://nepaleconomicforum.org/revitalizing-switzerland-nepal-connections/(accessed 20 March 2025).
82 PTI. 2022. Rs 15,477 Crore Spent to Construct 2,088 kms Road Along Border with China in Last 5 Years: Govt. *Economic Times*, (25 July), https://economictimes.indiatimes.com/news/defence/rs-15477-crore-spent-to-construct-2088-kms-road-along-border-with-china-in-last-5-years-govt/articleshow/93118438.cms (accessed 20 March 2025).
83 Rajat Pandit. 2024. Myanmar Border Fencing Gathers Pace, BRO to Complete Project in 10 Years. *Times of India*, (8 December), https://timesofindia.indiatimes.com/india/myanmar-border-fencing-gathers-pace-bro-to-complete-project-in-10-years/articleshow/116119190.cms (accessed 20 March 2025).

Chapter 3

1 Government of Nepal, Home Ministry notification.
2 Nepal Constitution, 1962.
3 Nepal Interim Constitution 1990, Part 17.
4 Government of Nepal, Local Self Governance Act 1999, Preamble.
5 Tika R. Pradhan. 2022. What's Enticing Some Central and Provincial Leaders into Local Politics. *Kathmandu Post*, (21 April), https://kathmandupost.com/politics/2022/04/21/what-s-enticing-some-central-and-provincial-leaders-into-local-politics (accessed 20 March 2025).

6 World Bank Group. 2020. Supporting Nepal's Historic Transition to Federalism. https://www.worldbank.org/en/results/2020/09/29/supporting-nepals-historic-transition-to-federalism (accessed 20 March 2025).
7 Karan Singh and Bhadra Sharma. 2022. How Nepal Grew Back Its Forests. *New York Times*, (11 November), https://www.nytimes.com/2022/11/11/world/asia/nepal-reforestation-climate.html (accessed 20 March 2025).
8 Ibid.
9 Kushan Pokhrel. (2025). East Asia Forum, Overcoming Hurdles to Effective Sub-National Governance in Nepal. East Asia Forum, (25 March), https://eastasiaforum.org/2024/03/25/overcoming-hurdles-to-effective-sub-national-governance-in-nepal/
10 Support to Post Legislation Review for Gandaki Province. 2024. Nepal Law Society, (1 May), https://nepallawsociety.org/2024-05-01-1714544087 (accessed 20 March 2025).
11 A Survey of the Nepali People in 2022. 2023. The Asia Foundation, (14 February), https://asiafoundation.org/publication/a-survey-of-the-nepali-people-in-2022/ (accessed 20 March 2025).
12 10,000 bridges. 2024. *Nepali Times*, (6 January), https://nepalitimes.com/here-now/10-000-bridges (accessed 20 March 2025).
13 The Himalayan Times. (n.d.). Total road length crosses 80,000 km. https://thehimalayantimes.com/business/total-road-length-crosses-80000km (accessed 20 March 2025).
14 Yimenu, Bizuneh. (2023). Federalism and State Restructuring in Africa: A Comparative Analysis of Origins, Rationales, and Challenges. Publius: *The Journal of Federalism*. 54. 10.1093/publius/pjad015.
15 World Bank Group. 2023. New World Bank Report Recommends Reforms to Strengthen Fiscal Federalism in Nepal. World Bank. https://www.worldbank.org/en/news/press-release/2023/06/15/new-world-bank-report-recommends-reforms-to-strengthen-fiscal-federalism-in-nepal (accessed 20 March 2025).

16. Yoshihiro Saito, Nayan Krishna Joshi and Rozo Rincon, Marcela. Nepal Fiscal Federalism Update 2024 (English). Washington, D.C.: World Bank Group. http://documents.worldbank.org/curated/en/099050924102027545 (accessed 20 March 2025).
17. 81 per cent of Chiefs of Local Bodies New Faces, Just 142 Get Reelected. (n.d.). Setopati. https://en.setopati.com/political/158723 (accessed 20 March 2025).
18. Sujeev Shakya. 2022. New Faces in Nepal's Politics, a Phase of Change. *The Hindu*, (4 December), https://www.thehindu.com/opinion/lead/new-faces-in-nepals-politics-a-phase-of-change/article66223342.ece (accessed 20 March 2025).
19. Onlinekhabar, (2017) Koirala Family Comeback: How Likely Is It? Online Khabar. https://www.onlinekhabar.com/2017/12/646915/
20. Ram Kumar Kamat. 2022. Gagan Thapa Lone Challenger to Sher Bahadur Deuba. *Himalayan Times*, (21 December), https://thehimalayantimes.com/nepal/gagan-thapa-lone-challenger-to-sher-bahadur-deuba (accessed 20 March 2025).
21. Purushottam Poudel. 2023. Deuba's Grip on Congress Firm Despite Losing Power. *Kathmandu Post*, (9 January), https://kathmandupost.com/politics/2023/01/09/deuba-s-grip-on-congress-firm-despite-losing-power (accessed 20 March 2025).
22. Who Will Succeed Deuba? (n.d.). *Annapurna Express*. https://theannapurnaexpress.com/story/51731/ (accessed 20 March 2025).
23. Sujeev Shakya. 2021. The Difference Between Communism in China and Nepal https://sujeevshakya.com/2021/07/the-difference-between-communism-in-china-andnepal (accessed 20 March 2025).
24. Anil Giri, Tika R. Pradhan and Binod Ghimire. 2021. President Dissolves House, Calls Snap Polls for November 12 and 19. Kathmandu Post, (22 May), https://kathmandupost.com/politics/2021/05/22/president-dissolves-house-calls-snap-polls-for-november-12-and-19 (accessed 20 March 2025).

25 UML Expels Bhim Rawal, Suspends Membership of Binda Pandey and Ushakiran Timsina. 2024. *Kathmandu Post*, (25 December), https://kathmandupost.com/national/2024/12/25/uml-expels-bhim-rawal-suspends-membership-of-binda-pandey-and-ushakiran-timsina (accessed 20 March 2025).

26 Dissatisfaction in CPN (US): Chair Nepal Engages Discontented Leaders. (n.d.). Ratopati. https://english.ratopati.com/story/34987 (accessed 20 March 2025).

27 Deutsche Welle. 2024. Nepal: Will New Laws Offer Closure to War Crime Victims? DW News, (March 20), https://www.dw.com/en/nepal-will-new-laws-offer-closure-to-war-crime-victims/a-70070899 (accessed 20 March 2025).

28 Binod Ghimire. 2024. Nepal Delays Reply to UN Concerns Over Transitional Justice. *Kathmandu Post*, (21 February), https://kathmandupost.com/national/2024/02/21/nepal-delays-reply-to-un-concerns-over-transitional-justice (accessed 20 March 2025).

29 Prashant Jha. 2024. Baburam Bhattarai's Exit a Body Blow to Nepal's Maoists. *Hindustan Times*, (20 March), https://www.hindustantimes.com/world/baburam-bhattarai-s-exit-a-body-blow-to-nepal-s-maoists/story-XtdVSDKN9rwqUpgC6iokxM.html (accessed 20 March 2025).

30 Deepak Thapa. 2023. Prachanda and Company. *Kathmandu Post*, (9 February), https://kathmandupost.com/columns/2023/02/09/prachanda-and-company (accessed 20 March 2025).

31 Ibid.

32 Anon. 2024. Out of power Maoist Leader Dahal Seeks Broader Unity to Build Strength. August 2024. https://kathmandupost.com/politics/2024/08/11/out-of-power-maoist-leader-dahal-seeks-broader-unity-to-build-strength (accessed 20 March 2025).

33 Rabindra Mishra joins RPP. Onlinekhabar, (September 2022), https://english.onlinekhabar.com/rabindra-mishra-joins-rpp.html (accessed 20 March 2025).

34 Santa Gaha Magar. 2024. Old Is Still Gold in Nepali Politics. *Nepali Times*, (20 March), https://nepalitimes.com/news/old-is-still-gold-in-nepali-politics (accessed 20 March 2025).

35 Advocate Pandey Held Over Controversial Remark. 2024. *Himalayan Times*, (20 March), https://thehimalayantimes.com/kathmandu/advocate-pandey-held-over-controversial-remark (accessed 20 March 2025).

36 Arpana Adhikari. 2022. Final Results of Elections Out NC Largest Party, UML Gets Highest Popular Votes. *Rising Nepal*, (8 December), https://risingnepaldaily.com/news/19749 (accessed 20 March 2025).

37 Dr Bhattarai alleges political vendetta behind Rabi's arrest. 2024. Khabarhub, (6 March), https://english.khabarhub.com/2024/06/417538/ (accessed 20 March 2025).

38 RSP Chair Lamichhane to Remain in Custody until Court Verdict. 2024. Nagariknetwork.com. (8 August), https://myrepublica.nagariknetwork.com/news/rsp-chair-lamichhane-to-remain-in-custody-until-court-verdict-71-45.html.

39 Prithivi Man Shrestha. 2024. Yearender 2023: Year of politically charged scams Kathmandu Post, (December 31), https://kathmandupost.com/special-supplement/2023/12/31/yearender-2023-year-of-politically-charged-scams (accessed 20 March 2025).

Chapter 4

1 Free Documentary. 2024. [Video]. Facebook. https://www.facebook.com/FreeDocumentaryOfficial/videos/1698499507345178/ (accessed 27 March 2025).

2 Resilience Capacities: Absorb, Adapt, Transform. 2017. Oxfam, (January 25), https://oxfamilibrary.openrepository.com/bitstream/handle/10546/620178/gd-resilience-capacities-absorb-adapt-transform-250117-en.pdf?sequence=4 (accessed 27 March 2025).

3   Guthis are collective community trusts popular with Newa community of the Kathmandu Valley that owns land, and the proceeds are utilized for the socio-economic benefit of the community.
4   Pulla, Venkat & Dhakal, Sandesh. (2018). Culture and Resilience to Earthquake Trauma: Nepal Newari Community Case Study.
5   Ibid.
6   Department for International Development. 2019. Resilience Measurement Literature Review. (March), https://assets.publishing.service.gov.uk/media/5cff7c18e5274a3cc494e7b1/Resilience_measurement_LitRev_FINAL-updated1_ML_June_2019.pdf (accessed 27 March 2025).
7   Durga Rana Magar. 2024. Jajarkot Survivors Show Collective Resilience. *Nepali Times*. (8 January), https://nepalitimes.com/here-now/jajarkot-survivors-show-collective-resilience (accessed 27 March 2025).
8   Ibid.
9   Ibid.
10 Purushottam Khatri. 2024. Roads Connecting Valley Disrupted at 57 Places. *Rising Nepal*, (30 September), https://risingnepaldaily.com/news/49752 (accessed 27 March 2025).
11 Blair Glencorse and Sujeev Shakya. 2015. Shaking Up the Status Quo in Nepal. *New York Times*, (1 June), https://www.nytimes.com/2015/06/02/opinion/shaking-up-the-status-quo-in-nepal.html (accessed 27 March 2025).
12 Ibid.
13 Bruno Philip. 2024. The World Champion of Political Instability. Le Monde, (16 July), https://www.lemonde.fr/en/international/article/2024/07/16/nepal-the-world-champion-of-political-instability_6686514_4.html (accessed 27 March 2025).
14 National Planning Commission. 2016. MDG Status Report 2016. https://www.npc.gov.np/images/category/MDG-Status-Report-2016_.pdf (accessed 27 March 2025).
15 World Bank Group. 2023. Evaluation of the World Bank Group in Nepal (2014-23): Chapter 6—Conclusions and Lessons.

https://ieg.worldbankgroup.org/evaluations/world-bank-group-nepal-2014-23/chapter-6-conclusions-and-lessons(accessed 27 March 2025).

16. Sujeev Shakya. 2021. Building Institutions. *Kathmandu Post*, (19 April), https://kathmandupost.com/columns/2021/04/19/building-institutions (accessed 27 March 2025).
17. Kul Chandra Gautam. 2021. Restructuring Nepali Army. *Kathmandu Post*, (21 November 1), https://kathmandupost.com/columns/2021/11/21/restructuring-nepali-army (accessed 27 March 2025).
18. Pushpa Kamal Dahal 'Prachanda'. 2021. *Kathmandu Post*. The Nepali Peace Process as a Global Model, (21 November), https://kathmandupost.com/columns/2021/11/20/the-nepali-peace-process-as-a-global-model (accessed 27 March 2025).
19. Ibid.
20. Rory McCarthy. 2001. Nepalese Regard New King with Suspicion. *Guardian*, (5 June), https://www.theguardian.com/world/2001/jun/05/nepal (accessed 27 March 2025).
21. South Asia Terrorism Portal (SATP). 2006. King Gyanendra's Proclamation. Institute for Conflict Management, (21 April), https://www.satp.org/satporgtp/countries/nepal/document/papers/King_Gyanendra per cent20Proclamation_Apr21.htm(accessed 27 March 2025).
22. Bal Gopal Shrestha. 2008. The End of Monarchy in Nepal and its Delicate Journey Towards a Republic. Contributions to Nepalese Studies. 35.1 (Jan. 2008): p. 63. https://himalaya.socanth.cam.ac.uk/collections/journals/contributions/pdf/CNAS_35_01_03.pdf (accessed 27 March 2025).
23. Simon Denyer and Gopal Sharma. 2008. Deposed King Quits Palace but Vows to Stay in Nepal. Reuters. (June 11), https://www.reuters.com/article/economy/deposed-king-quits-palace-but-vows-to-stay-in-nepal-idUS$EL197878/ (accessed 27 March 2025).

24. How They Kept Nepal in the Dark Ages. 2018. *Nepali Times*, (2 April), https://nepalitimes.com/here-now/how-they-kept-nepal-in-the-dark-ages (accessed 27 March 2025).
25. Ibid.
26. Shuvam Dhungana. 2021.The Nepal Banda Is Back. *Record Nepal*, (4 February 4), https://www.recordnepal.com/the-nepal-banda-is-back (accessed 27 March 2025).
27. Understanding Inflation; Why Are Prices Rising? 2010. *Nepali Times*, (10 September), https://archive.nepalitimes.com/news.php?id=17446 (accessed 27 March 2025).
28. Karuna Thapa. 2002. Maoists Announce Ceasefire. *Nepali Times*, (13 December), https://archive.nepalitimes.com/news.php?id=4396 (accessed 27 March 2025).
29. National Opinion Poll. 2025. Sharecast Initiative Nepal, https://sharecast.org.np/national-opinion-poll-2025/ (accessed 27 March 2025).
30. Ameet Dhakal. 2025. Nepal's Income Increased Threefold, Worries Doubled. LinkedIn Pulse, (18 February), https://www.linkedin.com/pulse/nepals-income-increased-threefold-worries-doubled-pfyff/ (accessed 27 March 2025).
31. Centers for Disease Control and Prevention (CDC). 2024. Ebola Virus Disease. CDC, https://www.cdc.gov/vhf/ebola/index.html (accessed 27 March 2025).
32. Severe Acute Respiratory Syndrome (SARS). 2024. WHO, https://www.who.int/health-topics/severe-acute-respiratory-syndrome (accessed 27 March 2025).
33. Public Health and COVID-19 Response. 2024. Wiley Online Library, https://onlinelibrary.wiley.com/doi/full/10.1002/puh2.127 (accessed 27 March 2025).
34. Allie Torgan. 2020. Nepal's Food Shortage Crisis During COVID-19 Quarantine. CNN, (23 April), https://edition.cnn.com/2020/04/23/world/coronavirus-nepal-food-shortage-quarantined-54-kids-cnnheroes/index.html (accessed 27 March 2025).

35 Nepal Volunteers Become Local Heroes During the Pandemic. 2020. Voice of America (VOA), (1 June), https://www.voanews.com/a/covid-19-pandemic_nepal-volunteers-become-local-heroes-during-pandemic/6190269.html (accessed 27 March 2025).

36 Bianca Caruana. 2021. How to Help Nepal Through the COVID-19 Pandemic. The Altruistic Traveller, (7 July), https://thealtruistictraveller.com/blog/how-to-help-nepal-through-the-covid-19-pandemic/ (accessed 27 March 2025).

37 Parag Karki, Lee Budhathoki, Manoj Khadka, Swojay Maharjan, Subodh Dhakal, Subashchandra Pokharel, Anita Poudel, Pooja Rokaya, Udit Raut, Sushma Rayamajhi. 2021. Willingness of Nepalese Medical and Nursing Students to Volunteer During COVID-19 Pandemic: A Single-Centered Cross-Sectional Study. *Annals of Medicine and Surgery*, 72, 103056. https://pubmed.ncbi.nlm.nih.gov/34812288/ (accessed 27 March 2025).

38 Nepal's Lockdown Leaves Many Hungry. 2020. Taipei Times, (14 April), https://www.taipeitimes.com/News/world/archives/2020/04/14/2003734595 (accessed 27 March 2025).

39 Nasana Bajracharya. 2020. Online Khabar. Nepal Lockdown Continues, Leaving Scores Hungry—But There Are a Few Who Feed Them. Online Khabar, (May 16), https://english.onlinekhabar.com/nepal-lockdown-continues-leaving-scores-hungry-but-there-are-a-few-who-feed-them.html (accessed 27 March 2025).

40 Feed the Hungry Nepal. 2020. Feed the Hungry Nepal Facebook Page. Facebook, https://www.facebook.com/feedthehungrynepal/ (accessed 27 March 2025).

41 Rabindra Ghimire. 2021. 65,000 Nepalis Went to UAE on a Visit Visa in 11 Months, but Most of Them Weren't Visitors. Online Khabar, (15 December), https://english.onlinekhabar.com/uae-visit-visa-trafficking.html (accessed 27 March 2025).

42 After Attending Kumbh Mela, Nepal's Former King Gyanendra & Queen Komal Test Positive for COVID-19. 2021. ThePrint, (20 April), https://theprint.in/world/after-attending-kumbh-

mela-nepals-former-king-gyanendra-queen-komal-test-positive-for-covid/642961/ (accessed 27 March 2025).

43 Machindranath Festival Concludes Amidst COVID-19. 2020. Nepali Times, (14 September), https://nepalitimes.com/news/machindranath-festival-concludes-amidst-covid-19-z9iscrwi (accessed 27 March 2025).

44 Bhadra Sharma. 2020. The Omni Scandal and Its Impacts. The Record Nepal, (29 September), https://www.recordnepal.com/the-omni-scandal-and-its-impacts (accessed 27 March 2025).

45 Sujeev Shakya. (n.d.) Center for International Private Enterprise (CIPE). Stalling the Pandemic of Corruption. CIPE, https://www.cipe.org/resources/stalling-the-pandemic-of-corruption/ (accessed 27 March 2025).

46 Prithivi Man Shrestha. 2020. Shankar Group Owner Sulabh Agrawal Arrested on Charges of Black Marketeering. The Kathmandu Post, (April 7), https://kathmandupost.com/national/2020/04/07/shankar-group-owner-sulabh-agrawal-arrested-on-charges-of-blackmarketeering (accessed 27 March 2025).

47 Prithivi Man Shrestha. 2021. Nepal Wanted to Buy Millions of Jabs. Here's How It Failed. Kathmandu Post, (May 8), https://kathmandupost.com/health/2021/05/08/nepal-wanted-to-buy-millions-of-jabs-here-s-how-it-failed (accessed 27 March 2025).

48 U4 Anti-Corruption Resource Centre. 2021. Corruption During COVID-19. U4, https://www.u4.no/publications/corruption-during-covid-19 (accessed 27 March 2025).

49 Procurement During the Pandemic: Responses and Failures. 2022. Nepal Economic Forum, (10 January), https://nepaleconomicforum.org/videos/procurement-during-pandemic-responses-and-failures/ (accessed 27 March 2025).

50 Procurement During the Pandemic: Responses and Failures. 2021. Nepal Economic Forum, (15 June), https://issuu.com/nepaleconomicforum/docs/procurement_during_pandemic_proceedings_report (accessed 27 March 2025).

51 Government of Nepal. 2024. Nagarik App. Government of Nepal, https://nagarikapp.gov.np/ (accessed 27 March 2025).
52 Sujeev Shakya. 2021. India-Nepal Open Borders and the Pandemic. Institute of South Asian Studies (ISAS), National University of Singapore. (September 9), https://www.isas.nus.edu.sg/papers/india-nepal-open-borders-and-the-pandemic/ (accessed 27 March 2025).

Chapter 5

1 Arnico Panday (n.d.) Places That Have Been Safe for Centuries Will Soon No Longer Be So. ICIMOD Blog, https://blog.icimod.org/regional-action/places-that-have-been-safe-for-centuries-will-soon-no-longer-be-so-arnico-panday/ (accessed 20 March 2025).
2 Ibid.
3 Ibid.
4 Disaster Task Force (n.d). The Melamchi Flood Disaster. ICIMOD, https://www.icimod.org/article/the-melamchi-flood-disaster/ (accessed 20 March 2025).
5 Rahul Karmakar and Suhasini Haidar. 2023. The Shadow from the Fallen Sikkim Dam Falls on India's Hydroelectric Projects in Bhutan. *The Hindu*, (5 January), https://www.thehindu.com/news/national/the-shadow-from-the-fallen-sikkim-dam-falls-on-indias-hydroelectric-projects-in-bhutan/article67420574.ece (accessed 23 March 2025).
6 Arnico Panday. (n.d.) Places That Have Been Safe for Centuries Will Soon No Longer Be So. ICIMOD Blog, https://blog.icimod.org/regional-action/places-that-have-been-safe-for-centuries-will-soon-no-longer-be-so-arnico-panday/ (accessed 20 March 2025).
7 Waning Winter Rains: A Burgeoning Crisis. 2025. Kathmandu Post, (20 January), https://kathmandupost.com/

columns/2025/01/20/waning-winter-rains-a-burgeoning-crisis (accessed 20 March 2025).

8 Ibid.

9 Intense late monsoon rain followed by a long, dry winter is a recipe for widespread wildfires. If these wildfires are followed by heavy early monsoon downpours, as has increasingly been the case in recent years; https://kathmandupost.com/columns/2025/01/20/waning-winter-rains-a-burgeoning-crisis

10 IPCC. (n.d.) About the IPCC. https://www.ipcc.ch/about (accessed 20 March 2025).

11 UNFCCC. (n.d.) What Is the United Nations Framework Convention on Climate Change? https://unfccc.int/process-and-meetings/what-is-the-united-nations-framework-convention-on-climate-change (accessed 20 March 2025).

12 UNFCCC. (n.d.) The Paris Agreement. https://unfccc.int/process-and-meetings/the-paris-agreement (accessed 20 March 2025).

13 Net Zero Climate. (n.d.) What Is Net Zero? https://netzeroclimate.org/what-is-net-zero-2/ (accessed 23 March 2025).

14 Ramesh Bhushal. 2023. IPCC Vice-Chair Vows to Give Himalayas Attention They Deserve. Dialogue Earth, (9 November), https://dialogue.earth/en/climate/interview-ipcc-vice-chair-nepal-give-himalayas-attention-they-deserve/ (accessed 23 March 2025).

15 National Trust for Nature Conservation (NTNC). 2024. Annual report 2023 (p. 62). https://ntnc.org.np/sites/default/files/doc_publication/2024-07/NTNC_AR_2023_print_.pdf, page 62 (accessed 23 March 2025).

16 NTNC. (n.d.) Achievements of NTNC. https://ntnc.org.np/achievements-ntnc (accessed 20 March 2025).

17 Annapurna Conservation: A Success Story. (n.d.) ECS Nepal, http://ecs.com.np/features/annapurna-conservation-a-success-story (accessed 23 March 2025).

18 ICIMOD. (n.d.) International Centre for Integrated Mountain Development. https://www.icimod.org/ (accessed 23 March 2025).
19 We Have Not Respected the Fragility of the Himalaya. 2022. *Nepali Times*, (2 September), https://nepalitimes.com/here-now/we-have-not-respected-the-fragility-of-the-himalaya (accessed 24 March 2025).
20 Niki Gribi. 2015. Nepalese Conservationist Wins Long Court Battle Using Economics Learned in CSF Course. Conservation Strategy Fund, (29 April), https://conservation-strategy.org/news/nepalese-conservationist-wins-long-court-battle-using-economics-learned-csf-course#:~:text\ (accessed 24 March 2025).
21 Aria Shree Parasai. 2022. Building Nijgad, Come What May. *Nepali Times*, (15 May), https://nepalitimes.com/here-now/building-nijgad-come-what-may (accessed 24 March 2025).
22 Aborted Landing in Nijgad. 2025. *Nepali Times*, (31 May), https://nepalitimes.com/editorial/aborted-landing-in-nijgad (accessed 24 March 2025).
23 Ananda Gautam. 2025. Pathibhara Cable Car Protest Resurges, Several Injured. *Kathmandu Post*, (21 February), https://kathmandupost.com/province-no-1/2025/02/21/pathibhara-cable-car-protest-resurges-several-injured (accessed 24 March 2025).
24 Drones to Airlift Mountain of Rubbish from Everest. 2025. *The Times*, https://www.thetimes.com/world/asia/article/drones-to-airlift-mountain-of-rubbish-from-everest-ljwk60rz8 (accessed 24 March 2025).
25 Bhadra Sharma and Alex Travelli. 2024. On Himalayan Hillsides Grows Japan's Cold, Hard Cash. *New York Times*, (15 April), https://www.nytimes.com/2024/04/15/world/asia/nepal-japan-yen-argeli.html (accessed 24 March 2025).
26 Integrating Climate Change into Nepal's Development Strategy Key to Build Resilience. 2022. World Bank Group.

(15 September), https://www.worldbank.org/en/news/press-release/2022/09/15/integrating-climate-change-into-nepal-s-development-strategy-key-to-build-resilience-says-new-world-bank-group-report (accessed 24 March 2025).

27 https://unfccc.int/sites/default/files/NDC/2022-06/Nepal per cent20First per cent20NDC.pdf

28 UNDP, Nepal Climate Change Support Programme Final Evaluation Report. 2019.

29 Bimal Khatiwada. 2014. EIA Report by Cut-Pasting Projects. Ekantipur, (24 December), https://ekantipur.com/en/business/2024/12/24/eia-report-by-cut-pasting-projects-39-27.html (accessed 24 March 2025).

30 Nepal Reforestation and Climate Change. 2022. *New York Times*, (11 November), https://www.nytimes.com/2022/11/11/world/asia/nepal-reforestration-climate.html (accessed 24 March 2025).

31 Reviving Nepal's Community Forestry Success Story. 2023. *Nepali Times*, (3 January), https://nepalitimes.com/banner/reviving-nepals-community-forestry-success-story (accessed 24 March 2025).

32 New Campaign Targets Food Wastage During Ramadan. (n.d.) Dubai Carbon Centre of Excellence, https://dcce.ae/press_releases/new-campaign-targets-food-wastage-during-ramadan/ (accessed 24 March 2025).

33 Sujeev Shakya. 2020. Reforming Religious Institutions. *Kathmandu Post*, (13 July), https://kathmandupost.com/columns/2020/07/13/reforming-religious-institutions (accessed 24 March 2025).

34 World religions pledge action on conservation—WWF and ARC celebrate Sacred Gifts. 2000. WWF, (15 November), https://wwf.panda.org/wwf_news/?2165/World-religions-pledge-action-on-conservation-WWF-and-ARC-celebrate-Sacred-Gifts (accessed 24 March 2025).

35 Ibid.

36 McAleer, Michael. 2017. Theravada Buddhism and Thai Luxury Fashion Consumption. *Journal of Reviews on Global Economics*. 6. 58-67. 10.6000/1929-7092.2017.06.05. https://www.researchgate.net/publication/313957681_Theravada_Buddhism_and_Thai_Luxury_Fashion_Consumption
37 Ashish Dhakal. 2021. Let's Only Buy Bio-Degradable Prayer Flags. *Nepali Times*, (16 December), https://nepalitimes.com/here-now/lets-only-buy-bio-degradable-prayer-flags (accessed 24 March 2025).
38 Confronting Climate Change to Save the Third Pole. 2021. UNDP, https://www.undp.org/sites/g/files/zskgke326/files/migration/asia_pacific_rbap/UNDP-RBAP-Policy-Brief-Confronting-Climate-Change-to-Save-the-Third-Pole-2021.pdf (accessed 24 March 2025).
39 Ramesh Bhushal. 2023. Uniquely Positioned to Be a Leader on Climate Change. Purak Asia, (5 June), https://purakasia.org/sustainable-future/uniquely-positioned-to-be-a-leader-on-climate-change/ (accessed 24 March 2025).
40 Nepal's Long-term Strategy for Net-zero Emissions. 2021. Government of Nepal. https://unfccc.int/sites/default/files/resource/NepalLTLEDS.pdf (accessed 24 March 2025).
41 Jill Colvin. 2017. Trump pulls US from global warming accord, to allies' dismay. AP News, (2 June), https://apnews.com/article/id.-0cafd1e56b124f5b9cf17ace7031d6d0 (accessed 24 March 2025).
42 Li Shuo. 2023. What Does China Want at COP28? 2025. Asia Society, (November 6), https://asiasociety.org/policy-institute/what-does-china-want-cop28 (accessed 24 March 2025).
43 Tashi Lhazom. (n.d.) Communities Hit Hardest by Climate Change. ICIMOD, https://saveoursnow.earth/videos/communities-that-have-contributed-nothing-to-climate-change-have-been-hit-the-hardest/ (accessed 24 March 2025).
44 S.D. Pradhan. 2023. China Building a Din Tibet: Aims at Acquiring Hydro-Hegemony. *Times of India*, (20 January),

https://timesofindia.indiatimes.com/blogs/ChanakyaCode/china-building-a-dam-in-tibet-aims-at-acquiring-hydro-hegemony / (accessed 24 March 2025).

45 Tariq Karim. 2024. The Seminal Importance of the Himalayan 'Third Pole' for Climate and Development Governance. ISAS, NUS, (21 March), https://www.isas.nus.edu.sg/papers/the-seminal-importance-of-the-himalayan-third-pole-for-climate-and-development-governance / (accessed 24 March 2025).

46 Ibid.

47 Government of Nepal and Development Partners Join Forces on Nepal's Green, Resilient, and Inclusive Development. 2021. World Bank, (September 24), https://www.worldbank.org/en/news/press-release/2021/09/24/government-of-nepal-and-development-partners-join-forces-on-nepal-s-green-resilient-and-inclusive-development (accessed 24 March 2025).

48 Ibid.

49 Joint Communiqué on GRID. 2023. World Bank, (November 2), https://thedocs.worldbank.org/en/doc/c4a8b716104eba07a79e4b44c332b684-0310012023/original/Joint-Communique-on-GRID-November-2023.pdf (accessed 24 March 2025).

50 Remarks by the Rt. Hon. Prime Minister. 2025. Ministry of Foreign Affairs, Nepal. https://mofa.gov.np/content/719/remarks-by-the-rt--hon--prime-minister/ (accessed 24 March 2025).

51 Mahendra P Lama. 2016. United We Stand. *Kathmandu Post*, (15 June), https://kathmandupost.com/opinion/2016/06/15/united-we-stand-20160615081551 (accessed 24 March 2025)

52 Ibid.

53 Sophia Kalantzakos and Kunda Dixit. 2023. The Global Climate System's Himalayan Hotspot. Project Syndicate, (11 May), https://www.project-syndicate.org/commentary/himalayan-mountains-climate-crisis-melting-glaciers-consequences-by-sophia-kalantzakos-and-kunda-dixit-2023-05 (accessed 24 March 2025).

54 Archana Darji. 2024. A flood of Tears on the Rosi. *Nepali Times*, (7 October), https://nepalitimes.com/multimedia/a-flood-of-tears-on-the-rosi (accessed 24 March 2025).

55 Sujeev Shakya. 2018. Replicating Chaos. *Kathmandu Post*, (2 January), https://kathmandupost.com/opinion/2018/01/02/replicating-chaos (accessed 24 March 2025).

56 Ramesh Bhushal. 2023. Uniquely Positioned to Be a Leader on Climate Change. Purak Asia, (5 June), https://purakasia.org/sustainable-future/uniquely-positioned-to-be-a-leader-on-climate-change/ (accessed 24 March 2025).

Chapter 6

1 Anil Giri. 2023. India Cabinet Okays Plan to Buy Nepal's 10,000 MW Power. *Kathmandu Post*, (6 September), https://kathmandupost.com/national/2023/09/06/india-cabinet-okays-plan-to-buy-nepal-s-10-000-mw-power

2 Anon. 2024. Blueprint for Nepal-India Electricity Trade, *Nepali Times*, (5 January), https://nepalitimes.com/news/blueprint-for-nepal-india-electricity-trade?%2F

3 Anon. 2024. PM Calls for Action on Plan to Generate 28,500 MW by 2035, *Kathmandu Post*, (8 October), https://kathmandupost.com/national/2024/10/08/pm-calls-for-action-on-plan-to-generate-28-500-mw-by-2035

4 Load Shedding Problem in Nepal: Pitch Black Past vs the Present. Earth and Human, (n.d.), https://earthandhuman.org/load-shedding-problem-in-nepal-pitch-black-past-vs-the-present/

5 Anon. 2023. Country Adds Around 500 Megawatts Power in 2079 BS. My Republica, (16 April), https://myrepublica.nagariknetwork.com/news/country-adds-around-500-megawatts-power-in-2079-bs

6 Bikash Pandey. 2024. Nepal turns to electric switch. *Nepali Times*, (2 August), https://nepalitimes.com/opinion/people-power/nepal-turns-on-the-electric-switch

7   Nepal Electricity Authority. Annual Report. (n.d.) https://www.nea.org.np/annual_report (accessed 16 April 2025).
8   Ibid.
9   Pravin Karki and Deepak Subedi. 2024. How World Bank support for a dam kept the lights on in Nepal. *World Bank Blogs*, (3 June), https://blogs.worldbank.org/en/endpovertyinsouthasia/how-world-bank-support-for-a-dam-kept-the-lights-on-in-nepal-
10 Nepal Electricity Authority. DCSD Book 2080/81 (2023/24). https://www.nea.org.np/admin/assets/uploads/annual_publications/DCSD_Book_2080_81.pdf
11 Chris Dickert. 2023. What Electricity Sources Power the World? Visual Capitalist. Electricity, (September 10), https://www.visualcapitalist.com/electricity-sources-by-fuel-in-2022/
12 Country Adds Around 500 Megawatts Power in 2079 BS. 2024. *Rising Nepal*, (22 December), https://risingnepaldaily.com/news/54093.
13 Anil Giri. 2025. Nepal-India Talks Today Aim to Boost Power Transmission. *Kathmandu Post*, (February 11), https://kathmandupost.com/national/2025/02/11/nepal-india-talks-today-aim-to-boost-power-transmission
14 Open Knowledge Repository: Power Sector Document. (n.d.) World Bank. https://openknowledge.worldbank.org/server/api/core/bitstreams/81e9c6a7-c342-5038-832a-4e1e17374200/content
15 India's Top Hydro Power Producers: A Profile. 2016. *Economic Times*, (August 11), https://energy.economictimes.indiatimes.com/news/renewable/indias-top-hydro-power-producers-a-profile/53632245
16 Economic Impact of Poor Power Quality in Nepal. 2023. Nexant SARI/Energy https://synergyforenergy.wordpress.com/wp-content/uploads/2011/06/economicimpact_poorpowerquality_nepal_complete.pdf
17 Dipak Gyawali and Sudhindra Sharma. 2025. Pump Water, Store Energy. *Nepali Times*, (8 February), https://nepalitimes.com/here-now/pump-water-store-energy

18 Per Capita Energy Consumption. (n.d.) World Bank https://data.worldbank.org/indicator/EG.USE.ELEC.KH.PC?locations=XD, https://www.statista.com/statistics/268151/per-capita-energy-consumption-in-selected-countries/
19 Smart Homes and Energy Management Systems. 2023. PR Newswire, (17 August), https://www.prnewswire.com/news-releases/pioneering-the-future-of-smart-homes-with-home-energy-management-system-301904231.html
20 Nepal Census 2021.
21 Ramchandra Bhandari and Surendra Pandit. 2018. Electricity as a Cooking Means in Nepal—A Modelling Tool Approach. MDPI, (10 August), https://www.mdpi.com/2071-1050/10/8/2841.
22 Nepal Census 2021.
23 Michele Robinson-Pontbriand. 2023. Quality Smart Home Systems Enable a Sustainable Future Through Power Consumption Management. CSRwire, (9 June), https://www.csrwire.com/press_releases/782811-quality-smart-home-systems-enable-sustainable-future-through-power
24 Steve. 2023. Haut volt. Noshaq, (9 November), https://noshaq.be/haut-volt/
25 Pete Pattisson. 2025. Leading the charge: how a drive for electric vehicles is cleaning up Nepal. *Guardian*, (4 Friday), https://www.theguardian.com/global-development/2025/apr/04/nepal-kathmandu-health-air-pollution-who-transport-electric-vehicles-
26 Mohd Sahil Ali and Rahul Tongia. 2018. Electrifying Mobility in India: Future Prospects for the Electric and EV Ecosystem. Brookings India IMPACT Series No. 052018. May 2018. https://www.brookings.edu/wp-content/uploads/2018/05/20180528_impact-series_ev_web.pdf
27 Second Nationally Determined Contribution (NDC). 2020. Government of Nepal, (8 December), http://climate.mohp.gov.np/attachments/article/167/Second%20Nationally%20Determined%20Contribution%20(NDC)%20-%202020.pdf

28. Kushal Gurung. 2023. Future-Proofing Nepal's Energy Sector. LinkedIn, (25 July), https://www.linkedin.com/pulse/future-proofing-nepals-energy-sector-kushal-gurung/
29. Establishing A Fertilizer Plant in Nepal: A Comparative Study and Analysis of Natural Gas Vs Water Electrolysis Technology. (n.d.) Government of Nepal. https://ibn.gov.np/uploads/documents/summary-reportchemical-fertilizer2021pdf-4182-401-1671614496.pdf
30. Lhakpa Quendren. 2025. Bitdeer Jigmeling's 500MW mining centre to go full-scale in 2026. Kuensel Online, (12 April), https://kuenselonline.com/news/bitdeer-jigmelings-500mw-mining-centre-to-go-full-scale-in-2026
31. Sushmita Pathak. 2025. A tiny Himalayan nation's big crypto gamble. World, (5 March), https://theworld.org/stories/2025/03/05/a-tiny-himalayan-nations-big-crypto-gamble
32. Amber Jackson. 2024. Top 10: Biggest Data Centres. Data Centre Magazine, (23 October), https://datacentremagazine.com/top10/top-10-biggest-data-centres
33. AI is Already Wreaking Havoc on Global Power Systems. 2024. Big Take, (21 June), https://www.bloomberg.com/graphics/2024-ai-data-centers-power-grids/
34. Global Green Finance Market Size to Exceed US$28.71 Trillion By 2033 | CAGR Of 4.18%. 2024. Spherical Insights, (22 February), https://www.globenewswire.com/news-release/2024/02/22/2833419/0/en/Global-Green-Finance-Market-Size-To-Exceed-USD-28-71-Trillion-By-2033-CAGR-Of-4-18.html
35. Papa Saliou DIOP, Vanessa Müller and Fabio Rocha. 2025. Green Finance: The role of the EU, US and China, and how Securitization can unlock the market potential. EY Insights, (17 January), https://www.ey.com/en_lu/insights/securitization/green-finance-the-role-of-the-eu-us-china
36. OPM. (2022). Capitalising Green Finance for Nepal, Oxford Policy Management Limited. https://www.opml.co.uk/

sites/default/files/migrated_bolt_files/capitalising-green-finance-report.pdf

37. Green Finance Taxonomy 2024. Nepal Rastra Bank. https://www.nrb.org.np/contents/uploads/2024/10/Nepal-Green-Finance-Taxonomy-2024.pdf
38. John Narayan Parajuli. (n.d.) Creating Waves to Achieve Sustainable Hydropower in Nepal. IFC, World Bank Group, https://www.ifc.org/en/stories/2023/creating-waves-to-achieve-sustainable-hydropower-in-nepal
39. Mark Liechty. 2022. What Went Right: Sustainability Versus Dependence in Nepal's Hydropower Development. New Delhi: Cambridge University Press.
40. Joti Giri. 2023. Nepal's hydropower goes international. Nepali Times, (6 November), https://nepalitimes.com/news/nepals-hydropower-goes-international
41. Prathik Desai. 2024. PM Modi Inaugurates Boeing's Largest Engineering & Technology Facility Outside US. Outlook Business, (21 January), https://business.outlookindia.com/corporate/pm-modi-inaugurates-boeings-largest-engineering-technology-facility-outside-us

Chapter 7

1. Agriculture, forestry, and fishing, value added (% of GDP)—Nepal. (n.d.) World Bank. https://data.worldbank.org/indicator/NV.AGR.TOTL.ZS?locations=NP
2. National Population and Housing Census 2021. (n.d.) Central Bureau of Statistics Nepal. https://docs.censusnepal.cbs.gov.np/Documents/e9f6d087-5f43-4e55-973e-b7e25cb213b9.pdf
3. Nepal census 2021.
4. How to Feed the World in 2050: Global Agriculture Towards 2050. (n.d.) FAO https://www.fao.org/fileadmin/templates/wsfs/docs/Issues_papers/HLEF2050_Global_Agriculture.pdf

5 Matsu. 2024. How Will Tea Production Sites Evolve with Agricultural Mechanization and Robotics? The Cutting Edge of Smart Agriculture [Horiguchi Seicha / Daisuke Horiguchi]. Global Japanese Tea Association, (24 September), https://gjtea.org/japanese-tea-innovators-19/.

6 An Overview of Agricultural Mechanization in Nepal. 2022. *Kathmandu University Journal of Science Engineering and Technology* 16(2):7 DOI:10.3126/kuset.v16i2.62626 https://www.researchgate.net/publication/366715029_An_overview_of_agricultural_mechanization_in_Nepal

7 Deepali Khanna and Mahendra Krishna Shrestha. 2024. Parametric insurance: How it can help Nepal build climate resilience. *Himalayan Times*, (26 December), https://thehimalayantimes.com/opinion/parametric-insurance-how-it-can-help-nepal-build-climate-resilience

8 https://www.agridigitechchallenge.com/

9 Water and Energy Commission Secretariat Singha Durbar, Kathmandu, Nepal Energy Sector Synopsis Report 2021/2022.

10 Bishal Thapa. 2022. Power to the farmer. *Kathmandu Post*, (29 December), https://kathmandupost.com/columns/2022/12/29/power-to-the-farmer

11 Benjamin Zimmerman. 2024. Helping Farmers Who Help Themselves. *Nepali Times*, (10 August), https://nepalitimes.com/here-now/helping-farmers-who-help-themselves

12 Sheilin Teo. 2019. Nepal's Yak Cheese is on World Map. *Nepali Times*, (11 June), https://nepalitimes.com/here-now/nepals-yak-cheese-is-on-world-map

13 Max Falkowitz. 2019. Don't Call It Darjeeling, It's Nepali Tea. *New York Times*, (28 May), https://www.nytimes.com/2019/05/28/dining/drinks/nepal-darjeeling-tea.html

14 Nepal Tea Collective—now available in the Nepali market. 2023. *Kathmandu Post*, (25 July), https://kathmandupost.com/money/2023/07/25/nepal-tea-collective-now-available-in-the-nepali-market

15 Laxman Dige. 2024. Health and Wellness Market Size to Reach US$9.4 Trillion by 2032. Lindkedin, (21 March), https://www.linkedin.com/pulse/health-wellness-market-laxman-dige-nyktf/
16 Krishana Prasain. 2025. India Recognises Nepal Food Lab for Exports After a Five-Year Wait. *Kathmandu Post*, (8 April), https://kathmandupost.com/money/2025/04/08/india-recognises-nepal-food-lab-for-exports-after-a-five-year-wait
17 Sanjukta Sen, Dipanjan Karati, Rosy Priyadarshini, Tarun Kumar Dua, Paramita Paul, Ranabir Sahu, Gouranga Nandi. (n.d.) Cordyceps sinensis (yarsagumba): Pharmacological properties of a mushroom; Pharmacological Research - *Modern Chinese Medicine* Volume 8 100294, ISSN 2667-1425, https://doi.org/10.1016/j.prmcm.2023.100294. https://www.sciencedirect.com/science/article/pii/S2667142523000805
18 Raj Bahadur Shahi. 2023. Price of yarsagumba surges after China re-opens border. The *Kathmandu Post*, (19 September), https://kathmandupost.com/money/2023/09/19/price-of-yarsagumba-surges-after-china-re-opens-border
19 Ibid.
20 Achyut Tiwari. 2022. Giving Yarsagumba a Chance for Regrowth. *Nepali Times*, (19 August), https://nepalitimes.com/banner/giving-yarsagumba-a-chance-for-regrowth
21 Nefport 52.
22 Agriculture Development Strategy (ADS) 2015 to 2035. Government of Nepal. https://faolex.fao.org/docs/pdf/nep171433.pdf

Chapter 8

1 Artha Beed. 2006. Trekking Through Time. *Nepali Times* archive, (13–19 January), https://archive.nepalitimes.com/news.php?id=10123
2 NLSS 2022.

3. Shristi Karki. 2024. Women on the Move. *Nepali Times*, (9 March), https://nepalitimes.com/here-now/women-on-the-move
4. Told in conversation to Riya Shrestha, in an interview, https://www.instagram.com/riyasthaa/
5. Sonia Awale. 2023. Behind the Cliff. *Nepali Times*, (20 December), https://nepalitimes.com/here-now/behind-the-cliff
6. Narayan Baral. 2025. Yatra Sansmaran: Nepal Has Progressed. Nepal Economic Forum, (11 March), https://nepaleconomicforum.org/yatra-sansmaran-nepal-has-progressed/
7. Sujeev Shakya. 2021. Digital Nomads. https://sujeevshakya.com/2021/07/digital-nomads/
8. Enika Rai. 2024. Travel Vlogs Promoting Nepal's Tourism. MyRepublica, (2 August), https://myrepublica.nagariknetwork.com/news/travel-vlogs-promoting-nepal-s-tourism/
9. Anon. (n.d.) First in: Shinta Mani Mustang – a Bensley Collection. CN Traveller. https://www.cntraveller.com/hotels/shinta-mani-mustang-a-bensley-collection.
10. Global Luxury Travel to Surge from $1.4 Trillion in 2024 to $2.2 Trillion by 2030. 2024. McKinsey & Company, (31 December), https://tourismbreakingnews.com/global-luxury-travel-to-surge-from-1-4-tn-in-2024-to-2-2-tn-by-2020-potential-to-grow-further-mckinsey/
11. Asia's 50 Best Bars. (n.d.) The World's 50 Best. https://www.theworlds50best.com/bars/asia/the-list/barc.html
12. Sangam Prasain. 2023. Everest Permit to Cost $15K from 2025. *Kathmandu Post*, (12 August), https://kathmandupost.com/money/2023/08/12/everest-permit-to-cost-15k-from-2025
13. Rwanda Development Board.
14. Divya Aggarwal, Margaux Constantin, Kanika Kalra, and Neelesh Mundra. 2023. From India to the World: Unleashing the Potential of India's Tourists. McKinsey & Company, (November 1), https://www.mckinsey.com/industries/travel-logistics-and-infrastructure/

our-insights/from-india-to-the-world-unleashing-the-potential-of-indias-tourists

15. Alex Dichter, Guang Chen, Steve Saxon, Jackey Yu, Peimin Suo. 2018. Chinese Tourists: Dispelling the Myths. McKinsey & Company, (September), https://www.mckinsey.com/~/media/mckinsey/industries/travel%20logistics%20and%20infrastructure/our%20insights/huanying%20to%20the%20new%20chinese%20traveler/chinese-tourists-dispelling-the-myths.pdf

16. Parulis Sienna-Cook. 2018. Women Dominate Chinese Outbound Tourism—What Does This Mean?. LinkedIn, (8 March), https://www.linkedin.com/pulse/women-dominate-chinese-outbound-tourism-what-does-sienna-parulis-cook/

17. Lauren Jackson. 2019. China Is Winning the War for Nepali Buddhism. *Diplomat*, (21 March), https://thediplomat.com/2019/03/china-is-winning-the-war-for-nepali-buddhism/

18. Lynn Hatem. 2023. Miaoying Temple: Celebrating Sino-Nepalese Cultural Heritage in Beijing. *Beijing Times*, (30 December), https://beijingtimes.com/culture/2023/12/30/miaoying-temple-celebrating-sino-nepalese-cultural-heritage-in-beijing/

19. World Bank, 2021, Buddhist Circuit in South Asia, https://documents1.worldbank.org/curated/en/387491563440124268/pdf/The-Buddhist-Circuit-A-Program-for-the-Development-of-the-Buddhist-Circuit-in-South-Asia.pdf

20. Kallol Bhattacherjee. 2022. India, Nepal to Speed Up Ramayana Circuit Projects. *The Hindu*, (14 September), https://www.thehindu.com/news/national/india-nepal-to-speed-up-ramayana-circuit-projects/article65887837.ece

21. Dinita Rishal. 2024. Tiny Australian Town Turns into 'Little Nepal' for Liam Neeson. SBS Nepali, (19 January), https://www.sbs.com.au/language/nepali/en/article/tiny-australian-town-turns-into-little-nepal-for-liam-neeson-but-how-taken-is-everyone/ojgpm476b

22 Razmig Bedirian. 2024. How a Hollywood-savvy animation studio in Nepal offers lessons in inclusivity. The National News, (February 15), https://www.thenationalnews.com/arts-culture/2024/02/15/hollywood-netflix-nepal-animation/
23 Alex Ritman. 2024. Tom Hiddleston, Willem Dafoe to Star in Biopic of Famed Everest Mountaineer Tenzing Norgay for See-Saw Films, Rocket Science. Variety, (May 9), https://variety.com/2024/film/global/tom-hiddleston-willem-dafoe-tenzing-norgay-biopic-1235997617/

Chapter 9

1 Global ideas will shape the Nepali mindset. 2023. The Kathmandu Post, (June 10), https://kathmandupost.com/money/2023/06/10/global-ideas-will-shape-the-nepali-mindset?hss_channel=fbp-1467318436849445 (accessed 22 May 2025).
2 USAID, Nepal Private Sector Assessment Report, 2020.
3 Nepal's Emerging Digital Economy: Trends and Opportunities. 2023. IIDS Report. https://iids.org.np/images/publications/15c4487b777dcf3239cd6af6dd15c2c1.pdf (accessed 22 May 2025).
4 Ibid.
5 Dilip Paudel. 2025. Govt Sets Ambitious IT Exports Target. MyRepublica, (2 February), https://myrepublica.nagariknetwork.com/news/govt-sets-ambitious-it-exports-target-17-70.html (accessed 22 May 2025).
6 Nepal's Emerging Digital Economy: Trends and Opportunities. 2023. IIDS Report. https://iids.org.np/images/publications/15c4487b777dcf3239cd6af6dd15c2c1.pdf (accessed 22 May 2025).

7. ICT Sector Profile. (n.d.) Investment Board Nepal. https://ibn.gov.np/wp-content/uploads/2020/04/ICT-Sector-Profile.pdf (accessed 21 April 2025).
8. Country profile—Nepal. (n.d.) Department of Home Affairs, Australian Government, https://www.homeaffairs.gov.au/research-and-statistics/statistics/country-profiles/profiles/nepal (accessed 22 May 2025).
9. Ryan Johnson. 2023. Home Loan Experts Rebrands Outsourcing Solution After Sustained Growth. Broker News, (Jul 25), https://www.brokernews.com.au/news/breaking-news/home-loan-experts-rebrands-outsourcing-solution-after-sustained-growth-282908.aspx (accessed 21 April 2025).
10. Nepal Economic Forum (2023). Nefport 54—Fueling Regional Connectivity.
11. Press Council Nepal. https://www.presscouncilnepal.gov.np/np/ (accessed 21 April 2025).
12. Krishna Prasain. 2023. Internet Traffic Grows Sharply in Nepal After TikTok Ban. *Kathmandu Post*, (20 November), https://kathmandupost.com/money/2023/11/20/internet-traffic-grows-sharply-in-nepal-after-tiktok-ban (accessed 21 April 2025).
13. Nepal Economic Forum. (2023). Proceedings Report—Digital Services at the Base of the Pyramid. https://nepaleconomicforum.org/reports/proceedings-report-neftalk-on-digital-services-at-the-base-of-the-pyramid/ (accessed 21 April 2025).
14. F1Soft Group, https://f1soft.com/about (accessed 22 May 2025).
15. QR Code Drives Nepal's Digital Payment Boom. 2025. *Kathmandu Post*, (11 April), https://kathmandupost.com/money/2025/04/11/qr-code-drives-nepal-s-digital-payment-boom (accessed 21 April 2025).
16. Securities Market Has More Than 42 Percent Women Investors. 2024. New Business Age, (8 March), https://www.newbusinessage.com/article/securities-market-has-more-than-42-percent-women-investors (accessed 21 April 2025).

17 Nishant Kumar. 2024. Women's Day 2024: Top 5 Women Investors in India, Their Portfolio Size & Key Holdings. LiveMint, (8 March), https://www.livemint.com/market/stock-market-news/womens-day-2024-top-5-women-investors-in-india-their-portfolio-size-key-holdings-11709873663075.html (accessed 21 April 2025).

18 Niraj Bhushal. 2025. X Post, (May 3), https://x.com/n7r9j/status/1918572722176532971

19 Fusemachines Company Profile. LinkedIn. https://www.linkedin.com/company/fusemachines/ (accessed 21 April 2025).

20 5G vs. 4G: What's the Difference? 2023. Thales Group. https://www.thalesgroup.com/en/worldwide-digital-identity-and-security/mobile/magazine/5g-vs-4g-whats-difference (accessed 21 April 2025).

21 Top 10 Energy Consuming Data Centers. n.d. Sunbird DCIM. https://www.sunbirddcim.com/infographic/top-10-energy-consuming-data-centers (accessed 22 May 2025).

22 Lambert Bu, Violet Chung, Nick Leung, Kevin Wei Wang, Bruce Xia and Chenan Xia. 2021. The Future of Digital Innovation in China. McKinsey Insights, (30 September), https://www.mckinsey.com/featured-insights/china/the-future-of-digital-innovation-in-china-megatrends-shaping-one-of-the-worlds-fastest-evolving-digital-ecosystems (accessed 22 May 2025).

23 Josh Ye and Julie Zhu. 2023. China Moves Towards Digital Economy Dream with National Data Bureau. Reuters, (8 March), https://www.reuters.com/world/china/china-moves-towards-digital-economy-dream-with-national-data-bureau-2023-03-08/ (accessed 22 May 2025).

24 ANI. 2023. India's Digital Economy to Grow Over Fivefold at $1 Trillion by 2030: Report. *Times of India*, (6 June), https://timesofindia.indiatimes.com/business/india-business/indias-digital-economy-to-grow-over-fivefold-at-1-trillion-by-2030-report/articleshow/100789668.cms (accessed 22 May 2025).

25 Mahesh Sachdev. 2020. The Differing Digital Journeys of India and China. *Hindustan Times*, (20 July), https://www.hindustantimes.com/analysis/the-differing-digital-journeys-of-india-china/story-nfCaSr6bn9RoJhb9CclNTN.html (accessed 22 May 2025).

26 Twenty Nepali startups take part in Startup Mahakumbh in India. 2025. *Kathmandu Post*, (4 April), https://kathmandupost.com/world/2025/04/04/twenty-nepali-startups-take-part-in-startup-mahakumbh-in-india (accessed 22 May 2025).

27 The Story of e-Estonia. e-Estonia. https://e-estonia.com/wp-content/uploads/story-of-e-estonia-nov2023-2.pdf (accessed 21 April 2025).

28 How Singapore Teaches Coding in Elementary Schools. Typeset.io. https://typeset.io/questions/how-singapore-teach-coding-in-elementary-schools-48i5rtet12 (accessed 22 May 2025).

29 Xinhua. 2025. China Unveils 2025 Plan to Boost Digital Literacy, Skills. ChinaDaily.com.cn, (27 April), https://www.chinadaily.com.cn/a/202504/27/WS680df25da3104d9fd3821d8c.html (accessed 22 May 2025).

30 Sumana Shrestha. (n.d.) Creating Tech Jobs in Nepal. https://sumanashrestha.com.np/en/priorities/creating-tech-jobs/ (accessed 22 May 2025).

31 Dima Syrothkin. 2021. The Next Trillion Dollar Startup Is Going to Be an Education Company. Medium, (28 May), https://medium.com/swlh/the-next-trillion-dollar-startup-is-going-to-be-an-education-company-3eecf764e8e6 (accessed 22 May 2025).

32 IT Colleges in Nepal. (n.d.) Colleges Nepal, https://www.collegesnepal.com/it/ (accessed 22 May 2025).

33 Kazi Arif Uz Zaman and Tapan Sarker. 2021. Demographic Dividend, Digital Innovation, and Economic Growth in Bangladesh. Asian Development Bank, (March), https://www.adb.org/publications/demographic-dividend-digital-innovation-economic-growth-bangladesh (accessed 22 May 2025).

Chapter 10

1. Prithvi Man Shrestha. 2023. Nepal could enjoy the demographic dividend for 40–60 years. The Kathmandu Post, (16 April), https://kathmandupost.com/interviews/2023/04/16/nepal-could-enjoy-the-demographic-dividend-for-40-60-years
2. Localizing investments: Demographic Dividend in Nepal. (n.d.). UNFPA Nepal. https://nepal.unfpa.org/en/publications/localizing-investments-demographic-dividend-nepal?page=13%2C0%2C2
3. Demographic dividend. 2024. UNFPA Arab States, (30 July), https://arabstates.unfpa.org/en/topics/demographic-dividend-6
4. Bloom, D.E., Canning, D., & Sevilla, J. (2003). The Demographic Dividend: A New Perspective on the Economic Consequences of Population Change. https://www.worldscientific.com/doi/10.1162/ADEV_a_00013
5. Economist Impact. (2018). Ready for 100: Whitepaper. https://impact.economist.com/projects/ready-for-100/wp-content/uploads/2019/07/20180924-ECO035-Ready-for-100-Whitepaper-Spread.pdf
6. Youth Demographic Dividend in Nepal. (n.d.). USAID. https://pdf.usaid.gov/pdf_docs/PBAAF234.pdf
7. National Planning Commission. (2017). Demographic dividend report—May 2017. https://www.npc.gov.np/images/category/Demographic_Dividend_Report_May_2017_final_for_circulation1.pdf
8. Nepal Economic Forum. 2025. Nepal's Income Increased Threefold; Worries Doubled [Translated From Setopati]. (18 February), https://www.linkedin.com/pulse/nepals-income-increased-threefold-worries-doubled-pfyff/
9. Ibid.
10. Ibid.
11. Krishana Prasain. Nepal's Banking Industry Is a Leader in South Asia in Employing Women. 2025. *Kathmandu Post*. 2025. https://

kathmandupost.com/money/2024/05/11/nepal-s-banking-industry-is-a-leader-in-south-asia-in-employing-women
12. Nepal Census 2021.
13. Nepal Census 2021.
14. https://npc.gov.np/images/category/Demographic_Dividend_Policy_Brief_Apr_2017_final.pdf
15. 'Nepal Female Literacy Rate, Ages 15-24 - Data, Chart | TheGlobalEconomy.com.'(n.d.)TheGlobalEconomy.Com. https://www.theglobaleconomy.com/Nepal/Female_literacy_rate_15_25/
16. Nefport 58.

Chapter 11

1. Tanka Subba. 1992. To Be or Not to Be 'Nepali'. Himal Southasian, (1 May), https://www.himalmag.com/cover/to-be-or-not-to-be-nepali
2. Bikram Sambat is also referred to as Nepali New Year outside Nepal and generally occurs on 13-15 April each year.
3. #DidYouKnowOutof100mostspokenlanguagesworldwide,Nepali stands in the 57th position. 2018. Facebook post - Nepal Economic Forum. https://www.facebook.com/nepaleconomicforum/posts/didyouknowout-of-100-most-spoken-languages-worldwide-nepali-stands-in-the-57th-p/1688002968016332/
4. Sujeev Shakya, *Unleashing the Vajra*, New Delhi: Penguin Random House India.
5. Ibid.
6. Sujeev Shakya. 2020. Will Nepali Remittance Bounce Back? ISAS NUS, (July 8), https://www.isas.nus.edu.sg/papers/will-nepali-remittance-bounce-back/
7. Revenue of Rs 50 million raised through passport camp in Portugal. 2023. Republica, (18 May), https://myrepublica.

nagariknetwork.com/news/revenue-of-rs-50-million-raised-through-passport-camp-in-portugal/

8 Getting passport in Nepal is pricey affair; costs highest in South Asia. 2013. Centre for the Study of Labour and Mobility, (16 April), https://ceslam.org/updates/getting-passport-in-nepal-is-pricey-affair-costs-highest-in-south-asia/

9 Government of Nepal, Ministry of Foreign Affairs, Department of Passports Website, https://nepalpassport.gov.np/

10 World Development Report 2023: Migrants, Refugees, and Societies. 2023. World Bank, https://www.worldbank.org/en/publication/wdr2023

11 Remittance flows grow in 2023 but at a slower pace—Migration and Development Brief. 2023. World Bank, (18 December), https://www.worldbank.org/en/news/press-release/2023/12/18/remittance-flows-grow-2023-slower-pace-migration-development-brief#:~:text=In%202023%2C%20remittance%20flows%20to,ability%20to%20send%20money%20home

12 Ibid.

13 Nepal Economic Forum. (2022). Proceedings report – Dissecting the world of remittances. https://nepaleconomicforum.org/reports/proceedings-report-dissecting-the-world-of-remittances

14 Human flight. 2023. *Nepali Times*, (10 May), https://nepalitimes.com/editorial/human-flight

15 Nepal Economic Forum, Understanding Remittance Market and Economy Report 2025.

16 Nepal-Japan relations. (n.d.). Ministry of Foreign Affairs Nepal. https://mofa.gov.np/content/1452/nepal-japan-relations/

17 Pinki Sris Rana. 2024. Japan-born Nepali children struggle to be Nepali. Nepali Times. (22 September), https://nepalitimes.com/multimedia/japan-born-nepali-children-struggle-to-be-nepali

18 Aseem Banstola. 2025. In limbo in Lisbon. *Nepali Times*, (4 April), https://nepalitimes.com/here-now/in-limbo-in-lisbon

Chapter 12

1. Daron Acemoglu, Suresh Naidu, Pascual Restrepo and James A. Robinson. 2019. Democracy does cause growth. Journal of Political Economy, https://economics.mit.edu/sites/default/files/publications/Democracy%20Does%20Cause%20Growth.pdf
2. Chung-in Moon and Song-min Kim. Democracy and Economic Performance in South Korea. Consolidating Democracy in South Korea, edited by Larry Diamond and Byung-Kook Kim, Boulder, USA: Lynne Rienner Publishers, 2000, pp. 139-172. https://www.degruyter.com/document/doi/10.1515/9781626373150-007/pdf?licenseType=restricted
3. Data compiled from Nepal Economic Forum Nefdata and World Bank.
4. Remarks by Deputy Secretary of Commerce Don Graves at the Center for Strategic and International Studies. 2023. U.S. Department of Commerce, (21 March), https://www.commerce.gov/news/speeches/2023/03/remarks-deputy-secretary-commerce-don-graves-center-strategic-and
5. Nepal should be open for South Asia. 2023. Nepali Times, (10 March), https://nepalitimes.com/news/nepal-should-be-open-for-south-asia
6. Tapendra Karki. 2024. Home Ministry backtracks its decision to increase media surveillance following protest from stakeholders. Republica, (22 March), https://myrepublica.nagariknetwork.com/news/home-ministry-backtracks-its-decision-to-increase-media-surveillance-following-protest-from-stakeholders
7. https://himalbooks.com/product/state-of-nepal/
8. Unleashing Nepal.
9. 'Impose Inheritance Tax to Change Politics.' 2025. @Kathmandupost. The Kathmandu Post. 2025. https://kathmandupost.com/columns/2021/08/23/impose-inheritance-tax-to-change-politics

10 Sujeev Shakya. 2021. 'Flourishing "Cartelpreneurship" | Sujeev Shakya.' Sujeev Shakya. July 14, 2021. https://sujeevshakya.com/2021/07/flourishing-cartelpreneurship/
11 Cartel reports.
12 'Nepali Firms to Be Allowed Foreign Investment; Individuals Eligible for Sweat Equity.' 2025. @Kathmandupost. The Kathmandu Post. 2025. https://kathmandupost.com/money/2025/05/29/nepali-firms-to-be-allowed-foreign-investment-individuals-eligible-for-sweat-equity
13 'Over Rs 8 Billion Paid from Social Security Fund so Far.' 2025. Nepal News. https://nepalnews.com/s/business/over-rs-8-billion-paid-from-social-security-fund-so-far
14 Cash balance of 75 billion 90 million in Military Welfare Fund. 2024. Ekantipur, (July 18), https://ekantipur.com/en/news/2024/07/18/cash-balance-of-75-billion-90-million-in-military-welfare-fund-05-56.html
15 Anon. 2022. Rs 75 Billion in Welfare Funds of Security Forces. New Business Age. Https://Newbusinessage.com/. new business age. July 30, 2022. https://newbusinessage.com/article/rs-75-billion-in-welfare-funds-of-security-forces
16 Reuters. 2024. India's richest 1% has highest concentration of wealth in decades, study shows. *Economic Times*, (21 March), https://economictimes.indiatimes.com/news/india/indias-richest-1-has-highest-concentration-of-wealth-in-decades-study-shows/articleshow/108650367.cms?from=mdr
17 World Bank. (2023). GRID Flyer – Nepal. https://thedocs.worldbank.org/en/doc/5f3ac1d71583fab500da942caea11dac-0310012023/original/GRID-Flyer-Nepal.pdf
18 World Trade Organization (WTO) 2023, Annual Report, Page 009, https://www.wto.org/english/res_e/booksp_e/anrep_e/ar23_e.pdf
19 Ghyanshyam Khadka. 2025. 11 percent increase in court case fees. Ekantipur, (13 March), https://ekantipur.com/

en/news/2025/03/13/11-percent-increase-in-court-case-fees-38-13.html

20 PTI. 2024. Nepal SC issues show cause notice over government's power trade deal with India. *Economic Times*, (1 February), https://energy.economictimes.indiatimes.com/news/power/nepal-sc-issues-show-cause-notice-over-governments-power-trade-deal-with-india/107376250

21 Brand Smile is Brand Nepal. (n.d). *Arthat Parivartan*. Thuprai. https://thuprai.com/read/brand-smile-is-brand-nepal/

22 Future of Compassion in the Context of Artificial Intelligence (AI) and Technology. (n.d). Nepal Economic Forum. https://issuu.com/nepaleconomicforum/docs/mr_report_-_final-min

Scan QR code to access the
Penguin Random House India website